Leavenworth Papers

Number 20

Russian-Soviet Unconventional Wars in the Caucasus, Central Asia, and Afghanistan

by Dr. Robert F. Baumann

Printed courtesy of the U.S. Army Center of Military History, Washington, D.C.

Combat Studies Institute
U.S. Army Command and General Staff College
Fort Leavenworth, Kansas 66027-6900

Contents

Illustrations v
Tables vii
Preface ix
Chapter
   1. Russian Subjugation of the Central Caucasus:
      The War Against the Mountaineers 1
   2. The Conquest of Central Asia 49
   3. The Liquidation of the Basmachi Resistance,
      1918—1933 91
   4. The Soviet-Afghan War 129
   5. Conclusions 211

Illustrations

Maps

1. Russia's southern frontier in the nineteenth century 4
2. The Caucasus and Transcaucasia, 1763—1914 6
3. The Akhulgo campaign, 1839 13
4. Russian positions, 4—22 August 1839 (up to the capture of Akhulgo) 18
5. The Dargo campaign, 1845 22
6. The Russians' linkup and final thrust into Dagestan, 1859 31
7. The Khivan campaign, 1873 64
8. The Akhal-Teke campaign, 1880—81 73
9. The storming of Geok Tepe fortress, 12 January 1881 75
10. The Red Army's capture of Bukhara, 1920 110
11. Afghanistan 130
12. Tactical combat in a green zone 162

Tables

1. Vorontsov's column order 24
2. Composition of Russian forces in the Khivan campaign 65
3. Composition of Russian garrisons outside Tashkent 95
4. Soviet losses in Afghanistan, 1979—89 148

Preface

Prior to the Bolshevik Revolution of October 1917, Russians adhered to the old Julian calendar, which during the nineteenth century was twelve days behind the modern Gregorian calendar that is in general use today. Nineteenth-century dates cited in this study are in accordance with the custom of that period. For twentieth-century dates, this study, of course, employs the modern calendar.

With regard to transliteration, this manuscript adheres to the Library of Congress system with a couple of exceptions. First, Russian "hard signs" are not transliterated into English. Second, for spellings of names and places, this manuscript uses accepted English spellings where applicable.

I would like to acknowledge the contributions of many individuals to the production of this manuscript. Special thanks are due to Robert H. Berlin, E. Willis Brooks, Jerry M. Cooper, Lester W. Grau, Jim Holbrook, Jacob W. Kipp, Bruce W. Menning, Roger J. Spiller, Colonel Richard M. Swain, Graham H. Turbiville, and Lawrence A. Yates for their suggestions and assistance in the research and writing of this study. The author also appreciates the thoughtful observations of colleagues in the Combat Studies Institute (CSI), as well as numerous USACGSC students who read draft versions of this book as part of their course work. Don Gilmore of CSI provided invaluable help in the editing of this manuscropt. Carolyn Conway and Marilyn Edwards also played important roles in guiding this Leavenworth Paper through the publication process. Robin Inojos and Al Dulin provided skillful assistance with graphics and maps. Librarians Mary Jo Nelson and Timothy L. Sanz again and again helped obtain difficult-to-locate materials. Cooperation from the Slavic Reference Service at the University of Illinois was also most appreciated.

Russian Subjugation of the Central Caucasus: The War Against the Mountaineers

The War Against the Mountaineers

Though little known, Russia's Caucasian campaigns from 1801 to 1864 constitute one of the most fascinating and instructive episodes in modern warfare. Pitted against the determined, resourceful Muslim tribes of the mountains and forests of the central Caucasus, Russia's military forces compiled a frustrating record that reflected many of the difficulties inherent in armed conflicts between Western-style, conventional armies and non-Western, unconventional forces in theaters lacking a highly developed transportation and communications infrastructure common to urbanized societies. Repeated Russian failures, the product of errors and the increasingly skillful leadership of the resistance, forced Russian military analysts to reexamine their approach. In the end, the conquest of the interior Caucasus depended upon the Russians' gradual recognition of the distinctive nature of their opponents and the local conditions, subsequent adaptations of their strategy and tactics in the face of intellectual and institutional inertia, and relentless and methodical prosecution of the war.

The southward extension of Russian imperial power into the Caucasus during the nineteenth century reflected the logic of political geography. Unchecked either by natural barriers or the once powerful empires of Ottoman Turkey and Persia, Russian penetration of the Caucasus was inevitable. Although Russian involvement in the Caucasus began in the sixteenth century when Ivan IV (the Terrible) established relations with the little kingdom of Kabarda at the northern edge of the Caucasus Mountains, only under Catherine II (1762—96), two centuries later, did Russia possess the might to assert direct influence in the region.[1] Thanks to the efforts of Prince Grigory Potemkin, appointed first viceroy of the Caucasus in 1785, and the gifted General Alexander Suvorov, Russian columns campaigned deep into the Caucasus to extend Russian power on the Caspian and Black Sea coasts. However, with Catherine's death, Russian forces withdrew northward to the so-called Caucasian Line—a string of forts, fortified points, and Cossack settlements following the Kuban and Terek Rivers across the northern tier of the Caucasus. The Caucasian Line defined the southernmost limit of effective Russian control over the land, populace, and lines of communication.

Catherine II (the Great)

A single event, Russia's annexation of the small Christian kingdom of Georgia in 1801, solidified Russia's long-term stake in the heart of the Caucasus. In 1799, Georgii XII, Georgia's ruler, sought Russian protection to avoid destruction of his kingdom by his more numerous Muslim neighbors, especially Persia and Turkey. By forcing reunification of the old Georgian lands and defeating Persia, Tsar Alexander I obtained title to a band of territory extending from the Black Sea to the Caspian Sea along the southern rim of the Caucasus Mountains. However, in asserting sovereignty over Georgia, Russia also claimed the intervening territories northward to the Caucasian Line (see map 1). But the predominantly Muslim tribes native to this area proved far less willing to give their allegiance to a Christian sovereign. Thus, in practical terms, Georgia formed an island of tsarist power in the southern Caucasus. Consolidation of Russia's position in the Caucasus required the subjugation of the tribes hemmed in between Georgia and the Caucasian Line.

Theater Overview

Home to a cluster of ancient peoples, the Caucasus region has served historically as a crossroads between Europe and Asia, a meeting ground of

Prince Grigory Potemkin

cultures, and, frequently, a battleground. By the early nineteenth century, the inhabitants of the region numbered about 2 million. Prominent among them were the Christian peoples of Georgia and Armenia in the south and the Muslim Azeris along the Caspian Sea shore. Less well known, but central to Russia's strategic problem, were the diverse tribesmen of the interior mountains and forests, with an aggregate population of about one-half million.[2] The chief bastions of resistance to the imposition of Russian rule proved to be in Dagestan, Chechnia, and Avaria in the east and the Kuban River basin in the west.

At its peak, the zone of struggle in the central Caucasus spanned a distance of about 600 kilometers from the Black Sea to the Caspian Sea and approximately 200 kilometers from the Groznaia fortress in the north to Tbilisi, the Georgian capital, in the south. The outstanding topographical feature of the region is the Caucasus Mountains, through which travel was often confined to steep trails and slender defiles. Rugged peaks and deep river gorges carved Dagestan into countless small, remote pockets of arable terrain characteristically flanked by thick forests, which dominated neighboring Chechnia, Avaria, and most of the periphery of the mountains. The isolation nature imposed on the mountain and forest tribes profoundly influenced their cultures. Speaking a variety of languages and dialects, they

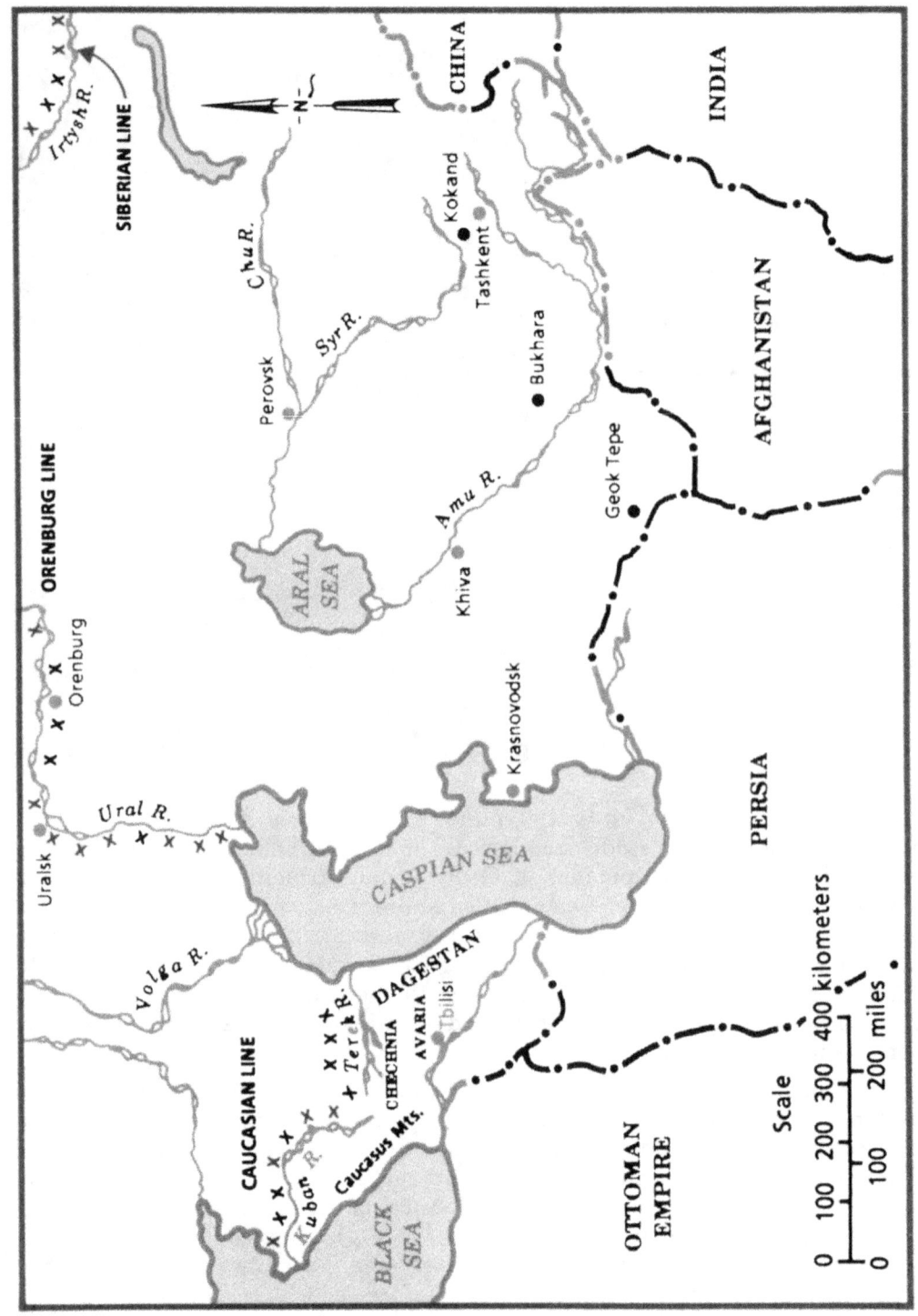

Map 1. Russia's southern frontier in the nineteenth century

lacked any semblance of unity—at least until driven to band together by the imminent threat of Russian control.

Russian military action in the interior of the Caucasus began on a modest scale. During the first two decades of the nineteenth century, Russian commanders in the Caucasus carried out campaigns against Turkey and Persia and secured the Caspian coast and portions of modern Azerbaijan (see map 2). Only gradually did the unruly tribes of the interior present an apparent threat to Russian rule. As their resistance intensified, Russia established a cordon of fortified points around the mountains to separate rebellious mountaineers from those more or less pacified tribes among the foothills. The latter, in close proximity to Russian outposts, had little capacity to resist Russian arms and even came to depend on Russia for defense against mountain raiders. However, successive Russian commanders found it increasingly difficult to contain the mountaineers and demanded a steady expansion of forces merely to maintain the status quo in the northern Caucasus. Russian General Aleksei Petrovich Ermolov viewed the mountains as a "great fortress," equally difficult to storm or besiege.[3]

Russia's subjugation of the central Caucasus is loosely divisible into three stages. During the first stage, from 1801 to 1832, Russia committed limited means to execute what it perceived as a police action that entailed the prevention of mountaineer raids on commercial traffic and friendly villages. During this period, the Caucasian Corps campaigned intermittently, remaining largely on the defensive while maintaining a network of small garrisons. From approximately 1832 to 1845, the mountaineer resistance, fired by the charismatic leadership of Shamil, grew tremendously and challenged the stability of Russian rule. Repeated Russian attempts to crush the mountaineers in a single, large-scale campaign ended in failure. From 1845 to 1859, Russia combined a more patient, methodical approach to the war with a larger commitment of forces. This stage witnessed relentless Russian campaigning along the edges of the mountaineers' strongholds that systematically reduced the territory and population under their control.

The expansion of Russian forces reflects the course of the Caucasian War. As of 1818, General Ermolov, commander of the Caucasus, had no more than 60,000 regulars at his disposal. Subsequent escalation of the struggle during the 1840s forced the expansion of Russian strength to about 200,000 men.[4] Ultimately, according to A. Zisserman, a contemporary observer as well as the biographer of General A. I Bariatinskii, the "conqueror of the Caucasus," all of that general's brilliant planning would have come to nothing had he not had nearly 300,000 men at his command.[5] Russian forces consisted of a mix of regular and irregular (mainly Cossack) units. The former were predominantly ethnic Russians, former peasants drawn from the interior of the empire and trained according to prevailing European norms. The Cossacks, in contrast, were members of a hereditary military class who frequently served on the frontier in the dual role of warriors and colonists. Small native militia formations, including some under the command of native officers, provided additional manpower and were employed

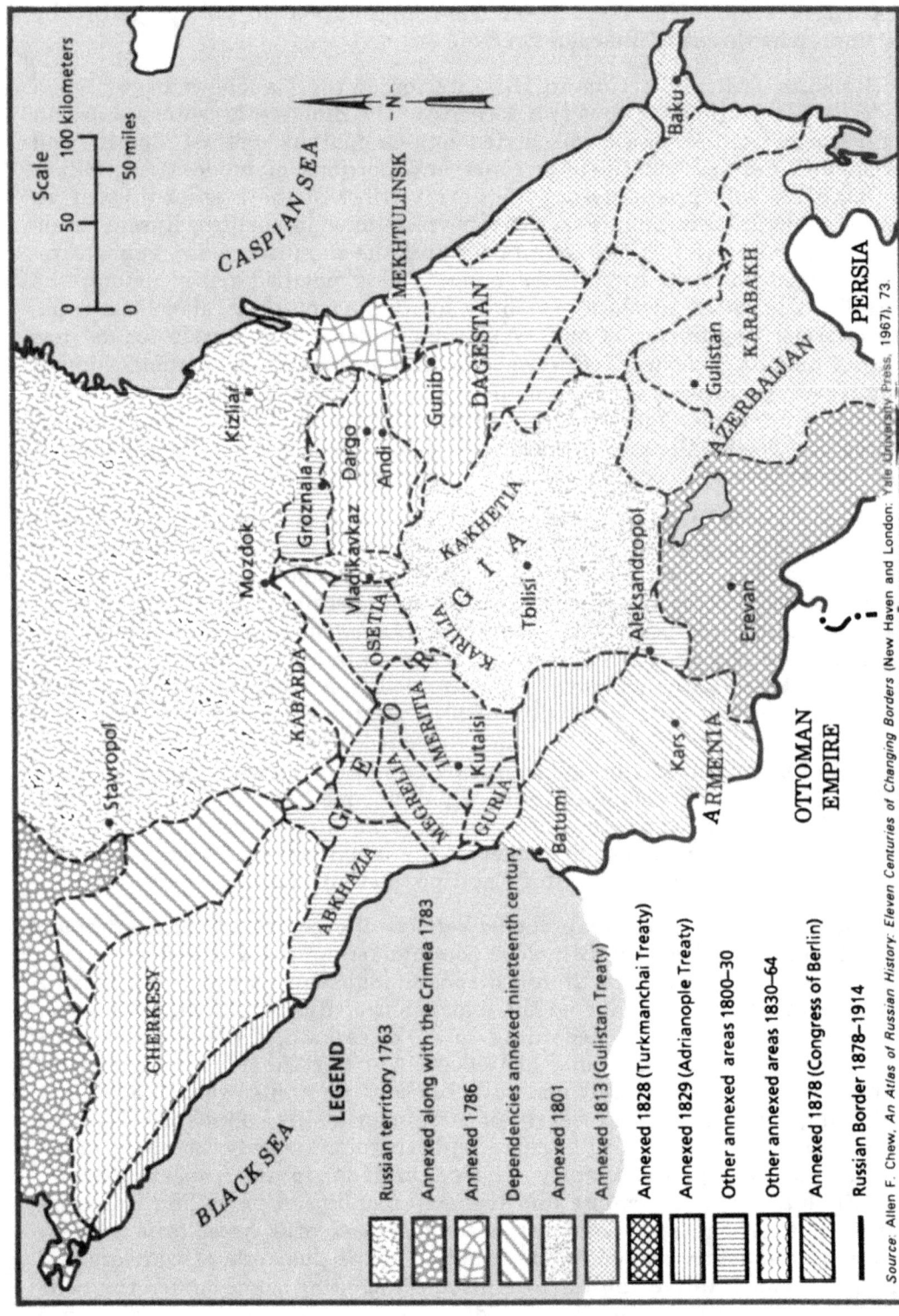

Map 2. The Caucasus and Transcaucasia, 1763—1914

General Aleksei Petrovich Ermolov, the first Russian commander in the Caucasus (1816—27) to confront the mountaineers

extensively for convoy duty. Georgians made up the largest share of the native irregulars.[6]

No one could envision in 1801 the scale of commitment that would be required to subjugate the seemingly backward populace of the mountains. Unknown to most Russians, centuries of struggle against one another and outside invaders had made the mountaineers masters of survival and nurtured among them a warrior tradition based on individual cunning and fearlessness. Until late in the war, when they obtained some modern rifles, the insurgents' arms included sabers, old muskets, and cannon. The mountaineers, however, were able tacticians on the defense or in staging small, guerrilla-style incursions. Experience taught them never to engage a superior enemy when he could bring his full power to bear but rather to use nature as their ally and lure the enemy into combat on unfavorable terms. Yet for all the mountaineers' martial virtues, shifting patterns of alliance and old rivalries restricted even the most elementary coordination of their efforts against a common adversary.

The Caucasian War

For three decades after the Georgian annexation, Russian authorities believed that the mountaineers posed little more than a nuisance to be subdued by scattered police actions. Then, the catalytic force of a religious movement, dubbed "muridism" by the Russians, and the appearance in 1834 of a shrewd and charismatic leader, Shamil, infused new strength into the resistance. (Indeed, the awkward term "muridism" was coined by the Russians from the word "murid," or disciple, as the leader's closest adherents were known.) Shamil combined religious appeal, uncommon political savvy, and the overt threat of force to weld together a military-political alliance of the mountain tribes under so-called *naibs*, or regional commanders. In so doing, Shamil changed the nature of the war—in actuality remaking the contest into a real war. Within a few years, he established a standing infantry and cavalry, raised by levy in each region, and his motley army increasingly resembled a regular European force. Shamil imposed a system of ranks and initiated the manufacture of cannon and gunpowder for his fledgling artillery.[7]

The strategic center of Shamil's power lay among the tribes of Dagestan in the eastern mountains, but his support by the Chechen tribes along the forested northern slopes and foothills was equally crucial in providing him manpower and essential supplies. Only slightly less important were the Lezgian tribes of the southern fringes of the mountains. This study will focus on the subjugation by the Russians of the eastern mountain region under Shamil's direct control.

The western Caucasus (comprising the Transkuban region and the Black Sea coast) was the scene of concurrent military actions, but from 1821, it constituted a separate theater. Though Shamil formed no alliance with the tribes of the Transkuban, his long-term fortunes depended, in part, on the dispersal of Russian forces there. Furthermore, it was the actions of the Abkhazians and other tribes along the Black Sea that raised the intermittent possibility of foreign intervention against Russia. Turkey, with diplomatic backing from Britain, saw in the uprising of the Caucasian tribes an opportunity to restore its former influence along the eastern shore of the Black Sea. Britain, meanwhile, viewed the Caucasus within the context of the great "Eastern Question," the contest for dominance of the Black Sea and the straits leading to it, which Britain hoped to deny to Russia.[8]

When he assumed command of the Caucasus in 1816, General Ermolov had little cause to expect that this would be the theater of the longest sustained conflict in Russian history. With the defeat of Napoleon in 1812–13 and the triumphant march of Russian forces to Paris still a vivid memory, the military might of the empire seemed irresistible. However, Ermolov was a sharp analyst of military and political situations and soon appreciated that the task before him would stretch his resources to the limit. Given the responsibility for defending the 700-mile Caucasian perimeter against raiders, who at any time might sally forth from hidden recesses, Ermolov responded by establishing forts such as Groznaia on the Terek River and Vnezapnaia beyond the Aksai River at the edge of Chechnia. In addition, he campaigned vigorously along the periphery of Dagestan, bringing Tarku, Kurin, the Kazikumukh khanates, Akusha, and most of Large and Small Chechnia under direct imperial authority.

Ermolov thereby became the first Russian chief of the Caucasus to thrust himself directly into the affairs of the mountaineers, who had scarcely ever been subject to interference by outsiders.[9] Historians dispute the effectiveness of Ermolov's military and administrative policies. To his credit, he was among the first Russian commanders to appreciate the importance of opening lines of communications with Russia itself and among key garrisons while maintaining pressure on hostile Chechen tribes by clearing roads into the forests to facilitate the rapid movement of Russian columns. By establishing a fort at Vnezapnaia in 1812, however, Russia alarmed the mountain chieftains with its encroachment. Ermolov also co-opted the elites of friendly tribes, making them officials in his administration. This approach contrasted sharply with his brutal, punitive raids against unsubmissive tribes. For insubordination, Ermolov exacted a stiff price through the wholesale destruction of crops, forests, and villages. In so doing, Ermolov acknowledged that he could not always distinguish between friendly and hostile tribes and that many villages were divided in their opinion of Russian rule. Meanwhile, by the late 1820s, resistance in Dagestan had grown dramatically.[10]

Ermolov reported in 1826 that the mountaineer rebellion was ever more assuming a religious character—a transformation of ominous portent.[11] An uprising among the Chechens in 1826—coinciding with a Persian invasion of Russian-held territory in the south—shattered the illusory calm and convinced Tsar Nicholas I that the advances of the preceding decade were insufficient. Ermolov soon relinquished command in the Caucasus to one of the tsar's favorites, General (Count) I. F. Paskevich. With Nicholas' mandate, Paskevich systematically Russified his administration. Such actions reflected the Russians' erroneous assumption that they could effectively govern peoples farther removed from them in culture and custom than Dagestan was from St. Petersburg and over whom Russia could not consistently assert its authority. If the Christian Georgians were pliable, the Muslim mountain tribes certainly were not. Yet Russia's military presence diminished throughout the remainder of the decade, as wars with Persia (1826) and Turkey (1828—29) held the attention of Russian commanders. During this time, a religious and political leader, Kazi-mullah, gained a following in the mountains and appealed for a holy war against the Russians in 1828. During the next several years, mountain tribesmen attacked Tarku, a small kingdom allied to Russia, as well as Russian fortresses at Vnezapnaia, Burnaia, and Derbent. His resources limited, Paskevich slightly strengthened Russian defenses in the region but concluded that Russia must eventually choose between appeasement or the annihilation of the mountain resistance.[12] Perhaps his greatest contribution was the undertaking of the first military topographical survey of the region, which resulted in the first reasonably complete maps of the Caucasus in 1834. Still, details of the interior mountainous regions remained sketchy.[13] The outbreak of revolt in Poland in 1831 further diverted Russian attention from the Caucasus and necessitated Field Marshal (as of 1829) Paskevich's departure. Thus, little progress was made in the pacification of the Caucasus under Paskevich.

Characteristic of military actions against the mountaineers during this period was an expedition mounted under Lieutenant General G. V. Rosen in 1830 to capture Kazi-mullah at his residence in the village of Gimri. Advancing into the mountains with a force of nearly 5,000 men, Rosen

Events elsewhere diverted General (Count) Paskevich's attention from the mountaineer problem

compelled area tribes to submit but failed to capture Kazi-mullah. Still, Rosen assumed that the point of Russian superiority in arms had been proven and withdrew his column. In reality, the tribes reverted to their past behavior, and the campaign achieved nothing. In the words of N. F. Dubrovin, a nineteenth-century Russian historian of the war in the Caucasus, "It [the expedition] remained only a testament to the absence of firmness, persistence and definition in the orders from our side."[14] Dubrovin's point was well taken in so far as Rosen labored under the contrary guidance that he must, on the one hand, bring the mountaineers to heel, while, on the other, minimize his use of force and encourage trade relations. In addition, Rosen lacked the power of theaterwide command vested in Paskevich. An 1835 directive from the war minister, Prince A. I. Chernyshev, specified objectives, the size of forces to be employed, and individual field commanders for the coming year.[15] Wise or not, the policy failed.

Immediately after Rosen's withdrawal from Gimri, Kazi-mullah summoned a council of mullahs and elders of area tribes and laid out his future plan to unify the tribes of the eastern Caucasus to drive out the Russians. Accordingly, Rosen reported to Chernyshev the futility of conducting scattered campaigns to places Russia had neither the capacity nor intent to hold. The result of such actions was to disperse the natives temporarily while antagonizing them in the long run. However, what most troubled Rosen was his belief that the menace was increasing. Given their warlike character and great resourcefulness, the mountaineers might be a menace to Russian rule if united by Kazi-mullah. Thus, to secure the Caucasian Line, Rosen required far more than the 15 infantry regiments (54,000 men) and garrison forces on hand.[16]

Though it briefly raised Russian hopes, the sudden death of Kazi-mullah during the Russian campaign on Gimri in 1832 did not spell the end of resistance. Rather, what followed belied all expectations. After a brief interim, Shamil, Kazi-mullah's deputy, succeeded as imam and surpassed his mentor both as a charismatic leader and as a pragmatic organizer. Well-educated in the traditions of the Islamic faith, Shamil had also absorbed essential lessons of warfare that made him a formidable strategic adversary. Through the preceding two decades of fighting, the mountaineers had lacked the concentration and coordination of forces needed to inflict any but minor defeats on the Russians. So deficient were the mountaineers in conducting offensive tactical operations more complex than an ordinary raid that the Russians considered a detachment of several companies sufficient to constitute an independent force. The mountaineers repeatedly proved unable to defeat a disciplined formation and showed no capacity whatever to cope effectively with artillery.[17]

The resulting complacency engendered among Russian commanders is evident in their failure to follow up the defeat of Kazi-mullah and press the attack aggressively against the rebels during the middle and late 1830s.[18] Unaware of the qualitative transformation taking place in the enemy in the mountains, the commander of the Caucasian Corps concentrated his attention on securing the Black Sea and Caspian Sea coastlines. In essence, the Russians assumed a reactive posture, responding to enemy raids but failing to engage the mountain tribes in any systematic fashion. The Russians' concomitant failure to strengthen imperial rule among the submissive tribes along the fringes of the mountains carried the seeds of great trouble to follow. Friendly peoples in the region were constantly exposed to the predations and intimidations of their more warlike neighbors in the mountains. For example, in 1834, the mountaineers struck at Khunzakh, center of the strategically positioned Avar khanate, and exterminated the ruling family, which had been loyal to Russia. Under such circumstances, stable rule was impossible.[19]

If the Russians failed to develop an overall approach to the struggle in the Caucasus, the same error cannot be attributed to Shamil. The new imam exploited the breathing space to consolidate his authority and organize a political-economic system as near to an overarching polity as the mountain tribes had ever known. Though he based his claim to power on religious authority, Shamil also was a consummate politician, drawing on every resource at his disposal to forge an alliance among the doggedly independent chieftains. Unswerving in his goals, he refused the offer of a pardon from the tsar in 1837 in exchange for his recognition of imperial authority. Instead, Shamil tended to the defense of the mountains. He urged the populace in exposed (to the Russians) parts of Chechnia to withdraw their villages deeper into the forests, both to reduce their vulnerability and to deny their food, property, and services to the Russian Army.[20] Furthermore, he created a support system by which the inhabitants of a village destroyed by the Russians would be sheltered by neighboring tribes until the next harvest.[21] Shamil established his own headquarters at the well-fortified village of Akhulgo, deep in the mountains along the Andi River (see map 3). Accessible only by difficult routes and perched atop rocky heights flanked on three sides by precipitous river gorges, Akhulgo enjoyed an ideal natural defensive position.

When the Russians resolved to mount an expedition to Akhulgo in 1839 to capture Shamil, the commander, General P. Kh. Grabbe, selected a route about fifty miles long, beginning at the fortress at Vnezapnaia and running through Salatau and Gumbet, both bastions of support for Shamil. Grabbe believed that the defeat of Shamil's forces on the way would weaken the morale of the garrison at Akhulgo and deny support from natives on the left bank of the Andi River. In addition, success along this axis would secure an exposed section of Russian defensive positions shielding Tarku and the Kumyk plain.[22] Then, upon arriving at Ashilta, a village near Akhulgo on the Andi River, the Russians would be able to establish communications lines through Khunzakh to Temir-Khan-Shura.

Departing from Vnezapnaia on 21 May, Grabbe's so-called Chechen detachment (*otriad*) passed through the mountain ridge separating Salatau from the Kumyk tribes and made camp in the Tala-su valley with 6,616 men and 16 field guns. The arrival of 2 additional battalions from the Apsheron Regiment—with 1 more to come later—brought the total strength of the force to 9 battalions or about 8,000 men. The column carried supplies with it sufficient for the trek through Gumbet, from which point, after crossing the Andi River, it would be essential to open communications lines to Temir-Khan-Shura for resupply. On 25—26 May, the column completed a perilous crossing of the pass at Sauk-bulakh. Every step of the cluttered trail had to be cleared of rocks and debris as the troops advanced along a steep incline for some twelve miles. Upon reaching the snowy top, the column was running short of water and fuel. The subsequent descent of the ponderous force toward Gumbet was no less trying, requiring single-file movement down the rocky slope.[23]

By 30 May, the column trudged ahead to the fortified village of Arguani, where Shamil waited with a force estimated at 16,000 tribesmen, most of them Lezgians. Shamil's decision to stand fast forced Grabbe's hand. Given the extreme difficulty and military risk of withdrawal as well as his own eagerness to engage the enemy, Grabbe resolved to take the mountaineer positions by storm. Grabbe divided his force, posing two-battalion columns

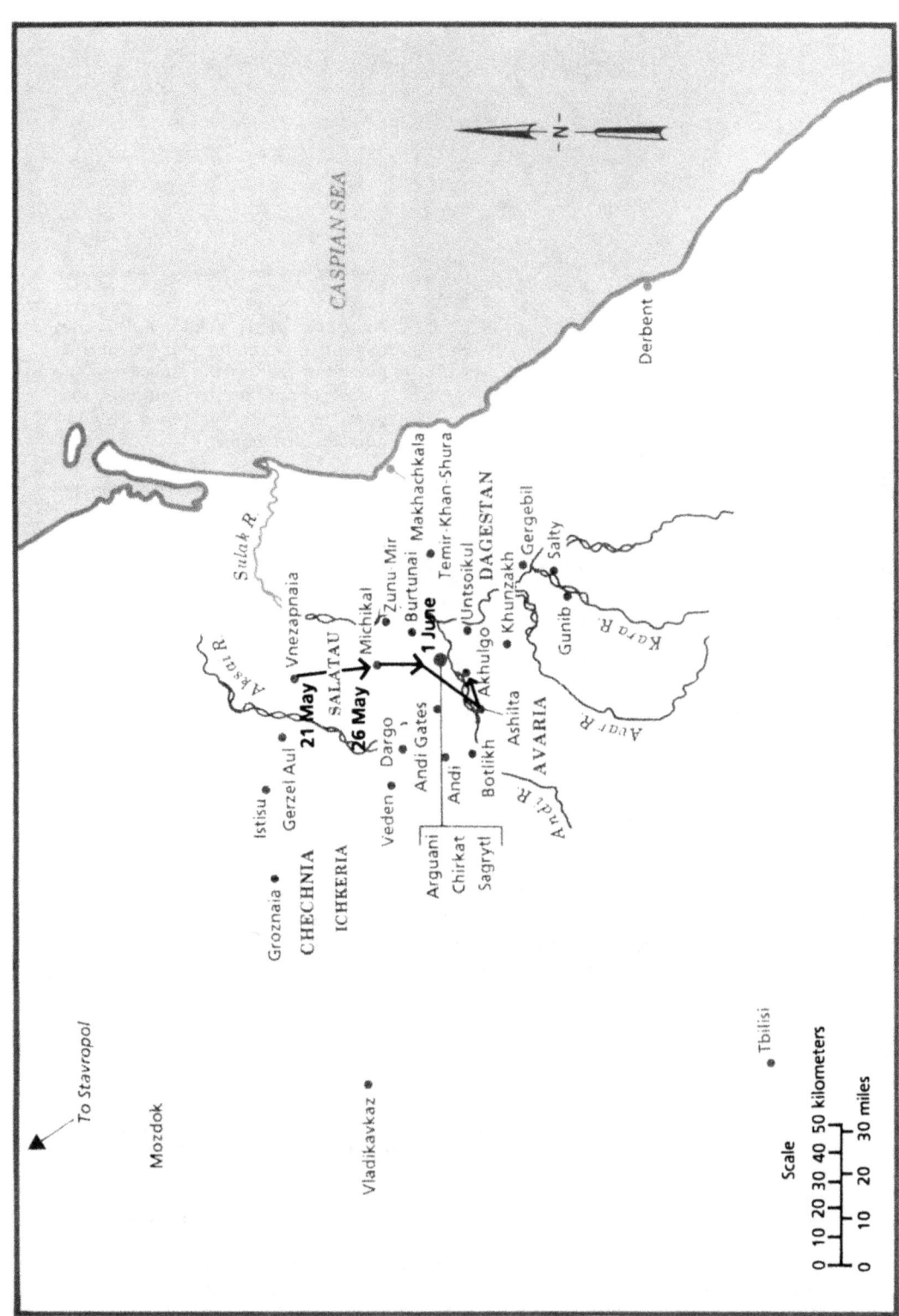

Map 3. The Akhulgo campaign, 1839

An early print shows a Russian column proceeding along a narrow mountain road in the Caucasus. The rugged terrain and fortified town suggest the difficulties faced by commanders and troops.

against the flanks of the fortified village. His column commanders personally reconnoitered the approaches to Arguani and at 1700 began their assault on a broad front. The Russians broke into the village on 1 June and cleared it building by building, as the battle quickly dissolved into countless small struggles.[24] Lieutenant Dmitrii A. Miliutin, an officer of the Russian General Staff (later a historian of this campaign and the Russian minister of war), recorded the following description:

> At 9 AM our troops were already in occupation of the greater part of the village, and even of the flat roofs of those houses where the Murids still defended themselves, but the bloodshed continued the whole day through until dark. The only way to drive the Murids out of the saklias [dwellings] was to break holes through the roofs and throw down burning substances, and so set fire to the beams. Even then they remained many hours in the houses, though sometimes they found means to break through and secretly pass from one dwelling to another but many bodies were found completely charred. In spite of their disadvantageous position ... the most fanatic amongst them were satisfied if they could destroy even some of the infidels.[25]

Shamil realized that his position was collapsing and retreated. The 2-day battle ended in the destruction of Arguani and cost Grabbe 30 officers and 611 men. Shamil lost perhaps 2,000 warriors in the desperate engagement.[26]

Before pressing on, the Russians systematically demolished the 500 or so stone dwellings that once made up the village. The fall of Arguani opened the way to Akhulgo, to which Shamil had withdrawn with his most dedicated followers. The Russians marched to the village of Chirkat, overlooking the Andi River, and paused to restore the bridge, which had been burned by the natives. While waiting for the engineers to finish their work (never actually completed for lack of materials), Grabbe dispatched a "flying detachment" (*letuchii otriad*—a highly mobile unit) consisting of two battalions of the Kurin Regiment and all of his cavalry to meet a supply column from Temir-Khan-Shura (traveling under the escort of friendly native militia) to assist it across the Andi River at Sagrytl. Securing the route toward Temir-Khan-Shura was now more critical because insurgents in Grabbe's rear had cut the road back to Vnezapnaia. Once new supplies were brought forward, Grabbe, now with a foothold on both sides of the river, advanced to Ashilta and then to Akhulgo.

At Akhulgo, which had a total population of only 4,000 (including not more than a thousand armed fighters), Shamil busied himself with the recruitment of additional warriors from other area villages. Akhulgo actually comprised three separate defensive positions. Old and New Akhulgo lay on the opposite sides of a deep river gorge (linked only by a few wooden bridges) and together occupied a notch in the Andi River that covered all approaches from the east, north, and west. To the south, or forward from New Akhulgo, stood Surkhai's "tower," a stone fortification atop a treacherously steep crag with a commanding view of the ground that any attacker must cross. The tower also served as the key communications link between the fortifications of Old and New Akhulgo. Having learned the value of artificial barriers, the mountaineers supplemented their natural defensive positions by erecting stone walls and connecting trench lines in front of the tower and the village.[27]

By the time he reached Akhulgo, Grabbe's effective force numbered about 6,000 men and several thousand native militia. Lacking the strength to impose a full blockade on Akhulgo, Grabbe made a futile effort to lay siege to the village from the southern side of the Andi River, establishing a cordon of small advance posts and moving them forward nightly (under cover of darkness) to tighten the noose. Yet as long as Shamil retained communications across the river, the attempt was doomed to failure. Each effort to tighten the blockade brought significant Russian losses, as many of the men had no idea how best to employ the terrain for cover. Furthermore, Grabbe lacked enough engineers, artillery, and shells to mount a full-scale effort.[28] Meanwhile, Shamil attempted to seize the initiative by placing a force on a ridge near Ashilta, thereby immediately threatening the Russian headquarters staff. Luckily for Grabbe, the Russians detected preparations for an attack and drove the mountaineers off.

Shortly, Grabbe refocused his efforts on the blockade of Akhulgo, establishing six battery positions and deploying sapper units along the river banks. His success depended first of all on the capture of Surkhai's tower, which, though defended by a mere hundred men, proved an extremely difficult objective. On 29 June, three batteries of light field guns opened fire on the tower but, due to the steep angle of fire, had little effect against the rock piles obscuring the fortifications.[29] After this brief and useless preparation, 2 battalions of the Kurin Regiment and one each from the Apsheron and Kabardian Regiments attempted to scale the heights and storm the tower but were driven back at a cost of 315 casualties.[30] The mountaineers paid a high price as well, losing the fiery commander of the position, Ali Bek. Grabbe immediately resolved to try again, this time shifting four field guns to the eastern side of the crag where he knew the angle of fire was less steep and the possible result more favorable.[31] Continuous pounding here, made possible by ammunition resupply from a caravan from Temir-Khan-Shura, eventually drove the defenders from their positions.

The fall of Surkhai's tower altered the tactical situation sharply. The Russians were now able to draw in their siege lines tightly around Akhulgo and mount two light guns on the rubble atop the tower. With the arrival of three additional battalions on 12 July, Grabbe made the abrupt decision to storm Akhulgo on the 16th. This decision, based in part on intelligence reports that enemy morale was poor,[32] greatly surprised Miliutin, who at the general's request had just completed a new scheme for the placement of Russian forces in anticipation of continuing the siege:

> We could not explain to ourselves what aroused our command to set about such an important, difficult feat so suddenly, without any advance preparatory measures. We had hardly even succeeded in forming our dispositions and distributing our forces; at our batteries there were not stored sufficient shells; there was not time by means of our preliminary artillery fire to ease the path of the infantry.[33]

Grabbe, nonetheless, organized three attack columns, the strongest consisting of three battalions under Lieutenant General (Baron) Vrangel, and struck directly at New Akhulgo, while the others did just enough to tie up enemy forces and sow confusion. The second column, a single battalion, moved against Old Akhulgo, and the third, one and one-half battalions, occupied the gorge of the Ashilta River to ensure the isolation of respective enemy garrisons in Old and New Akhulgo. After an artillery preparation, the assault began. Vrangel's battalions encountered many obstacles and deadly cross fire in the narrow sector in front of New Akhulgo and were soon pinned down, managing to withdraw only under the cover of night with over 800 casualties. Every officer in Vrangel's command was killed or wounded. The Russians estimated Shamil's losses at 150 after the first day of fighting.[34]

Undeterred, Grabbe resumed his blockade and sent 4 squadrons of cavalry (of varying size) to seal off the left bank of the river opposite Akhulgo, thereby curtailing further supply or escape for Shamil, who had evacuated his wounded and had perhaps 1,800 men remaining at his disposal. A standoff persisted for the next several weeks, during which living conditions in Akhulgo deteriorated rapidly and disease tore into the strength of the defenders. Groping for an escape from his predicament, Shamil offered to negotiate and even delivered his own twelve-year-old son to Grabbe as proof of his earnest desire for a settlement. However, a brief meeting with Grabbe—who would accept no terms short of surrender—achieved nothing. By mid-August, the ravages of poor sanitation and illness took a toll on the Russians as well, reducing the average battalion to a strength of about 450 able men (for Russian deployments, see map 4).[35]

Grabbe now realized that delay was costly and planned another general assault for 17 August. Once again, he dispatched three columns against the mountaineer stronghold. The main force of three battalions struck the walls of New Akhulgo and easily pierced the outer defenses. A desperate Shamil sent out his son one more time under a white flag, and talks resumed briefly but to no effect. The antagonists rejoined the battle on 21 August. Amid fierce fighting, Shamil managed to slip away with his family. The Russians took 900 prisoners, most of them women and children, some of whom, in the end, opted for death over captivity. In all, the 80-day campaign for Akhulgo cost Russia over 3,000 casualties and produced a deceptive result. Strictly speaking, the capture of Akhulgo had been a military success. The enemy stronghold had fallen, Grabbe had demonstrated Russia's ability to drive deep into the mountains against great obstacles, and Shamil had lost many of his staunchest warriors. Moreover, the imam himself had barely escaped. But as Dubrovin observed, the "brilliant action of [Russian] forces and the huge loss in men brought no result and did not impress the mountaineers with our strength."[36]

In the wake of Russia's "victory" at Akhulgo, Shamil emerged stronger than before. His prestige fortified by the inevitable retreat of Russian troops, he rallied the mountain tribes and carried out a series of offensive actions heretofore unthinkable. Russian influence in Dagestan, Chechnia, and Avaria plummeted, but the damage was not confined to the eastern Caucasus. The Cherkes tribes in the west also rose and devastated Russia's Black Sea garrisons.[37] In 1842, Grabbe mounted an expedition against Shamil's new center at Dargo and this time failed utterly. Short of water, badly strung out over a soggy trail in inclement weather, and constantly harassed by enemy fire in the thick Chechen forests, the Russian column had to turn back without reaching its objective. The resulting consternation in St. Petersburg was so great that the war minister, Prince Chernyshev, suspended military operations and visited the Caucasus to make a personal assessment. The mountaineers exploited the pause to overrun Avaria, and in 1843, Shamil launched a broad offensive.

Shamil's campaign against Russian forts in Avaria marked his maturation as a military planner and, in particular, his ability to grasp the strategic situation and implement a broad plan.[38] Undetected by the Russians, on 28 August 1843, 3 separate forces of mountaineers, numbering about 10,000 men in all, suddenly converged on Untsoikul, where they outmaneuvered a

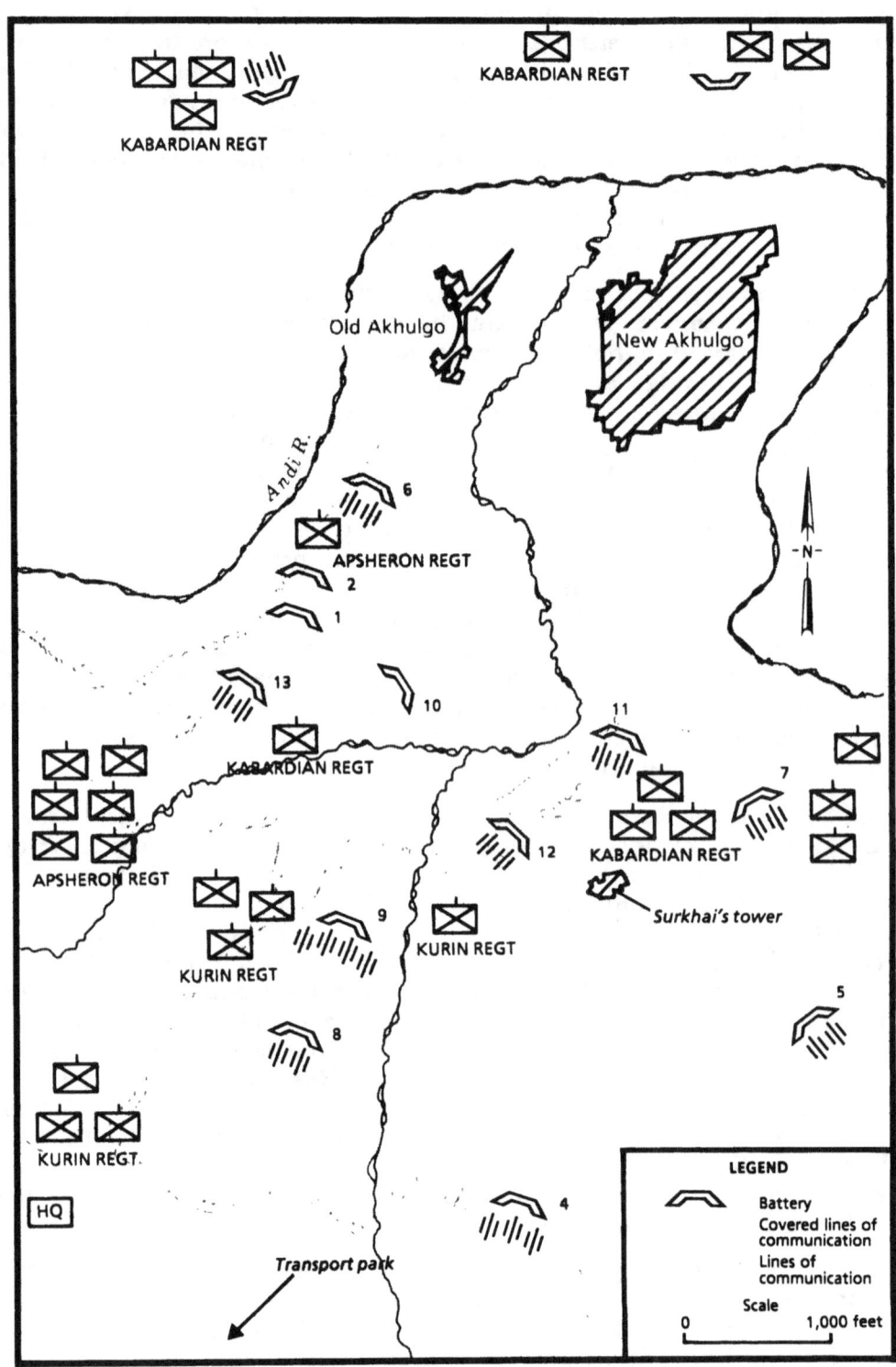

Map 4. Russian positions, 4—22 August 1839 (up to the capture of Akhulgo)

Russian column and killed 486 officers and men. Two days later, they captured the local garrison. Within the next 4 weeks, Shamil laid waste to every Russian outpost in Avaria save one and inflicted a total of over 2,000 casualties.[39] While the Russians were still in disarray, but assuming that the worst had passed, Shamil seized Gergebil at the junction of the Avar and Kazi-kumuch Rivers, from which he could command the only communications route linking Avaria to the Russian base at Temir-Khan-Shura. By feigning preparations for an invasion of the Kumyk plain, Shamil succeeded in drawing Russian forces away from Gergebil, which fell into his hands after a protracted struggle.[40] Such rapid, well-disguised, and skillfully executed movements enabled Shamil's guerrilla army to seize and hold the initiative and befuddle the Russians.

Russian Analysis and Reassessment

The disasters of 1840—43 did not bring about an immediate change in Russia's conduct of the war in the Caucasus, but the foundation for a new approach was being developed. In fact, the central elements that might contribute to a methodical reduction of the Caucasus had been identified years before. Ermolov himself once observed that "not the bayonet but the axe" would prove the key to pacification of the region.[41] The key was to clear and hold a road net through the Caucasus. Ermolov, however, never possessed the manpower necessary to implement such a policy. Another who foresaw, to some degree, the ultimate methods of subjugation was General A. A. Veliaminov, who wrote a lengthy commentary in 1832 in which he advocated the gradual extension of forts into enemy territory as well as the establishment of settlements by the Cossacks. This expedient would block the path of invading mountaineers. Yet, he cautioned, this method alone would not yield victory for another thirty years. Rapid progress required the creation of 5 independent military columns about 7,000 strong to carry out relentless campaigns against the sanctuaries and economic base of the mountaineers. Only when deprived of the material means to carry on would they submit.[42]

One fact apparent to analysts of the late 1830s and early 1840s was that the Russians could not pacify the mountaineers until they were able to strike at their villages with impunity. Two of the most insightful observers of the situation were young officers of the General Staff, Captain (after his first Caucasus tour) Dmitrii Miliutin and Captain I. Mochulskii, who accepted temporary assignments in the Caucasus to gain a better practical understanding of their craft. Indeed, there being no active theater of conventional combat, the Academy of the General Staff looked upon the Caucasus as a "combat school" for young officers.[43]

Mochulskii spent a tour of duty in the Caucasus in 1837. Miliutin followed in 1839 and again in 1843. Mochulskii wrote a study on his return that identified the principal causes of Russian failure in the Caucasus. Mochulskii noted the advantages afforded the enemy by the extremely difficult terrain as well as the potent blend of spiritual and military power inherent in the resistance movement. Nevertheless, Mochulskii attributed most causes of failure directly to Russian shortcomings. For example, he believed Russian officers were inexperienced and had inadequate tactical training for mountain warfare. They neither knew the terrain of the Caucasus nor understood how to use it for such purposes as setting up an ambush. In addition, Russian forces were not properly equipped and wore the same woolen coats, socks, and boot linings through winter and summer alike. They also suffered from boredom and poor morale. Furthermore, given their European-style training, commanders were intellectually wedded to heavy artillery and cumbersome supply trains that left them too dependent on a poor road system.[44]

Both Mochulskii and Miliutin emphasized the absence of any coherent policy by the Russians in the Caucasus as a crucial factor in the squandering of past efforts. Diverging from Veliaminov's appraisal, each lamented the maintenance of over 150 forts, which they saw as a hopeless dispersal of available manpower. They believed such small garrisons could not control substantial territory and often were not secure themselves.[45] Advancing suggestions of his own in a memorandum titled "Thoughts About the Means of Establishing Russian Rule in the Caucasus," Miliutin called for a reduction in the number of forts, preserving only those in strategic locations to control the main tribes and guarantee principal communications routes. Given large garrisons, such forts could serve as bases from which powerful mobile columns could move at any time to restore order or extend a zone of Russian control. Miliutin hoped that through a more systematic military penetration of the Caucasus, a cultural policy less antagonistic to local customs, and the promotion of trade and industry, Russia ultimately could persuade most of the Caucasian population of the advantages—not to mention the inevitability—of imperial rule.[46]

Notwithstanding such analysis, the Russian command in St. Petersburg and the Caucasus failed to craft a systematic approach to conquest. Still, the Russians had by 1840 made significant tactical adjustments. Recognizing the vulnerability of columns extended on the march, commanders, wherever conditions permitted, came to employ a close, rectangular formation, the length of which depended on the size of the supply train and other factors. The sides of the column reached from the advance guard to the rear guard. Cavalry, artillery, and transport moved within the rectangle, while groups of sharpshooters formed an outer security cordon.[47] The Russians also made a practice of forming square encampments, placing the infantry and artillery on the sides. Smaller forces often formed their supply wagons into a laager. In addition, given the importance they placed on mobility, the Russians developed a light mountain gun (a portable artillery piece) for use in the Caucasus, and the Caucasian Corps deployed Russia's first mountain gun battery in its organization in 1842.[48]

Final Phase of the War

Count M. S. Vorontsov assumed command in the Caucasus in 1844 and, though named viceroy with full military and civil authority, found himself under immediate pressure from Tsar Nicholas to annihilate Shamil's forces in a single, decisive campaign of the very type the army had been unable to execute in the past.[49] Veteran commanders in the Caucasus were skeptical. General Adjutant Neidhart, Vorontsov's predecessor, asserted that Shamil would probably withdraw from his new headquarters at Dargo rather than offer the decisive battle the tsar sought. Furthermore, Shamil might take the opportunity to make incursions elsewhere, where Russian forces would be weak.[50] Still, the campaign went forward, and Neidhart himself worked to secure the system of supply—a critical function in view of the fact that provisions could not be obtained on the way (see map 5). In the end, native bearers moved half of the requisite supplies.[51]

Vorontsov took 42 guns; 21 battalions, supported by 4 sapper companies; 1,600 irregular cavalry; and about 1,000 native militia—a total of about 18,000 men. Some were to remain at advanced supply points along the way, and a force estimated at thirteen battalions would actually enter the mountains.[52] The forces assembled in Salatau in May and moved toward Andi with the appearance of the first grass in the mountains. Vorontsov occupied Kyrk Pass on 5 June, leaving an occupying force of five battalions. Soon, he ran into foul weather.

On 6 June, General Passek led the advance guard in pursuit of an enemy force about ten miles ahead of the main column. Without orders and neglecting to send word back to the main column, Passek proceeded to the heights of Zunu-Mir. The problem with this move was that Vorontsov intended to take the column to Andi via Michikal, not Zunu-Mir.

Thus, by the time Passek halted in the bitter cold at Zunu-Mir, he faced a dilemma. Though short of supplies and out of contact with the main column, he dared not withdraw for fear that the appearance of a retreat would rally more of the native populace around Shamil. When Vorontsov finally learned of the situation, he directed Passek to send back only his cavalry and mounted native militia, there being no forage for the horses at Zunu-Mir.[53] The action came too late, however, to save some 500 horses from breakdown. In addition, approximately 450 men suffered frostbite before Vorontsov reached Passek on 11 June.[54]

All the while, Shamil remained just out of reach of the Russian advance and refused to give battle even at the so-called Andi Gates, a principal passageway into hostile Lezgian territory. Instead, the wily guerrilla leader pulled back the remaining ten miles to Dargo. Finally, on 4 July, with only a six-day supply of provisions remaining,[55] Vorontsov decided to march on Dargo with his main force. At about the same time, he relayed word to General Freitag, commander of the Left Flank of the Caucasian Line (at the northern edge of Dagestan), to be prepared to lead a column in support of a possible exit of the expedition from Dargo in that direction. On 7 July, after a brief but fierce fight, the Russians took Dargo but, as in the past, not Shamil. Nor, with a total force of 7,940 infantry, 1,218 cavalry, 342 artillerymen and 16 guns, had they managed to administer a sound beating to the enemy. The mountaineers (mostly Chechens) vanished into

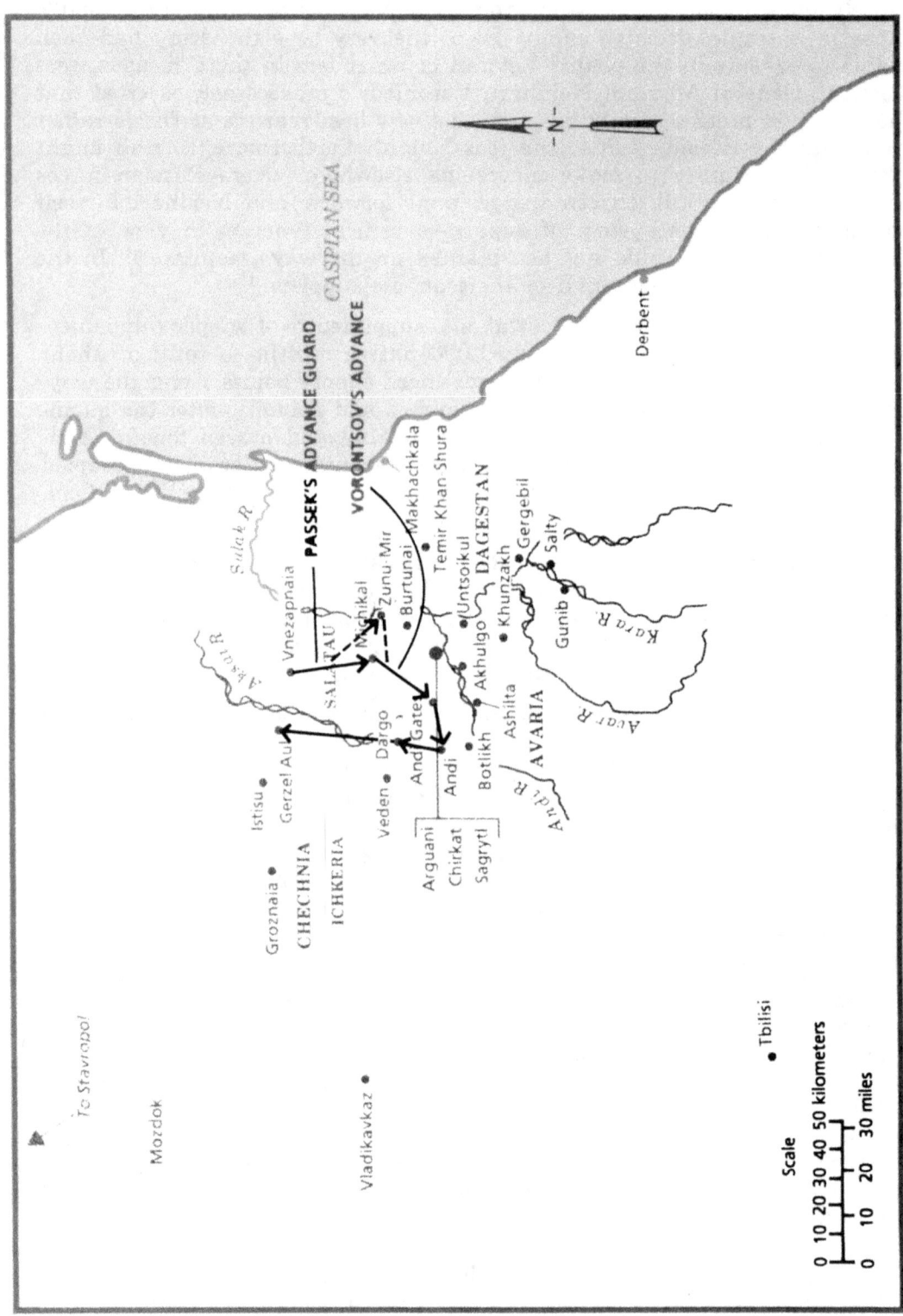

Map 5. The Dargo campaign, 1845

the forest—but remained nearby, convinced that an opportunity to destroy Vorontsov's column would come as it departed through Ichkeria.[56]

Having raised the flag at Dargo, Vorontsov's immediate concern was to ensure the arrival of his latest, and urgently awaited, supply column. On 9 July, he split his force, sending half his infantry, cavalry, and artillery in a detachment under Lieutenant General K. von Klugenau to meet the train and lead it through the forests. In particular, Vorontsov's decision to encumber the escort force with artillery and cavalry in unsuitable forest terrain drew criticism from later analysts. Passek blazed the trail for Klugenau with the advance guard, encountering many obstacles (such as piles of felled trees) erected by the mountaineers to impede any Russian withdrawal. In the process of clearing the barriers of enemy fighters and struggling with unseen snipers in the forests, the column began to disintegrate, presenting just the opportunity the mountaineers sought. In the disaster that followed, the guerrillas swarmed around isolated groups of men, killing Passek along with 556 officers and men.[57] A dispirited Klugenau almost abandoned the attempt to return to Dargo in favor of a retreat through Dagestan, but after a grim march, he rejoined Vorontsov and the main column.

On 11 July, the reunited force embarked on a difficult journey, not over the route by which it had come, but in the direction of the village of Gerzel Aul so as to prevent, as before, the appearance of a retreat. On the first day of the march, repeating the mistake of Passek's advance guard, the 3d Battalion of the Lublin Jaeger Regiment rushed ahead to attack hastily formed enemy positions along the road, which resulted in its own temporary isolation and left a unit of sappers exposed whose task it was to clear the road. Soon, the supply train of the main column was under attack. By the time Klugenau (entrusted by Vorontsov with operational control of the column) restored order, his losses after two days of fighting mounted to 553 killed and almost 800 wounded.[58]

On the night of 12 July, Vorontsov sent five copies of an order to General Freitag by five different routes requesting that he come immediately to meet the expedition in the vicinity of Gerzel Aul.[59] The next day, Vorontsov's column, with eleven badly depleted battalions, advanced along the Aksai River in textbook fashion, with advance and rear guards drawn in close to the main column and an infantry cordon on either side (see table 1). The Russian column encountered resistance en route, and a serious action on 16 July cost Vorontsov 103 men killed and an additional 372 wounded.[60]

By now, Vorontsov could go on no longer. His strongest battalion was reduced to 300 combat-ready infantrymen, and he had 1,500 sick and wounded to care for. Moreover, his artillery had lost 400 of 635 horses and most of its guns had to be destroyed. As of 17 July, Vorontsov's remaining artillery consisted of two light field guns and six mountain guns.[61] Luckily, his messengers had successfully slipped through guerrilla lines, and on 18 July, a relief column under Freitag's command arrived. The expedition was

TABLE 1
Vorontsov's Column Order

Advance guard under Major General Beliavskii
    3d Battalion, Apsheron Regiment
    1st Battalion, Lublin Jaeger Regiment
    5th Sapper Battalion
    3 companies, Caucasian Rifle Battalion
    4 mountain guns, Number 3 Battery
    Assorted mounted militia

Main column under Lieutenant General von Klugenau
    1st Battalion, Lithuanian Jaeger Regiment
    2d Battalion, Zamotsk Jaeger Regiment
    3d Battalion, Lublin Jaeger Regiment
    2 light field guns, Number 7 Battery
    2 mountain guns, Number 1 Battery
    3 mountain guns, Number 3 Battery
    Supply train and the wounded

Rear Guard under Major General Labyntsov
    1st and 2d Battalions, Prince Chernyshev Regiment
    2 mountain guns, Number 3 Battery
    Assorted Cossacks

Right Cordon
    3d and 4th Battalions, Navagin Infantry Regiment
    Gurian Militia
    Tiflis Druzhina (troop), Georgian Militia

Left Cordon
    Composite (*svodnyi*) Battalion, Kurin Regiment
    Guria Druzhina, Georgian Militia

Source: L.-D.G., "Pokhod 1845 goda," 56.

saved, but only after total casualties of 3 generals, 186 officers, and 3,321 men.[62]

Despite its tragic dimensions, the Dargo expedition provided the impetus for a crucial change in Russia's approach to the war. Never again would a large Russian column drive into the mountains without first having completely secured its rear and lines of communication.[63] Vorontsov resolved that Russia must henceforth move forward slowly, securing the plains and foothills before trying to corner Shamil in the mountains. In particular, Large and Small Chechnia now stood out as the focal point of Russian operations. Reduction of the Chechnian forests and foothills would eventually deprive Shamil of a critical source of manpower and provisions and make possible a direct advance into deepest Dagestan.[64]

The year 1846 marked the beginning of a new phase in the Caucasian War—in no small measure because Nicholas refrained from further interference. Vorontsov now blended patience in military policy with decentralized administration, which entailed greater reliance on native officials. He also did much to restore the privileges of tribal leaders, whose powers had eroded under the influence of "muridism," and oversaw completion of the strategic Georgian Military Road joining Tbilisi and the Caucasian Line. Although the Russians had yet to crystallize a coherent military plan, Vorontsov sensibly confined himself to limited, achievable objectives and denied Shamil further victories. In tribute to Vorontsov's measured advance, General Staff historian, D. I. Romanovskii, later wrote that "Russia did not make a single sacrifice or suffer a single casualty that did not advance the great enterprise of pacification of the Caucasus." Yet Romanovskii and others questioned Vorontsov's lack of energy and failure to exploit opportunities.[65]

Generals Freitag and Bariatinskii, in succession, served as executors of Vorontsov's policy on the Left Flank facing the Chechen forests. Each proved a capable and ruthless executor of a cut-and-burn policy to clear the zone as a base for future operations while placing the natives in a state of unquestioning submission. The recapture of Salty in 1847 and Gergebil in 1848 marked the consolidation of Russian gains and foreshadowed greater triumphs to come. Shamil, fearing a decline in his influence, tried to rekindle the fire of muridism by threatening to resign as imam. But by 1852, Chechnia offered no sanctuary from Russian onslaughts, and large numbers of natives were forcibly resettled in areas under Russian control. Vorontsov also organized native militias in Kabarda and elsewhere.[66] Systematic deforestation and the destruction of crops and villages in Chechnia continued in a series of winter campaigns until the outbreak of the Crimean War in 1853.

As Russia's fortunes rose, Shamil's began a corresponding, if at first imperceptible, decline. His military efforts to win Kabarda away from Russian control failed, and political setbacks compounded his frustration. In particular, he alienated much of the mountain population with his attempt in 1846 to have his own son recognized as his heir.[67] The tribes that had accepted Shamil as imam and head of the resistance were not yet willing to grant him dynastic succession. According to the early Soviet Marxist historian, M. N. Pokrovskii, the great successes of the period 1840—45 bred complacency among the mountaineers, and many chieftains began to chafe under the draconian discipline demanded by Shamil.[68] Thus, due to the combined effects of increasing pressure by the Russians and diminishing cohesiveness among the mountain tribes, Shamil was not in a position to take advantage of the increased strain on Russian military resources brought on by the Crimean War. While he received ample encouragement from the Turks and English, who in 1854 shipped him late-model rifles, he hoped in vain for an allied landing in the Caucasus.[69] Shamil did mount one major offensive in 1854, when he assembled a force of 15,000 to 20,000 warriors to drive on the Russian headquarters at Tbilisi. But facing popular resistance by the Christian Georgians and threatened by a Chechen uprising in his rear, Shamil's campaign faltered against the Russians after a bitter defeat near the village of Istisu.[70]

From this point forward in the war, the major protagonist in the Caucasian drama was General Bariatinskii. A participant in the Dargo campaign in 1845 and a highly successful commander of the Left Flank of the Caucasian Line against the Chechens beginning in 1851, Bariatinskii believed in aggressive prosecution of the struggle. Much impressed and no doubt influenced by Miliutin's 1854 study titled *Thoughts on the Means for the Establishment of Russian Domination in the Caucasus*, the general selected Miliutin as his chief of staff upon his own appointment as viceroy of the Caucasus in 1856 by Tsar Alexander II.[71] Bariatinskii intended to subdue the mountaineers by the same relentless pressure he had employed in Chechnia. The general had forests cut and villages and crops burned,[72] leaving the Chechens to choose between death, flight, or settlement on Russian territory. A thorough and systematic Russian campaign of resettlement began in 1855.[73] Bariatinskii's mandate was to conclude the war quickly and at minimum cost. As War Minister I. O. Sukhozanet reminded the general, "To achieve a significant reduction of [Russian] forces would be a service surpassing glorious victories."[74]

As viceroy, Bariatinskii enjoyed unprecedented latitude and resources, including two divisions fresh from service against Turkey. Further, his reputation as an aggressive leader bolstered the morale of the troops. Bariatinskii immediately rearranged the theater's command structure, which had remained in place since the emergence of muridism in the 1830s and was based on a defensive concept.[75] Bariatinskii's scheme, worked out in detail by Miliutin, consisted of five corps-level commands: two directed against the western Caucasus (beyond the purview of this study) and three against the eastern mountaineers—the Left Wing facing Chechnia and extending from the Terek to the Andi mountain range; the Pricaspian command, embracing all forces in Dagestan; and the Lezgian Line along the southeastern edge of the mountains. Although the geographical responsibilities of the commands changed little, the overall lines of command were made more efficient. In the past, for example, the army of the Left Flank (henceforth the Left Wing) was administratively controlled all the way from Stavropol. Further, the previous dispersal of forces all but ensured the superiority of the enemy in any given sector of the theater. Miliutin's task as chief of staff was to make certain that each command had the means (including logistical support and engineers) to operate independently and the organizational capability to undertake campaigns jointly with other commands.[76]

Bariatinskii's objective was the complete reduction of Dagestan and the territories shielding it. Comparing the campaign to the "regular siege of a fortress,"[77] Bariatinskii grasped that the key to the defense of the mountains lay not deep in their interior, the object of failed campaigns of past years, but along the periphery. By capturing the approaches to the mountains and advancing methodically on several axes, Russia could force the collapse of the center.[78] Bariatinskii tied down minimal forces in garrison duty and sought to occupy only the most strategic positions. The most crucial tasks in this offensive plan fell to the energetic commander of the Left Wing, General N. I. Evdokimov, who would deny the guerrillas any respite in

As viceroy of the Caucasus, Prince Bariatinskii directed the conquest of the mountaineers from 1856 to 1859

coming years. In marked contrast to past practice, Evdokimov did not seek to engage the enemy, even along the periphery of the mountains. Rather, he concentrated his forces in clearing the approaches to the mountains and relied on maneuver—made possible by the act of clearing roads—to avoid battles in conditions favoring the guerrillas.[79] By encroaching ever deeper, Evdokimov forced the enemy to come to him. Chechnia remained the focus of Russian operations because it offered, once cleared, the easiest access to the mountaineers' sanctuaries in Dagestan. Further, the Chechen tribes were no longer unified in their support for Shamil. (Meanwhile, along the Lezgian Line in the south, the accumulation of snow in the mountain passes limited campaigning to the summer months.)[80]

From November 1856 through April 1857, Evdokimov conducted four campaigns into Large Chechnia. Though encountering stiff opposition, not only from the Chechens but from allied Dagestani tribes, he succeeded in clearing the way for actions into Dagestan during the succeeding summer. In March, Evdokimov significantly advanced Russia's position with the establishment of two new forts, Shalin on the Bass River and Khobi-Shavdonskaia at the edge of Dagestan. Thus, behind him lay the entire Chechen plain, which Evdokimov intended to bring under his control as soon as possible, while before him lay his main objective, the Argun ravine that offered passage into the mountains. Hoping to keep his next move a secret, Evdokimov leaked word in the late fall of 1857 that he planned to march on Avtura, in Large Chechnia, to draw Shamil's forces out of Little Chechnia and away from Argun. Accordingly, a Russian column moved in the direction of Avtura, thereby prompting Shamil to assemble forces for its defense. Then, the column abruptly turned along the right bank of the Argun River toward the ravine, where it linked up with a second column under Evdokimov coming from Vozdvizhensk. Together, the columns entered the ravine and proceeded through its thick forests. Part of the force went to Izmail, while the remainder stayed behind to work on road construction and establish defensive positions. Under Evdokimov, the forward column moved along the Sharo-Argun River into the mountains and established Fort Argun near the village of Dacha-Borza. In a single stroke, Evdokimov occupied the Argun ravine with a minimum of bloodshed, and the conquest of Little Chechnia was, for all practical purposes, complete. Evdokimov burned existing villages and resettled about 15,000 Chechens to ensure they could never again be of use to Shamil.[81]

Having gained a clear approach to the mountains and secured his rear, Evdokimov in the summer of 1858 began a series of expeditions deep into the mountains that would result in the final defeat of Shamil. In June, operating as one of three columns converging along different axes, Evdokimov's Chechen detachment advanced along the Chanta-Argun gorge to conduct the main attack. The Dagestan detachment, which in 1857 had captured the strategic position of Burtunai (the new staff headquarters of the Dagestan Infantry Regiment), moved to Machik, while the Lezgian detachment moved through Kanuch, to the inner mountains of Lezgia to carry out the burning and destruction of unsubmissive villages in southern Lezgia. Shamil made valiant attempts to rally the tribes throughout the region to rise in the rear of the Russian columns, but in sad contrast to the 1840s, his appeals drew little response. Lacking victories and looking more and more like a beaten figure, Shamil found his support evaporating.[82] Russian control of the upper Argun valleys and gorges vastly reduced the territory under Shamil's control, leaving him with only part of northern Dagestan and the regions of Andi and Ichkeria. Those tribes west of the

Tbilisi, ca. 1890

Argun, primarily the Chechens and Ingush, had little choice but to capitulate.[83] The decision to do so seemed all the more rational to the inhabitants because it was at last clear that the Russians could guarantee their security against Shamil's retaliation.

With a force of seven and three-quarter battalions, four mountain guns, and a squadron of militia, Evdokimov next advanced along the Argun and surprised the mountaineers, seizing the village of Shata and occupying the Varaden meadow. In accord with standard practice, the troops immediately began cutting a path back through the forest and working on a bridge over the Argun, as well as erecting an intermediate fortification. The mountaineers, aware of the Russian presence, began preparing positions at the stronghold of Akh, about two miles in front of the Russian column. A guerrilla force of about 9,000 gathered there, but when the Russians arrived, the defense collapsed, virtually without a fight, offering compelling evidence of the moral decline of the resistance movement.[84] Within days, Russia controlled the right bank of the Argun and the western portion of Large Chechnia. By late October, the tribes of the mountainous expanse from the Georgian Military Road (running from Tbilisi to Mozdok) to the Sharo-Argun River recognized Russian power.[85]

Shamil's last gasp came later in the summer of 1858 following a revolt by resettled Ingush tribesmen living in the vicinity of Nazran. Ordinarily submissive, the Ingush had been crowded together into a few large settlements, and resentment soon exploded into violence.[86] Shamil crossed the Chanti-Argun River in force hoping to rekindle the lost fervor of his movement but in two attempts was unable to defeat the garrison at Nazran.

For Shamil, there was no recourse but to withdraw and defend his last sanctuaries in the mountains. In February 1859, Evdokimov led a large column to Shamil's capital at Veden, acting without direction from Bariatinskii. Having failed to block the Russian advance along the Argun, Shamil was in no position to rescue Veden, which fell after a two-month siege. After the war, Bariatinskii praised Evdokimov's initiative and aggressiveness:

> [Evdokimov] never once gave the enemy a chance of fighting where they meant to and where the advantage might have been on their side. The strongest positions held by Shamil and his hordes fell almost without resistance as a result of well-planned movements.... Three things—a systematic conduct of the war, the able dispositions of the chief leaders, and the arming of the troops with rifles—reduced our losses in the Caucasus to a minimum, and this, in turn, coupled with the fact that engagements were decided by tactical movements, was the chief cause of our success.[87]

The moral impact of the fall of Veden was as great as the practical result. Entire tribes and many of Shamil's most devoted allies now gave up and offered their submission to Russia.[88] Rostislav A. Fadeev, a Russian officer (who retired as a general and became an outspoken publicist), observed in his own reflections about the war in the Caucasus that Shamil's once fanatical followers lost their faith and became mere "soldiers." No longer willing to fight and die for every inch of ground, they gave more consideration to their families and property. The Russians, as a consequence, were now able to deal with them more in the manner of a conventional foe and decide the prolonged struggle with swift military incisions into Dagestan.[89]

Nevertheless, as of 1859, few other than Bariatinskii could see that the fall of Dagestan was imminent. Most anticipated that the reduction of Shamil's mountain stronghold would unfold over a series of years in the manner of Chechnia.[90] Bariatinskii's plan for the final conquest entailed offensive action against Dagestan from three general directions (see map 6). General Evdokimov's Chechen detachment would play the main role. Consisting of 14,000 men (12 1/2 battalions of infantry, a unit of dragoons, 900 Cossacks, 2 "hundreds" of native militia, 16 field guns, and 8 rocket launchers), Evdokimov's detachment proceeded from Veden along the Andi ridge (via Mt. Arzhi-lam) to Tikhnuntsal and then eastward to the Andi River, where it would await supporting columns.[91]

At the same time, Lieutenant General Baron Vrangel's advance southward from Burtunai with 9,000 men of the Pricaspian detachment greatly alarmed Shamil, thereby enabling the Chechen detachment to march to the valley of the Andi River virtually unimpeded. Shamil had assembled a considerable force of several thousand warriors in fortified positions on the eastern bank of the Andi. The mountaineers could have made any crossing extremely costly, but Vrangel's advance foiled their efforts. On 15 July, Vrangel's column reached the river between Chirkat and Sagrytl and, using bridging materials lugged the entire distance from Burtunai, established a crossing on the 17th. Kazi Muhamed realized that Vrangel now threatened not only his northern flank but his line of retreat and fled to rejoin his

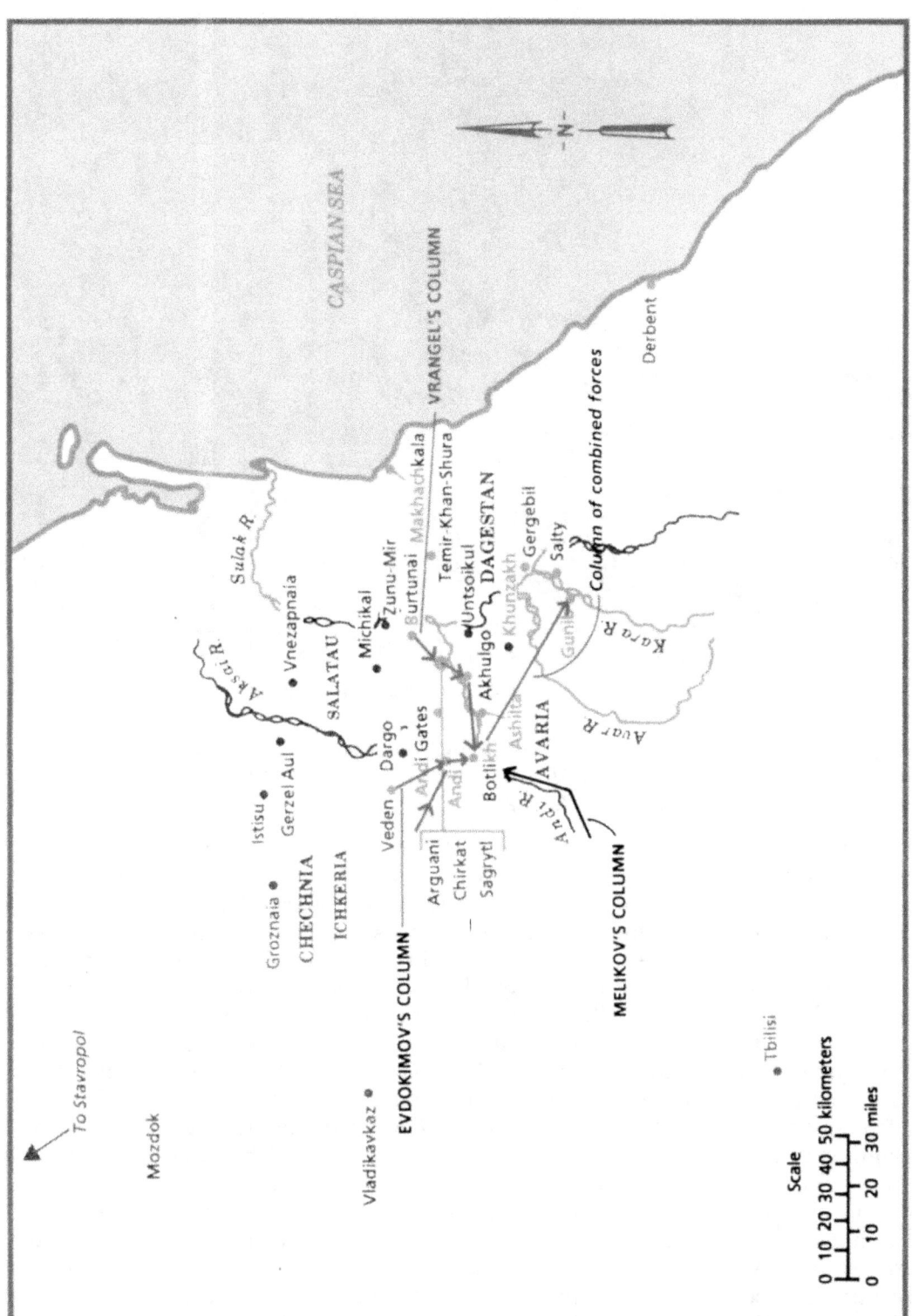

Map 6. The Russians' linkup and final thrust into Dagestan, 1859

Shamil's surrender to Bariatinskii (as depicted by a Russian artist)

father. Shamil now had no recourse but to withdraw farther east to the Gunib plateau. In his wake, the tribes west of the Avar River rushed to proclaim their submission to Russia.[92]

With the arrival of Prince Levan Melikov's Lezgian detachment (7,000 men) from the south at Botlikh on the Andi River in early August, Bariatinskii had successfully grouped his forces and prepared for the final march to Gunib. Victory in sight, the Russian commanders were besieged by tribal delegations pledging their fealty, and Bariatinskii felt sufficiently confident to undertake an inspection tour of the area before conducting the final assault. In village after village, eager throngs greeted the viceroy of the Caucasus to demonstrate their loyalty. Satisfied with the situation in his rear, Bariatinskii opened the siege of Gunib, which like so many other fortified positions in the mountains offered great advantages to the imaginative defender. A broad stretch of high ground surrounded by rugged cliffs descending at angles as sharp as 45 degrees, Gunib could have been defended almost indefinitely by a reasonably large force. Such was Shamil's misfortune that his loyal following had dwindled to a mere 400 men, who despite the most valiant efforts could not protect the entire defensive perimeter against Russian attack.[93] Though Shamil refused an invitation to surrender, Bariatinskii issued strict orders that the gallant leader of the "murids" be taken alive. Only when Russian forces had broken through to the interior of his last sanctuary did Shamil (perhaps for the sake of family members present with him) give up the struggle he had led for a quarter of a century.

Conclusions

Among the sources of Russian triumph in the Caucasus, a general superiority in manpower and resources was of indisputable importance. The Russians could not have continued the war in the face of numerous setbacks and overcome a highly motivated and skillfully directed resistance had they not possessed the resources of a great empire. But these assets did not make victory inevitable. Essential to success was the conviction of successive tsars that the strategic significance of the Caucasus made it an objective worthy of the costs in subjugating it. The prolongation of the war never particularly disturbed members of the court, and the popular press, still in its infancy, lacked the stature and confidence (not to mention the freedom under Nicholas I) to raise serious questions about the imperial policy. As Fadeev observed, "Russia became accustomed little by little to the thought that such a situation of affairs was natural and must continue almost forever..."[94]

Only by means of well-chosen application of its resources could Russia work its will in the Caucasus. Romanovskii asserts that Russian success was achievable only through a skillful blend of military and nonmilitary methods: "But if it is difficult to imagine the subjugation of the Caucasian tribes without the use of arms, it is also not easy to imagine how and when their subjugation could have been completed if our actions were based solely on arms."[95] The Russians' unfamiliarity with the region and its peoples combined with constant reversals of policy to hamper Russian administration of the Caucasus. As the events of Shamil's rise and decline demonstrate, the war was at heart a struggle for domination of the forested mountain periphery. Shamil understood that control of Chechnia and the Lezgian territories expanded his resources and provided forward bases for his incursions against chieftains siding with Russia. Russian success, therefore, necessarily depended on effective military administration of the border zones. Until the peoples of Dagestan's periphery were either won over or subjugated, effective action against Shamil was impossible.

Ermolov took a gradualist point of view toward the implementation of Russian laws and customs and relied heavily on native elites in his own bureaucracy. His successor, Paskevich, however, systematically purged native officials and Russified the administrative apparatus. General G. V. Rosen, in turn, adopted a middle point of view, supporting the abolition of native customs but accommodating himself to existing realities.[96] Following the complete disintegration of Russian rule outside of Georgia and Stavropol in the 1830s, Nicholas permitted Vorontsov sweeping authority to act as he saw fit. Vorontsov's more competent and relatively humane administration reduced antagonism among tribes already in submission and ensured greater stability in areas to the rear of the Russian forces. Yet even Vorontsov, though making substantial progress, was unable to find a consistently effective mix of repression and tolerance and of administrative modernization and respect for custom.[97]

In time, the Russians adopted innovative techniques for working their will in the Caucasus. For example, during his tenure as commander of the Left Flank in Chechnia, Bariatinskii deftly attempted to reinforce separatist tendencies among the Chechens to make them less receptive to Shamil's claims of absolute authority.[98] Bariatinskii, like Ermolov long before him, employed a system of native courts for the arbitration of disputes within and among the tribes under Russian control.[99] He also sought to alleviate specific grievances, such as in 1859, when he lifted an imperial ban to allow small numbers of tribesmen to make a pilgrimage to Mecca.[100] In addition, the Russians had long made a practice of hiring local informants, although many chieftains became alert to this method and were careful to watch anyone suspected of pro-Russian leanings.[101]

What appeared to many Russians to be the greatest potential instrument of assimilation in the long run was the cultivation of economic relationships, which would give the natives an inducement to accept Russian power and eventually to depend on it. Even in this, however, Russia lacked continuity in its policy. Though Russia forged a stronger relationship with the tribes on the periphery of Chechnia and Dagestan through commercial inducements, the self-sufficient tribes of the interior remained largely unaffected.[102]

The Russians' search for a military means to victory hinged on the recognition of a single, crucial truth: the mountainous eastern Caucasus region could not be reduced in a lightning campaign of destruction but only through years of patient and methodical effort. The refusal of tsars and, therefore, generals to accept such a view led to much wasted time and sacrifice. Moreover, the Russians could not maintain control over any portion of the region without adequate lines of communication, a virtual impossibility given the scarcity of secure roads and the difficult terrain conventional forces must march through. Therefore, from 1846, the development of a comprehensive and workable system for reducing the Caucasus was, in the view of most observers, the key to success.

Pokrovskii departs from this analysis, contending that chance, rather than operational planning, was the primary determinant of the outcome.[103] He notes, for example, that Shamil's rule progressively alienated the independent-minded chieftains of the Caucasus by his absolute insistence on religious discipline among peoples accustomed to observing Islam on their own terms. Relying on a class analysis, Pokrovskii also claims the mountaineer cause was betrayed by the native nobility, to whom Bariatinskii promised restoration of pre-Shamil privileges.[104] Pokrovskii's argument is not without merit, but it devalues the fraying of Shamil's coalition, which occurred in conjunction with his military demise. The authority of the imam was based on a general belief in his infallible leadership. When events shattered that confidence and Shamil lost the physical means to enforce his will, his moral authority evaporated.

To deal with Shamil effectively, the Russians first adapted their tactics, then their strategy. The appearance of the rifle at the very end of the war, which made conventional units substantially stronger, came too late to influence dramatically the course of events in the eastern Caucasus, and in any case, the mountaineers had already procured a few modern weapons of their own.[105] Even the unequivocal superiority of Russian tactical firepower, the product of the combined force of separate military arms and disciplined maneuver, only achieved telling effect when the enemy was forced to wage battle on conventional terms. Yet though painfully accumulated, battle experience improved Russian efficiency. The understanding of the tactical importance of a close column order and the discipline to maintain it under all conditions left Russian forces less susceptible to ambushes, so favored by the mountaineers.

Beyond the tactical level, Bariatinskii's plan for Shamil's final defeat reflected a grasp of objective steps that would lead to a successful strategic decision. The separate but coordinated movements of independent columns in different parts of the theater were carefully calculated toward a greater end. When in July 1859 three columns linked near Botlikh, they had so thoroughly liquidated the opposition in their rear that the leaders of Avaria scurried to capitulate. Under Bariatinskii and Evdokimov, the Russians demonstrated that well-planned maneuver and deception could neutralize the superior mobility of Shamil's guerrillas and deny the mountaineers the initiative.

The cornerstone of the Russian method of conquest was the reshaping of the physical and human environment, enabling Bariatinskii to dictate the terms of combat. Surpassing by far the destructive effects of William Sherman's "march to the sea" in the American Civil War, Russia's scorched earth policy, coupled with a massive campaign of forced resettlement, stripped Shamil of his greatest assets and permanently transformed the central Caucasus. Pokrovskii estimates that 400,000 tribesmen emigrated to Turkey under Russian pressure,[106] and many more resettled within imperial boundaries. Population movement was especially high in the western Caucasus, and as many as half a million Cherkes were eventually driven from their ancestral lands.[107] In their place came Cossacks and other colonists from Russia's interior. The construction of a network of roads and, ultimately, a railroad brought the Caucasus into regular communication with the empire. In such a way, Russia came to dominate the land if not the spirits of the natives who remained. Popular uprisings against Russian rule during the Russo-Turkish War of 1877—78 and again following the Revolution of 1917 served as a reminder that conquest did not necessarily mean final assimilation.

The Caucasian experience left only a modest legacy for the Russian Army. From an institutional perspective, no systematic effort was made to preserve and disseminate the lessons of the Caucasian theater, which had little relevance to European warfare. Even Miliutin, who served as war minister from 1861 to 1881 and whose own analysis of the war proved so vital, subsequently became preoccupied with modernization of the Russian

Army in a desperate effort to achieve parity with Germany and Austria. Furthermore, the long and bloody struggle in the Caucasus soiled many more reputations than it enhanced. Yet as historian John Sheldon Curtiss contends, the neglect of the Caucasian experience may have been costly. Years of combat against guerrilla fighters in the mountains "taught the commanders there to stress mobility and agility rather than parade-ground technique and to value soldiers with initiative and élan."[108]

Some veterans of the Caucasus were able to transfer the lessons of the war to the increasingly active theater in Central Asia. Further, the appointment of Miliutin as war minister in 1861 ensured that valuable knowledge would not only survive but would be employed. During and after Miliutin's tenure, articles and full histories devoted to the Caucasian War achieved wide circulation, although it would be fair to say that the average Russian officer probably did not read them. In any case, Russia remained preoccupied with the greater threat of warfare on the European continent, and the events of the Caucasus did not become an essential part of the army's institutional memory. Within two generations, vital tenets of irregular and mountain warfare would have to be learned anew.

Notes

Chapter 1

1. For a detailed account of the early years of Russian involvement in the Caucasus, see N. E. Dubrovin, *Istoriia voiny i vladychestva russkikh na Kavkaze*, 4 vols. (St. Petersburg, 1887); and V. Potto, *Istoricheskii ocherk kavkazskikh voin ot ikh nachala do prisoedineniia Gruzii* (Tiflis, 1899). For a good, brief historical sketch of Russian imperial activity in the Caucasus until the revolution, see Firuz Kazemzadeh, "Russian Penetration of the Caucasus," in *Russian Imperialism: From Ivan the Great to the Revolution*, ed. Taras Hunczak (New Brunswick, NJ: Rutgers University Press, 1974), 239—63. Unfortunately for our understanding of the Caucasian War, we are almost entirely dependent for data upon Russian sources, some of which have not yet become available to Western scholars.

2. D. I. Romanovskii, "General Fel'dmarshal Kniaz' Aleksandr Ivanovich Bariatinskii i kavkazskaia voina, 1815—1879 gg.," *Russkaia starina*, no. 2 (1881):290; and D. A. Miliutin, *Opisanie voennykh deistvii 1839 goda na severnom Dagestane* (St. Petersburg, 1860), 11.

3. M. I. Shishkevich, "Pokorenie Kavkaza, Persidskaia i kavkazskaia voiny," in *Istoriia russkoi armii i flota*, vol. 6 (Moscow, 1911—13), 53.

4. S. K. Bushuev, *Bor'ba gortsev za nezavisimost' pod rukovodstvom Shamilia* (Moscow: Akademiia nauk soiuza S.S.R., 1939), 98—99. R. A. Fadeev contends in "Shest'desiat' let Kavkazskoi voiny," part of his *Sobranie sochinenii R. A. Fadeeva*, vol. 1 (St. Petersburg, 1889), 18, that Ermolov never had in excess of 45,000 men under his control. In his own notes on the war, published in *Zapiski A. P. Ermolova, 1798—1826* (Moscow: Vysshaia shkola, 1991), Ermolov listed his forces in 1816 as follows: 19th and 20th Infantry Divisions (30,336 men), reserve brigade and 3 grenadier regiments (7,024 men), garrison regiments and battalions (5,920 men), the Nizhegorod Dragoon Regiment (711 men), line Cossack regiments (5,302 men), Don Cossack regiments (5,237 men), Astrakhan Cossack regiments (1,634 men), and artillery (48 battery guns, 60 light guns, and 24 horse Cossack guns).

5. A. Zisserman, "Kriticheskie zametki," *Russkii arkhiv*, no. 2 (1885):567.

6. "Predpisanie gen.-adiut. kn. Bariatinskogo nachal'niku grazhdanskogo upravlenii na Kavkaze i za Kavkazom, gen. Kn. Bebutova, ot 25-go ianvaria 1857 goda," in *Akty sobrannye Kavkazskoi arkheograficheskoi kommissiei*, vol. 11, pt. 3 (Tiflis, 1893), 187—90.

7. Kazemzadeh, "Russian Penetration of the Caucasus," 256; and Bushuev, *Bor'ba gortsev za nezavisimost'*, 110—12, 124—29. See also M. D. Bagirov, *K voprosu o kharaktere dvizheniia miuridizma i Shamilia* (Moscow: Gosizdat Politlit, 1950).

8. G. H. Bolsover, "David Urquhart and the Eastern Question, 1833—37: A Study in Publicity and Diplomacy," *Journal of Modern History* 8 (December 1936):444—67; Paul Henze, "Circassia in the Nineteenth Century: The Futile Fight for Freedom," in *Turko-Tatar Past, Soviet Present*, ed. Ch. Lemercier-Quelquejay (Paris, 1986), 193—94; and N. S. Kiniapina, M. M. Bliev, and V. V. Degoev, *Kavkaz i sredniaia Aziia vo vneshnei politike Rossii, Vtoraia polovina XVIII-80-e gody XIX 6.* (Moscow: Izdatel'stvo Moskovskogo Universiteta, 1984), 138—58.

9. L. Hamilton Rhinelander, "Russia's Imperial Policy: The Administration of the Caucasus in the First Half of the Nineteenth Century," *Canadian Slavonic Papers*, nos. 2—3 (1975):226—27.

10. E. Willis Brooks, "Nicholas as Reformer: Russian Attempts to Conquer the Caucasus, 1825—1855," in *Nation and Ideology: Essays in Honor of Wayne S. Vucinich* (Boulder, CO: 1981), 229; Kazemzadeh, "Russian Penetration of the Caucasus," 255—63; Ermolov, *Zapiski A. P. Ermolova*, 304—85; and John F. Baddeley, *The Russian Conquest of the Caucasus* (New York: Longmans, Green & Co., 1908), 124. Baddeley places the blame for this on Ermolov.

11. D. I. Romanovskii, *Kavkaz i kavkazskaia voina* (St. Petersburg, 1860), 212—16; and John Sheldon Curtiss, *The Russian Army Under Nicholas I* (Durham, NC: Duke University Press, 1965), 153—54.

12. N. Sh., "General Veliaminov i ego znachenie dlia istorii kavkazskoi voiny," in *Kavkazskii sbornik*, vol. 7 (Tiflis, 1883), 4; N. E. Dubrovin, *Kavkazskaia voina v tsarstvovanie imperatorov Nikolaia I i Aleksandra II (1825—1864 g.)*, in the series *Ot Petra Velikogo do nashikh dnei*, pt. 4, bk. 2, gen. ed. Lieutenant General Leer (St. Petersburg: Izdanie glavnogo upravleniia voenno-uchebnykh zavedenii, 1896), 16; V. I. Ivanenko, *Grazhdanskoe upravlenie Zakavkazem ot prisoedineniia Gruzii do namestnichestva Velikogo Kniazia Mikhaila Nikolaevicha* (Tbilisi, 1901), 161; and A. P. Scherbatov, *General-Fel'dmarshal Kniaz' Paskevich. Ego zhizn' i deiatelmost'* (St. Petersburg, 1891), 246—50.

13. "O fortifikatsionnoi oborone Zakavkazskogo kraia ustroistvom dorog i voobshche o predpriiatiiakh v stroitelnoi chasti," in *Akty sobrannye*, vol. 8, 379.

14. Dubrovin, *Kavkazskaia voina*, 16.

15. Curtiss, *The Russian Army*, 157; "Otnoshenie gr. Chernysheva k baronu Rozenu, ot 26-go fevralia 1835-go goda," in *Akty sobrannye*, vol. 8, 353—54; and Romanovskii, *Kavkaz i kavkazskaia voina*, 222.

16. "Otnoshenie baron Rozena K gr. Chernysheva, ot 12-go noiabria 1831 goda," in *Akty sobrannye*, vol. 8, 340—41.

17. Fadeev, "Shest'desiat' let kavkazskoi voiny," 17.

18. Dubrovin, *Kavkazskaia voina*, 12.

19. Miliutin, *Opisanie voennykh deistvii*, 16.

20. Bushuev, *Bor'ba gortsev za nezavisimost'*, 92; and Miliutin, *Opisanie voennykh deistvii*, 7—17. Miliutin estimates the entire Chechnian population at between 80,000 and 100,000.

21. Curtiss, *The Russian Army*, 161.

22. Miliutin, *Opisanie voennykh deistvii*, 45—47; and Dubrovin, *Kavkazskaia voina*, 116.

23. Dubrovin, *Kavkazskaia voina*, 116—17.

24. Ibid., 118.

25. As translated in Baddeley, *The Russian Conquest*, 319—20. The original text appears in Miliutin, *Opisanie voennykh deistvii*, 62—63.

26. Dubrovin, *Kavkazskaia voina*, 118; and Miliutin, *Opisanie voennykh deistvii*, 64.

27. Dubrovin, *Kavkazskaia voina*, 120; and Miliutin, *Opisanie voennykh deistvii*, 70—75.

28. Baddeley, *The Russian Conquest*, 325; and Miliutin, *Opisanie voennykh deistvii*, 80.

29. Baddeley, *The Russian Conquest*, 328.

30. Dubrovin, *Kavkazskaia voina*, 124.

31. Baddeley, *The Russian Conquest*, 330.

32. Miliutin, *Opisanie voennykh deistvii*, 99—100.

33. Miliutin, *Vospominaniia* (Tomsk, 1919); reprint (Newtonville, MA: Oriental Research Partners, 1979), 226.

34. Dubrovin, *Kavkazskaia voina*, 125—26; and Miliutin, *Opisanie voennykh deistvii*, 102—3.
35. Miliutin, *Opisanie voennykh deistvii*, 104—12; and Baddeley, *The Russian Conquest*, 336.
36. Miliutin, *Opisanie voennykh deistvii*, 114—21; and Dubrovin, *Kavkazskaia voina*, 130.
37. Dubrovin, *Kavkazskaia voina*, 133—40; and Baddeley, *The Russian Conquest*, 356—59; and Curtiss, *The Russian Army*, 164.
38. N. Okolnichii, "Perechen' poslednikh voennykh sobytii v Dagestane," pt. 3, *Voennyi sbornik*, no. 3 (1859):47.
39. Baddeley, *The Russian Conquest*, 365—67.
40. Ibid., 369—70.
41. M. N. Pokrovskii, "Zavoevanie Kavkaza," in *Istoriia Rossii v XIX veke*, vol. 5 (St. Petersburg, 1907—11), 326.
42. A. A. Veliaminov, "Zamechanie na pis'mo glavnokomanduiushchego deistvuiushchei armiei k voennomu ministru ot 27 Iulia 1832 goda," in *Kavkazskii sbornik*, vol. 7 (Tiflis, 1883), 142—43; and Romanovskii, *Kavkaz i kavkazskaia voina*, 229—30.
43. D. A. Skalon, *Glavnyi shtab: istoricheskii ocherk vozniknoveniia i razvitiia v Rossii general'nogo shtaba v 1825—1902 gg.*, in the series *Stoletie voennogo ministerstva, 1802—1902*, vol. 3, pt. 2 (St. Petersburg, 1910), 251. See also A. Kersnovskii, *Istoriia russkoi armii*, pt. 2 (1814—81) (Belgrade, 1934), 348—49.
44. Bushuev, *Bor'ba gortsev za nezavisimost'*, 99—100; and Kazemzadeh, "Russian Penetration of the Caucasus," 259—60. See also Skalon, *Glavnyi shtab*, 252.
45. Miliutin, *Vospominaniia*, 305; and E. Willis Brooks, "D. A. Miliutin: Life and Activity to 1856," dissertation, Stanford University, 1970, 78. See also Bushuev, *Bor'ba gortsev za nezavisimost'*, 99—100.
46. Miliutin, *Vospominaniia*, 305; and Brooks, "D. A. Miliutin," 78—79.
47. M. Ol'shevskii, "Kavkaz s 1841 po 1866 god," pt. 4, *Russkaia starina*, no. 7 (1893):98; and Baddeley, *The Russian Conquest*, 268—70.
48. "Gornaia artilleriia," *Voennaia entsiklopediia*, vol. 8 (St. Petersburg, 1912), 403—4.
49. Bushuev, *Bor'ba gortsev za nezavisimost'*, 97; A. Rzhevskii, "1845-i god na Kavkaze," in *Kavkazskii sbornik*, vol. 6 (Tiflis, 1882), 231. Rzhevskii provides a transcript of Nicholas' instructions to the war minister on 235—39. For a good discussion of the powers vested in the viceroy, see L. Hamilton Rhinelander, *Prince Michael Vorontsov: Viceroy to the Tsar* (Montreal: McGill-Queens University Press, 1990), 141—43.
50. L.—D.G., "Pokhod 1845 goda v Dargo," *Voennyi sbornik*, no. 7 (1859):5.
51. Ibid., 9.
52. Ibid., 10.
53. Ibid., 25—26; and Rzhevskii, "1845-i god na Kavkaze," 299—300.
54. Baddeley, *The Russian Conquest*, 389.
55. Dubrovin, *Kavkazskaia voina*, 215.
56. Ibid., 218.
57. For a vivid account, see Baddeley, *The Russian Conquest*, 396—402. Also, see Dubrovin, *Kavkazskaia voina*, 221.
58. L.—D.G., "Pokhod 1845 goda," 44—47; and Dubrovin, *Kavkazskaia voina*, 219.
59. L.—D.G., "Pokhod 1845 goda," 47—48.
60. Ibid., 55—56; and Dubrovin, *Kavkazskaia voina*, 219.
61. L.—D.G., "Pokhod 1845 goda," 56.
62. Shishkevich, "Pokorenie Kavkaza," 91. Baddeley, *The Russian Conquest*, 410, claims

casualty totals of 195 officers and 3,433 men. Kersnovskii, *Istoriia russkoi armii*, 344—45, gives casualty totals of 3 generals, 141 officers, and 2,831 men.

63. Rzhevskii, "1845-i god na Kavkaze," 231.
64. Dubrovin, *Kavkazskaia voina*, 221.
65. Romanovskii, *Kavkaz i kavkazskaia voina*, 382; and Central State Historical Archive, St. Petersburg, Russia, fund 1100 (Fadeev), 1860, index 1, no. 39, sheet 3. This document is a letter from General E. V. Brimmer to General R. A. Fadeev.
66. Zisserman, "Kriticheskie zametki," 562; Skalon, *Glavnyi shtab*, 284; Bushuev, *Bor'ba gortsev za nezavisimost'*, 139; and Shishkevich, "Pokorenie Kavkaza," 93.
67. Fadeev, "Shest'desiat' let Kavkazskoi voiny," 36—37.
68. Pokrovskii, "Zavoevanie Kavkaza," 336.
69. John Sheldon Curtiss, *Russia's Crimean War* (Durham, NC: Duke University Press, 1979), 414—19.
70. Zisserman, "Kriticheskie zametki," 565.
71. Brooks, "D. A. Miliutin," 146; and Romanovskii, "General Fel'dmarshal Kniaz'," 279. Romanovskii credits Bariatinskii with great originality on these matters and suggests that the basic scheme was the general's own. Zisserman makes the same point forcefully in "Po povodu zapisok M. Ia. Ol'shevskogo," *Russkaia starina*, no. 1 (1885):124. For more of the same, see Ivan Kravtsov, "Kavkaz i ego voenachal'niki," "Russkaia starina", no. 6 (1886):566. Kravtsov also praises Bariatinskii for his choice of Evdokimov, the son of a peasant, as a field commander. For an account of Bariatinskii's prior service, see the memoirs of Prince Gagarin, "Vospominaniia o fel'dmarshale kniaze Aleksandr Ivanovich Bariatinskii," *Russkii vestnik*, no. 8 (1888).
72. Zisserman, "Kriticheskie zametki," 562.
73. Dubrovin, *Kavkazskaia voina*, 326—29.
74. "Pis'mo voennogo ministra, gen. adiut. Sukhozaneta, k gen. adiut. kn. Bariatinskomu, ot 29 iiunia 1857 goda," *Akty sobrannye*, vol. 12, pt. 3, 199—200.
75. Fadeev, "Shest'desiat' let Kavkazskoi voiny," 41, 43; A. L. Zisserman, *Feldmarshal Kniaz' Aleksandr Ivanovich Bariatinskii 1815—1879*, vol. 2 (Moscow, 1890), 88.
76. Ibid., 84, 88—90; and Forrestt Miller, *Dmitrii Miliutin and the Reform Era in Russia* (Nashville, TN: Vanderbilt, 1968), 20—31.
77. Fadeev, "Shest'desiat' let Kavkazskoi voiny," 46. Veliaminov made the same observation in 1828. See Baddeley, *The Russian Conquest*, 112; and "1843-i god na Kavkaze," *Kavkazskii sbornik*, vol. 8 (Tiflis, 1884), 335—97.
78. Fadeev, "Shest'desiat' let Kavkazskoi voiny," 46—47.
79. Ibid., 48; and Zisserman, *Fel'dmarshal kniaz'*, vol. 2, 95—98.
80. Fadeev, "Shest'desiat' let Kavkazskoi voiny," 48.
81. "Pis'mo gen. adiut. kn. Bariatinskogo k voennomu ministru, gen. adiut. Sukhozanetu, ot 7-go fevralia 1858 goda," *Akty sobrannye*, vol. 7, pt. 3, 216; Dubrovin, *Kavkazskaia voina*, 329—32; Fadeev, "Shest'desiat' let Kavkazskoi voiny," 53—55; and Romanovskii, *Kavkaz i kavkazskaia voina*, 428—29.
82. "Otnoshenie gen.-adiut. kn. Bariatinskogo k upravliaiushchemu voennym ministerstvom, gen. adiut. kn. Vasilchikovu, ot 29-go iulia 1858 goda," *Akty sobrannye*, vol. 12, pt. 3, 243; and Fadeev, "Shest'desiat' let Kavkazskoi voiny," 56—57. For a good account of the capture of Salatau, see V. Soltan, "Zaniatie Salatavii v 1857 godu," in *Kavkazskii sbornik*, vol. 8 (Tiflis, 1884), 335—97.
83. Baddeley, *The Russian Conquest*, 461.
84. Dubrovin, *Kavkazskaia voina*, 332—33.

85. Fadeev, "Shest'desiat' let Kavkazskoi voiny," 59.
86. Baddeley, *The Russian Conquest*, 471.
87. Ibid.
88. Ibid., 472; Dubrovin, *Kavkazskaia voina*, 348. See also Apolon Shpakovskii, "Zapiski starogo kazaka," *Voennyi sbornik*, no. 2 (1874):365—66.
89. Fadeev, "Shest'desiat' let Kavkazskoi voiny," 66—67.
90. Ibid., 68. See also *Akty sobrannye*, vol. 12, pt. 3, 241—48, for a transcript of Bariatinskii's plan, which does not specifically foresee the collapse of Shamil but does presume rapid advances are possible.
91. Ibid., 68—69; and Dubrovin, *Kavkazskaia voina*, 352—60.
92. Ibid.
93. Baddeley, *The Russian Conquest*, 476—77; and Fadeev, "Shest'desiat' let Kavkazskoi voiny," 82—83.
94. Fadeev, "Shest'desiat' let Kavkazskoi voiny," 1.
95. Romanovskii, *Kavkaz i kavkazskaia voina*, 366.
96. Brooks, "Nicholas as Reformer," 234—38.
97. Ibid., 248—49.
98. Zisserman, "Fel'dmarshal kniaz' Aleksandr Ivanovich Bariatinskii 1815—1879," *Russkii arkhiv*, no. 1 (1888):192—93. See also *Akty sobrannye*, vol. 12, pt. 3, 248—64.
99. Romanovskii, "General Fel'dmarshal Kniaz'," 283—84.
100. "Otzyv glavnokomanduiushchego Kavkazskoi Armiei k. Ministru inostrannykh del," 19 November 1859, *Akty sobrannye*, vol. 12, pt. 1, 167—71.
101. V. I. Pisarev, "Metody zavoevaniia adygeiskogo naroda tsarizmom v pervoi polovine XIX v.," in *Istoricheskie zapiski*, vol. 9 (Moscow: Akademiia Nauk, 1940), 163; and Pokrovskii, "Zavoevanie Kavkaza," 327.
102. Pisarev, "Metody zavoevaniia," 163; and Romanovskii, *Kavkaz i Kavkazskaia voina*, 357.
103. Pokrovskii, "Zavoevanie Kavkaza," 325.
104. Ibid.
105. Zisserman, *Fel'dmarshal kniaz'*, vol. 2, 185. Bariatinskii reports this fact in a letter to War Minister N. O. Sukhozanet in October 1859.
106. Pokrovskii, "Zavoevanie Kavkaza," 339. See P. Berzhe, "Vyselenie gortsev s Kavkaza," *Russkaia starina*, no. 1 (1882):161—76; no. 2 (1882):337—63; no. 10 (1882):1—32. For details of the war in the Transkuban region, see a series of articles by P. P. Korolenko, "Transkubanskii krai," *Voennyi sbornik*, nos. 2, 4—9 (1893).
107. W. E. D. Allen and Paul Muratoff, *Caucasian Battlefields: A History of the Wars on the Turco-Caucasian Border, 1828—1921* (Cambridge, MA: Cambridge University Press, 1953), 107. Data on resettlements or exiles are rough, and such estimates may be inflated or include a variety of tribal groups. At the peak period, 1858—65, 493,000 persons relocated to Turkey through the Black Sea ports. See V. G. Gadzhiev, "Narody severnogo Kavkaza vo vremia i posle Krymskoi voiny. Porazhenie gortsev pod predvoditel'stvom Shamilia," in *Istoriia narodov Severnogo Kavkaza: Konets XVIII V.—1917 g.*, ed. A. L. Narochnitskii (Moscow: Nauka, 1988), 207.
108. Curtiss, *The Russian Army*, 174.

Bibliography

Chapter 1

Archival Documents

Central State Historical Archive. Fund 1100 (Fadeev), 1860. St. Petersburg.

Published Memoirs and Documents

Akty sobrannye Kavkazskoi arkheograficheskoi kommissiei. 12 vols. Tiflis, 1867—93.

Ermolov, A. P. *Zapiski A. P. Ermolova, 1798—1826.* Moscow: Vysshaia shkola, 1991.

"Ermolov, Dibich i Paskevich v 1826—1827 gg. Perepiska imperatora Nikolaia." *Russkaia starina*, no. 11 (1880):617—26.

Fadeev, R. A. "Pis'ma s Kavkaza." *Sobranie sochineniia R. A. Fadeeva.* 2 vols. St. Petersburg, 1889.

Gagarin, Prince. "Vospominaniia o fel'dmarshale kniaze Aleksandr Ivanovich Bariatinskii." *Russkii vestnik*, no. 8 (1888).

Miliutin, D. A. *Opisanie voennykh deistvii 1839 goda na severnom Dagestane.* St. Petersburg, 1860.

——. *Vospominaniia.* Tomsk, 1919. Reprint. Newtonville, MA: Oriental Research Partners, 1979.

Shpakovskii, Apolon. "Zapiski starogo kazaka." *Voennyi sbornik*, no. 2 (1874).

Veliaminov, A. A. "Sposob uskorit' pokorenie gortsev (Memoriia general-leitenant Veliaminova, predstavlennaia v 1828-m gody)." In *Kavkazskii sbornik.* Vol. 7. Tiflis, 1883, 67—77.

——. "Zamechanie na pis'mo glavnokomanduiushchego deistvuiushchei armiei k voennomu ministru ot 27 Iulia 1832 goda." In *Kavkazskii sbornik.* Vol. 7. Tiflis, 1883, 78—155.

Vorontsov, M. S. *Vypiski iz dnevnika s 1845 po 1854.* St. Petersburg, 1902.

Books

Allen, W. E. D., and Paul Muratoff. *Caucasian Battlefields: A History of the Wars on the Turco-Caucasian Border, 1828—1921.* Cambridge, MA: Cambridge University Press, 1953.

Baddeley, John F. *The Russian Conquest of the Caucasus.* New York: Longmans, Green & Co., 1908.

Bagirov, M. D. *K voprosu o kharaktere dvizheniia miuridizma i Shamilia.* Moscow: Gosizdat Politlit, 1950.

Bushuev, S. K. *Bor'ba gortsev za nezavisimost' pod rukovodstvom Shamilia.* Moscow: Akademiia Nauk Soiuza S.S.R., 1939.

Chew, A. N. *An Atlas of Russian History.* Revised edition. New Haven, CT: Yale University Press, 1970.

Curtiss, John Sheldon. *The Russian Army Under Nicholas I.* Durham, NC: Duke University Press, 1965.

──── . *Russia's Crimean War.* Durham, NC: Duke University Press, 1979.

Dubrovin, N. E. *Istoriia voiny i vladychestva russkikh na Kavkaze.* 4 vols. St. Petersburg, 1887.

──── . *Kavkazskaia voina v tsarstvovanie imperatorov Nikolaia I i Aleksandra II (1825—1864 g.).* In the series *Ot Petra Velikogo do nashikh dnei.* Gen. ed. Lieutenant General Leer. St. Petersburg: Izdanie glavnogo upravleniia voenno-uchebnykh zavedenii, 1896.

Fadeev, A. V. *Rossiia i Kavkaz pervoi treti xix v.* Moscow: Izdatel'stvo Akademii Nauk, 1960.

Fadeev, R. A. *Sobranie sochinenii R. A. Fadeeva.* 2 vols. St. Petersburg, 1889.

Gadzhiev, V. G. *Rol' Rossii v istorii Dagestana.* Moscow, 1965.

Gizetti, A. L. *Sbornik svedenii o poterakh Kavkazskikh voisk vo vremia voin Kavkazsko-gorskoi, persidskikh, turetskikh i v Zakaspiiskom Krae.* Tiflis, 1901.

Hunczak, Taras, ed. *Russian Imperialism: From Ivan the Great to the Revolution.* New Brunswick, NJ: Rutgers University Press, 1974.

Ibragimbeili, Khadzhi Murat. *Kavkaz v Krymskoi voine 1853—1856 gg. i mezhdunarodnye otnosheniia.* Moscow: Nauka, 1971.

Ivanenko, V. I. *Grazhdanskoe upravlenie Zakavkazem ot prisoedineniia Gruzii do namestnichestva Velikogo Kniazia Mikhaila Nikolaevicha.* Tbilisi, 1901.

Kersnovskii, A. *Istoriia russkoi armii.* Belgrade, 1934.

Kiniapina, N. S., M. M. Bliev, and B. B. Degoev. *Kavkaz i Sredniaia Aziia vo vneshnei politike Rossii, Vtoraia polovina XVIII-80-e gody XIX b.* Moscow: Izdatel'stvo Moskovskogo Universiteta, 1984.

Miller, Forrestt. *Dmitrii Miliutin and the Reform Era in Russia.* Nashville, TN: Vanderbilt, 1968.

Narochnitskii, A. L., ed. *Istoriia narodov Severnogo Kavkaza: Konets XVIII V.-1917 g.* Moscow: Nauka, 1988.

Potto, V. *Istoricheskii ocherk kavkazskikh voin ot ikh nachala do prisoedineniia Gruzii.* Tiflis, 1899.

Rhinelander, L. Hamilton. *Prince Mikhail Vorontsov: Viceroy to the Tsar.* Montreal: McGill-Queens University Press, 1990.

Romanovskii, D. I. *Kavkaz i kavkazskaia voina.* St. Petersburg, 1860.

Runovskii, A. *Zapiski o Shamile.* St. Petersburg, 1960.

Skalon, D. A. *Glavnyi shtab: istoricheskii ocherk vozniknoveniia i razvitiia v Rossii general'nogo shtaba v 1825—1902 gg.* In the series *Stoletie voennogo ministerstva, 1802—1902.* Vol. 3, pt. 2. St. Petersburg, 1910.

Smirnov, N. A. *Miuridizm na Kavkaze.* Moscow, 1963.

Zaionchkovskii, A. M. *Vostochnaia voina 1853—1856 gg. v sviazi s sovremennoi ei politicheskoi obstanovkoi.* St. Petersburg, 1908.

Zisserman, A. L. *Dvadtsat'piat'let na Kavkaze (1842—1867).* St. Petersburg, 1879.

——. *Fel'dmarshal Kniaz' Aleksandr Ivanovich Bariatinskii 1815—1879.* 3 vols. Moscow, 1890.

Selected Articles

Allen, W. E. D. "The Operations of the Allies in the Caucasus, 1853—1855." *The Army Quarterly* 6 (April and July 1923):113—21.

Avtorkhanov, Abdurakhman. "Kavkaz, kavkazskaia voina, i imam Shamil." *Sovetskii Dagestan*, no. 1 (1991):33—40.

Bariatinskii, V. I. "Shamil i Fel'dmarshal Kniaz' Bariatinskii i pis'ma Shamilia i evo zhen." *Russkaia starina*, no. 4 (1880):801—12.

Berzhe, P. "Vyselenie gortsev s Kavkaza." *Russkaia starina*, no. 1 (1882): 161—76; no. 2 (1882):337—63; no. 10 (1882):1—32.

Bolsover, G. H. "David Urquhart and the Eastern Question, 1833—37: A Study in Publicity and Diplomacy." *Journal of Modern History* 8 (December 1936):444—67.

Brooks, E. Willis. "Nicholas as Reformer: Russian Attempts to Conquer the Caucasus, 1825—1855." In *Nation and Ideology: Essays in Honor of Wayne S. Vucinich.* Boulder, CO, 1981.

Bushuev, P. P. "O Kavkazskom miuridizme." *Voprosy istorii*, no. 12 (1956).

"1843-i god na Kavkaze." In *Kavkazskii sbornik.* Vol. 8. Tiflis, 1884, 335—97.

"From Ottoman Archives." *Central Asian Survey*, no. 4 (1985):7—12.

Gammer, Moshe. "Vorontsov's 1845 Expedition Against Shamil: A British Report." *Central Asian Survey* 4, no. 4 (1985):13—33.

"Gornaia artilleriia." *Voennaia entsiklopediia*. Vol. 8. St. Petersburg, 1912, 403—4.

Henze, Paul. "Circassia in the Nineteenth Century: The Futile Flight for Freedom." In *Turko-Tatar Past, Soviet Present*. Ed. Ch. Lemercier-Quelquejay. Paris, 1986.

———. "Fire and Sword in the Caucasus: The 19th Century Resistance of the North Caucasian Mountaineers." *Central Asian Survey* 2, no. 1 (1983):5—44.

Iurov, A. "1843-i god na Kavkaze." In *Kavkazskii sbornik*. Vol. 6. Tiflis, 1882, 1—219.

Kazemzadeh, Firuz. "Russian Penetration of the Caucasus." In *Russian Imperialism: From Ivan the Great to the Revolution*. Ed. Taras Hunczak. New Brunswick, NJ: Rutgers University Press, 1974.

Korolenko, P. O. "Transkubanskii krai." *Voennyi sbornik*, nos. 2, 4—9 (1893).

Kostemirovskii, I. S. "Istoricheskii ocherke. 1. Temir-khan-shura." *Sovetskii Dagestan*, no. 1 (1991):24—28.

Kravtsov, Ivan. "Kavkaz i ego voenachal'niki." *Russkaia starina,* no. 6 (1886).

L.—D. G. "Pokhod 1845 goda v Dargo." *Voennyi sbornik*, no. 7 (1859): 1—63.

N. Sh. "General Veliaminov i ego znachenie dlia istorii kavkazskoi voiny." In *Kavkazskii sbornik*. Vol. 7. Tbilisi, 1883, 1—155.

Okol'nichii, N. "Perechen' poslednikh voennykh sobytii v Dagestane." *Voennyi sbornik*, no. 3, pt. 3 (1859):1—54; no. 4, pt. 4 (1859):305—18; no. 6, pt. 5 (1859):341—80.

Ol'shevskii, M. "Kavkaz s 1841 po 1866 god." *Russkaia starina*, no. 7 (1893).

Pisarev, V. I. "Metody zavoevaniia adygeiskogo naroda tsarizmom v pervoi polovine XIX v." In *Istoricheskie zapiski*. Vol. 9. Moscow: Akademiia Nauk, 1940, 154—85.

Pokrovskii, M. N. "Zavoevanie Kavkaza." In *Istoriia Rossii v XIX veke*. Vol. 5. St. Petersburg, 1907—11, 272—338.

Rhinelander, L. Hamilton. "Russia's Imperial Policy: The Administration of the Caucasus in the First Half of the Nineteenth Century." *Canadian Slavonic Papers*, nos. 2—3 (1975):218—35.

Romanovskii, D. I. "General Fel'dmarshal Kniaz' Aleksandr Ivanovich Bariatinskii i Kavkazskaia voina 1815—1879 gg." *Russkaia starina*, no. 2 (1881):247—318.

———. "Kn. M. S. Vorontsov i Kn. A. I. Bariatinskii." *Russkaia starina*, no. 4 (1881):908—11.

Runovskii, A. "Shamil." *Voennyi sbornik*, no. 11 (1860):529—82.

Rzhevskii, A. "1845-i god na Kavkaze." In *Kavkazskii sbornik*. Vol. 6. Tiflis, 1882, 221—476. Vol. 7. Tiflis, 1883, 383—479.

Shishkevich, M. I. "Pokorenie Kavkaza, Persidskaia i kavkazskaia voiny." In *Istoriia russkoi armii i flota*. Vol. 6. Moscow, 1911—13.

Soltan, V. "Zaniatie Salatavii v 1857 godu." In *Kavkazskii sbornik*. Vol. 8. Tiflis, 1884, 335—97.

Zisserman, A. L. "Khadzhi-Murat. Pis'ma o nem Kn. M. S. Vorontsova i rasskazy Kavkavtsev, 1851—1852 gg." *Russkaia starina*, no. 3 (1881): 655—92.

———. "Kriticheskie zametki." *Russkii arkhiv*, no. 2 (1885):558—69.

———. "Po povodu zapisok M. Ia. Ol'shevskogo." *Russkaia starina*, no. 1 (1885).

Unpublished Manuscripts

Brooks, E. Willis. "D. A. Miliutin: Life and Activity to 1856." Dissertation. Stanford University, 1970.

The Conquest of Central Asia

The conquest of the Caucasus helped set the stage for further Russian expansion. From a geopolitical perspective, Russia's advance into Central Asia was a logical extension of the Anglo-Russian theater of competition from the Turkish straits, to the Caucasus, to the northern fringes of Persia and Afghanistan. The rivalry with England served more as a stimulant than a deterrent to Russian expansion, impelling Russia to move preemptively in Central Asia. Even as he completed his work in the Caucasus, General A. I. Bariatinskii advocated creation of a railroad linking Russian ports on the eastern shore of the Caspian Sea with the Aral Sea, a step necessarily entailing the assertion of Russian power over the khanate of Khiva. Delay, he contended, would "not facilitate our success in the future, but would give freedom to our enemies to strengthen their influence and dominion in Asia."[1]

Bariatinskii would not participate in the conquest of Central Asia, but among those who did were a number of officers who, like him, had served in the Caucasus. Bariatinskii's former chief of staff, Dmitrii Miliutin, would preside over the decisive phase of the conquest during his twenty-year tenure as minister of war from 1861 to 1881. By virtue of his Caucasian experience, Miliutin recognized the complexities of unconventional war, the need for patience, and the challenges of imperial administration. When he assumed office, the immediate task in Central Asia was the assertion of Russian power over the weak but troublesome oasis khanates south of the steppe. The tsar's ministers, however, were by no means united in pursuit of this objective, the costs and risks of which were uncertain. Indeed, in 1868, Governor General Konstantin P. von Kaufman, newly appointed governor general of Turkestan, felt compelled to write a memorandum assuring critics that the costs would not surpass the benefits of ruling Central Asia.[2] Russia would consolidate its grip on the entire region in only two decades, propelled by a variable mixture of lust for conquest, desire for commercial advantages, and the ambitions of local commanders. In so doing, the army would learn a new style of warfare dictated by the harsh climate and vast deserts of Central Asia.

Dmitrii Miliutin served as a young officer in the Caucasus and as minister of war from 1861 to 1881

Governor General K. P. von Kaufman

A Kazakh tribesman (an illustration from a design by Vereshchagin)

Theater Overview

As of 1800, Central Asia was divisible into two distinct geographical and cultural zones. Its northern half was a vast steppe, subject to climatic extremes in summer and winter and populated chiefly by some 2 million nomadic Kazakhs.[3] These people ranged along the upper tier of Central Asia from the edge of the Caspian Sea in the west to the Altai Mountains along the Chinese frontier in the east. Kazakh life necessarily centered around the annual cycle of migration customary to plains herders. The Kazakhs' horses were small and not especially fast, but they were perfectly adapted to the harsh conditions of the steppe and could easily outlast even Cossack mounts over extended marches. Their lives ordered by nature, the Kazakhs needed little formal political structure and invested no more authority in their chiefs than was essential to maintain a semblance of control within and among the tribes. The Kazakhs displayed similar informality in observing the rules of Sunnite Islam.[4]

Within the context of Russia's Central Asian designs, the Kazakh steppe represented the frontier zone dividing the Russian empire from the ancient oasis kingdoms bordering Persia and Afghanistan (see map 1). Faced with unrelenting political, demographic, and military pressure from Russia, the Kazakhs found themselves in a position resembling that of the plains tribes of North America at about the same time. Inexorable encroachment by Russian Cossacks and settlers drove the tribes first to resist the Russians and then to collapse under the weight of relentless demographic and military pressure. The conscious designs of Russian officials and generals aside, the unbridgeable difference between the Russian and Kazakh cultures precluded any chance of stable coexistence.

The second major zone in Central Asia was the desert expanse to the south of the Aral Sea, an area divided by several major rivers and bounded in its southeastern extremity by imposing mountain ranges. The culture in the area centered for many centuries around a cluster of fertile oases linked together by ancient caravan routes. Three so-called khanates—Bukhara (population 3 million), Kokand (population 1.5 million), and Khiva (population 500,000)[5]—dominated the desert and often extended their influence far into the steppe.

The Uzbeks, who enjoyed a long Islamic cultural tradition, an elaborate social structure, and advanced systems of agriculture and commerce, constituted the dominant ethnic group in the khanates. Slightly less influential were the Tajiks and Kirghiz, residing largely in the mountainous, southeastern corner of the region along the Chinese frontier. In the opposite, or western, corner, along the southern shore of the Caspian Sea, the predominantly nomadic Turkomans lived by means of herding, fishing, and plundering.

The khans of Khiva and Kokand and the emir of Bukhara ruled as despots. Their armies, though large, were poorly equipped and organized by contemporary European standards. Kokand and Bukhara, in particular, had developed economies and found foreign buyers for their cotton, textiles, silks, dyes, and fruits.[6] Khiva, though less prosperous, enjoyed the most secure frontiers and greater political stability. Because it was not, like its counterparts, an agglomeration of trade centers with independent traditions, but rather a discrete kingdom buffered on all sides by desert, Khiva proved less susceptible to diplomatic pressures and invasion.[7]

Russia's conquest of Central Asia unfolded in three stages, reflecting the political geography of the region. During the 105-year span from 1735, when it pushed its southern frontier to Orenburg at the northern edge of the Kazakh steppe, to approximately 1840, the Russian empire busied itself with settlement and consolidation of its borderlands in the southeast Volga region and Western Siberia. From 1840 to 1864, Russian forces enveloped the Kazakh steppe. The next step was subjugation of the three Central Asian khanates, which concluded with the fall of Khiva in 1873. Defeat of the Teke Turkomans in the 1880s constituted the final phase of conquest and brought Russian dominion to the modern borders of Iran and Afghanistan.

For the Russians in Central Asia, combat with the enemy did not in itself pose a formidable challenge once its terms were fully understood. Rather, as one contemporary Russian observer put it, the organization of supply and the acquisition of transport constituted "the most important difficulties in the preparation of a campaign."[8]

As in the Caucasus, however, military triumphs alone did not assure political stability. Pacification of the independent Central Asian tribes demanded a skillful blend of coercion, diplomacy, and patient military administration. The latter, in particular, demanded a capacity for subtle judgment and compromise by army commanders that transcended their routine concerns.

The Conquest of Central Asia

At the turn of the nineteenth century, the Orenburg and Siberian Lines (analogous to the Caucasian Line) formally delimited Russian territory in Central Asia (see map 1). Each comprised a string of Cossack settlements and forts intended both to keep the Kazakhs from raiding across the border and to serve as bases for retaliatory raids into the steppe.[9] In the 1820s, Russia organized the steppe into administrative zones. Kazakh tribes in the west fell under the supervision of the governor general of Orenburg, who selected native chieftains (termed sultans) to rule in Russia's name. Each sultan received a Cossack bodyguard of about 200 men—a necessary asset since most did not dare venture into the steppe except under heavy escort. The administration of the Kazakhs farther east by the government of Western Siberia proceeded more smoothly perhaps because of their relative remoteness from the anti-Russian instigations of the khanates.[10]

Kazakh resistance to Russian domination exploded sporadically but suddenly intensified in the 1840s when a Kazakh chieftain by the name of Kenisary Kasimov began to organize the tribes against Russian rule, thereby earning the nickname of the "Kazakh Shamil." The Kazakh bands (usually less than 1,000 strong) were able practitioners of hit-and-run attacks against Russian outposts and caravans. Beginning in 1843, Russia mounted small unsuccessful expeditions (less than 2,000 men) from the Orenburg and West Siberian Lines to trap Kenisary. When pursued, Kenisary shunned battle, electing instead to disappear into the vast steppe. Army detachments foolhardy enough to pursue mounted Kazakh warriors across the prairie risked becoming lost or exhausted, thus becoming easy prey themselves. To camouflage their failures with the area tribes (knowledge of which might send other tribes flocking to Kenisary's standard), the Russians circulated declarations of brilliant victories over a fleeing adversary.[11]

In 1847, conflict on the steppe subsided when Kenisary perished at the hands of rival tribesmen. This turn of fortune presented Russia an opportunity to consolidate its political and military presence through the establishment of imperial outposts deep in Central Asia. Russian commanders, not unlike their Indian-fighting counterparts on the American plains, soon learned to direct their punitive raids against Kazakh villages and encampments for the purpose of driving off cattle, destroying property, and demoralizing the populace. Still, notwithstanding Russian gains, experience showed the futility of attempting to police the steppe from its

A Kazakh winter encampment (this illustration is from a design by Vereshchagin, a prominent Russian artist who accompanied General Skobelev on a campaign in Central Asia)

northern periphery, especially given the disruptive influence of Kokand and Khiva to the south.[12]

Khiva, long a thorn in Russia's side, intermittently seized Russian subjects from merchant caravans bound for Bukhara or from fishing vessels anchored along the Caspian coast. Peter I (the Great) engineered the first attempt to conquer Khiva in 1717, sending a force of 3,727 men under Prince Bekovich-Cherkasskii to make the long and perilous march to Khiva. The prince subsequently defeated a much larger Khivan army in battle but committed the fatal error of entering into negotiations. Feigning submission, the khan persuaded the prince to divide his force into five encampments within the city. As soon as the Russians had settled in, the khan's army swarmed over the isolated detachments and annihilated them.[13]

Russia's second attempt at conquest followed over a century later and met an almost equally disastrous fate. The genesis of the failure of the 1839 expedition under General V. A. Perovskii lay in a punitive expedition undertaken in the winter of 1825—26 against Kazakh raiders along the Emba River, a few hundred miles north of Khiva. A column of 2,310 men departed Orenburg in December and succeeded in striking the Kazakh winter encampments with complete surprise. Rather than face the certain doom of a hasty retreat into the snowy steppe, the Kazakhs capitulated quickly.[14] The experience of this campaign convinced the Russians of the suitability of movement across the steppe during winter.

The proximate cause of the 1839 expedition was the repeated breakdown of relations between Orenburg and Khiva. In 1836, furious Russian authorities had detained all Khivan traders along the Orenburg and Siberian frontiers and demanded the release of Russians held in Khiva. An exchange followed shortly, entailing the return of 105 Russian prisoners. But no sooner had the transaction been completed than the khan seized 200 more Russians on the Mangyshlak Peninsula (an expanse of land jutting into the Caspian Sea and the site of some imperial fishing stations). Thus, in March 1839, Russian military planners proposed an expedition to force the absolute submission of the khan.[15]

The original campaign plan called for a column of 5,000 men to depart in the spring, concealing its military intent under the guise of a scientific expedition to the Aral Sea coast.[16] Perovskii selected a route from Orenburg to the upper Emba River, through the Ust Urt plateau, and along the west bank of the Aral Sea (about 1,000 miles in extent). Two considerations, however, led him to depart in the fall of 1839 rather than the spring of 1840: the readier availability of water during the winter and the precedent of the winter campaign of 1825—26.[17] Preparations, including establishment of two forward supply posts, began in total secrecy. Nevertheless, the khan learned of the unfolding operation and directed Kazakh tribes in the path of the invading army to migrate east and south so that the Russians could not requisition camels and drivers.[18]

The expedition required the procurement of about 2 camels for each soldier and over 2,000 native drivers, one for each 4 or 5 camels.[19] In the end, the Russians employed over 9,000 camels and over 2,000 horses, for which forage alone would tie up half of the supply train.[20] To ease the movement of the huge column, the Russians moved out in four separate detachments between 14 and 17 September. The detachments always stopped at least two hours before sunset to permit the animals to graze. Small groups of Cossacks deployed around the detachments at night to form a security perimeter about a kilometer from the camp.[21] After only a few days, the weather turned cold, and snowstorms, which were to plague Perovskii throughout the campaign, began to take a toll on men and animals. Upon reaching the Emba River supply station on 19 December, the column had already lost approximately 3,000 camels, and the rest could only carry reduced loads.[22]

The journey onward to the Ak Bulak supply station took fifteen days and entailed the loss of still more transport animals. Scarcely over 5,000 camels were now able to continue. Conditions in Ak Bulak itself were miserable, as the disease-ravaged garrison had been forced to withstand several Khivan attacks. His force melting away before his eyes, Perovskii realized he had no option but to retreat, though he was still over 500 miles from Khiva. During the column's return, men and animals suffered still more, and by their arrival, 1,054 men, about 10,000 camels, and a large majority of the horses had perished. Though it did not fundamentally affect Russo-Khivan relations, the expedition so alarmed the khan that he subsequently returned over 400 Russian prisoners.[23]

In the 1840s, Kokand usurped Khiva's place as Russia's foremost challenger in Central Asia by attempting to solidify its influence among the Kazakh tribes north of the Syr River. In the process, Kokand's aspirations to regional hegemony collided directly with those of Russia. Even after Kenisary's death, the Russian policymakers found that "to take nomads as subjects is much easier than to hold them in obedience."[24]

Thus began a concerted Russian drive to secure a position at the southern fringe of the steppe. In 1845, Nicholas I approved a general strategy for a systematic Russian advance employing forward based fortifications and mobile "flying detachments" to subdue local resistance.[25] Converging from Orenburg to the northwest and Western Siberia to the northeast, Russian forces secured a forward frontier line at Kokand's expense. In 1847, they founded the fortress of Aralsk at the mouth of the Syr River on the Caspian Sea. Aralsk became the home base of the Aral Sea flotilla, employed in 1848—49 to map the Aral Sea and the approaches to Khiva. In 1853, the Russians captured Ak Mechet, farther south along the Syr River, and there founded Fort Perovsk. A separate force, advancing from Siberia in 1854, established the fortified outpost of Vernoe (site of modern Alma Ata) south of the Ili River and Lake Issyk Kul.

The outbreak of the Crimean War (1853—56) briefly forestalled further progress, but Russia had by this time nearly enveloped the steppe, although Kirghiz tribes beyond Vernoe remained a problem. A case in point was that of the Bugu Kirghiz. Under the domination of Kokand since the 1820s, the Bugus (numbering about 10,000 households) gave their allegiance to Russia in 1855. In response, Kokand instigated other tribes to attack the Bugus, and intermittent warfare continued until 1860 when a Russian expedition secured the newly proclaimed Alatav district. The campaigns of the mid-1860s aimed at closure of the gap in Russia's frontier between the Syr River outposts and Vernoe.[26]

In 1864, an ambitious colonel, M. G. Cherniaev, led a column from Vernoe and captured the Kokandian fortress of Aulie Ata at little cost. Almost concurrently, a detachment under Colonel N. A. Verevkin captured the town of Turkestan. The two forces then linked up under Cherniaev's command and took Chimkent by siege, thereby giving Russia a continuous line of garrisons across its southern frontier with the territories of Kokand and Bukhara.[27]

Despite their importance, such outposts bore little likeness, in design or purpose, to the border fortresses of Europe, a fact noted by a visiting foreign observer, who said, "All the steppe forts which I have seen throughout the length and breadth of Central Asia—Karabutak, Uralsk, Forts No. 1 and 2, Fort Perovskii, Djulak—are on the same pattern, a mud wall sufficient to resist any force without discipline or cannon, manned by a few hundred seasoned Cossacks."[28] No matter how simple and primitive, such permanent positions assumed tremendous psychological as well as military significance in the advancement of Russian rule. As in the Caucasus, the Russians found that the indigenous populace paid scant heed to rulers who lacked visible military strength.

The Russian conquests of 1863—64 thrust the Central Asian question to the fore of international politics—at least as far as Russia and Britain

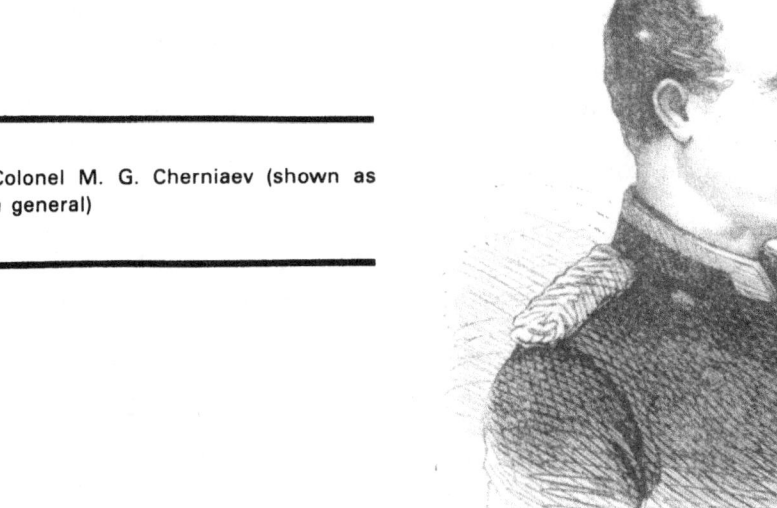

Colonel M. G. Cherniaev (shown as a general)

were concerned. The growth of British diplomatic and commercial contacts in Central Asia during the 1840s sparked a strong competitive response from Russia. In turn, the British viewed Afghanistan as the shield for their Indian Empire and feared that continued southward advancement by Russia might jeopardize their position. Sensitive to such concerns, Russian Foreign Minister Mikhail Gorchakov issued a famous memorandum in 1864 summarizing the state of affairs in Asia and the limits of Russia's aims:

> The position of Russia in Cental Asia is that of all civilized societies which are brought into contact with half-savage, nomad populations, possessing no fixed social organization ... the more civilized state is forced, in the interests of the security of its frontier and its commercial relations, to exercise a certain ascendancy over those whom their turbulent and unsettled character make most undesirable neighbors.[29]

In other words, Russia contended that circumstances, rather than any grand design of conquest, were at the source of Russian expansion. All Russia sought was a stable border with a responsible state and, having achieved this, would seek no further conquests.[30] Gorchakov, who wanted no clash with the British, was not wholly insincere but undoubtedly understood that there were many in his own government who fully expected, sooner or later, to make war on the khanates. Contrary views among the various ministries undoubtedly helped sow confusion at home and abroad. Russian diplomats explained their nation's subsequent military advances as the direct result of treachery by the khanates or the unauthorized actions of overzealous commanders, a calculated fiction termed by one scholar as the "legend of insubordination."[31] In reality, ambitious commanders, acting in the absence of direct supervision and timely communications with St. Petersburg, did hasten Russian expansion, but there is little reason to conclude that they fundamentally altered its course.[32] Had Miliutin, or above all Alexander II, ever firmly intended to stop Central Asian expansion they could have done so. In fact, they generally approved advances, so long as no crisis developed in relations with Britain.

Within months of his 1864 statement, however, Gorchakov was made to look a fool or a liar. Cherniaev, promoted to major general, advanced with a small force on Tashkent, a commercial center under Kokandian rule. His first attempt to take the city failed but, undaunted, he returned to seize Tashkent in 1865. The resultant destabilization in Central Asian politics drew Russia inexorably into the affairs of Bukhara as well as Kokand. While the Kokandian khan was expending his strength in a futile attempt to hold back the tide of Russian arms, Bukhara had begun to maneuver for its own advantage, taking the cities of Kokand and Khodzhent, and might have moved on Tashkent as well had Cherniaev not positioned Russian forces there. Having established Russian authority in Tashkent, where his first act of popular diplomacy was to free the city from taxes for an entire year, Cherniaev turned in 1866 to deal with Bukhara. Before he could do so, however, Miliutin replaced him with the more responsible General D. I. Romanovskii.[33] Yet even after Cherniaev's replacement, the course of affairs changed little. Later the same year, General Romanovskii took Khodzhent from Bukhara, placing Russia in control of the rich Fergana Valley. The fall of Ura-tiube, along the Kokand-Bukhara frontier, soon followed.

General Romanovskii explained both his motives and methods in a message of 7 October 1866 to General N. Kryzhanovskii, commander of the Orenburg district: Ura-tiube, a place where no European had ever set foot, was the most important fortress of the Bukharan emir in the valley of the Syr River, and its capture was a warning to the emir to cease his recent anti-Russian behavior. Romanovskii's column departed on 7 September with a force of nineteen and one-half companies of infantry (organized into two ad hoc battalions), five "hundreds" of Cossack cavalry, a rocket command, eight mountain guns, and four 18-pound mortars. On the 23d, a reconnaissance detachment went ahead to examine the environs of Ura-tiube and entered into talks with the garrison commander. Establishing that the northern face of the fortress was the strongest, the Russians resolved to conduct their main attack from the south, the approaches to which were not obstructed by any natural barriers. Russian artillery easily blew gaps in the walls. The attackers seized the walls in half an hour, and the battle ended an hour later. Only seventeen Russians fell in combat.[34] Because it was unauthorized, the seizure of Ura-tiube displeased Miliutin, whose next communication to Kryzhanovskii directed that no further military actions in the region be undertaken.[35]

By 1868, Russian actions triggered the emergence of a strongly anti-Russian clerical faction in Bukhara that pressed the emir to orchestrate a diplomatic coalition with Kokand, Khiva, Kashgar, and Afghanistan. Given Bukhara's growing influence and central position in the region, the emir's quest might have imperiled the integrity of Russia's newly acquired territories (the district of Turkestan). Therefore, Governor General K. P. von Kaufman immediately mounted a preemptive attack against the ancient commercial city of Samarkand and routed a Bukharan army. Then, leaving a garrison of 700 at nearby Katy-kurgan, Kaufman marched off in search of the main Bukharan army with a column of 3,500 men. In late spring, he cornered his quarry—6,000 Bukharan infantry, 15,000 cavalry, and 14 light cannons (by Russian claims). Better led and far better armed, the Russians disposed of their foe easily. In the meantime, the garrison at Katy-kurgan found itself facing a full-scale insurrection within the city supported by about 40,000 attackers from outside. The beleaguered Russians held out for an entire week before Kaufman returned to restore the situation.[36]

His armies defeated, the emir acceded in 1868 to a treaty granting extensive privileges to Russia. Not only was Bukhara subject to an indemnity, but it ceded unlimited access to its markets to Russian merchants on favorable terms. Thoroughly humiliated, the emir sought to relinquish his title, but the Russians insisted that he remain as a pliable figurehead. The Russians also gained a considerable tract of territory, henceforth to be administered as the Zeravshan district under a military commandant.[37]

Russia's rapid thrusts south of the Syr River during the 1850s and 1860s were positive proof of the superiority of Russian military power over the outmoded armies of the khanates. Though much better organized politically and militarily than the steppe tribes, the khanates proved much easier to subdue because they represented inferior versions of what the Russians considered a conventional adversary. Their cities, upon which all wealth and power depended, constituted fixed objectives, and their armies repeatedly engaged the Russians in open battle, for which they had neither adequate firepower nor discipline. Even with great numerical advantages, the Central Asians of the oasis khanates had little chance of victory, a fact that emerges clearly in the record of their losses to the Russians. Through the course of hundreds of military actions during the entire period from 1847 to 1873, the Russians suffered an incredibly low 2,000 battle casualties.[38]

The Nature of Combat in Central Asia

It would be a mistake to assume that the conquest of Central Asia did not pose distinct and serious military problems. Some of these the Russians overcame on the basis of their long experience in the Caucasus. The order of column movements and the pattern of defense of the supply trains, for example, were products of the Russian Caucasus experience. As in the Caucasus, a large expedition had to be virtually self-sufficient, though it would establish forward supply points where possible. Communication between cities and garrisons or among forces in the field was extremely difficult to maintain. The division of large forces into echelons often proved essential because the number of wells along even the best routes was seldom sufficient to accommodate an entire expedition at one time. For instance, in 1873, the Mangyshlak detachment, part of the great Khivan campaign, crossed the desert in three echelons. The first moved from 0300 to 0900, and again from 1600 to 2000. The second and third echelons were each staggered one phase back. Thus, the second echelon departed at 1600 and always remained one stop back on the trail. The third echelon followed behind the second. As a general rule, the echelons never moved beyond six hours' range from one another.[39]

Even in Central Asia, the enemy was dangerous if precautions were not strictly observed. When a column was in movement, the supply train required constant protection on all sides by the infantry. In the train itself, camels bearing wooden crates of food and other items were arranged on the outside so that their loads might hastily be employed in the construction of a laager. The advance and rear guards, consisting of cavalry (usually Cossacks), stayed within one to two miles of the main force. Cossacks also patrolled alongside the column at close range.

Russian columns in Turkestan, including vast numbers of horses and camels, could sometimes move over thirty miles in a day before stopping to establish an encampment.[40] Because of its flat, open expanses, the steppe afforded few satisfactory defensive positions for night encampments. Thus, Russian forces at rest normally organized themselves into a square formation, sometimes using packs and wagons to form breastworks. Cossacks and infantry held the outer faces, with guns and rockets situated at the corners. The horses and camels were kept inside the square, as were any livestock brought along.[41]

As adversaries, the nomads were daring and resourceful but lacked the discipline to break Russian formations or to sustain an assault. One of the nomads' preferred modes of attack was to surround a Russian column and strike its flanks and rear. But experience had shown that if the Russians held formation and maintained a strong reserve to prevent a breakthrough— the result of which could indeed be catastrophic against a numerically superior foe—they had little to fear.[42] In addition, the armies of the khanates, like the war parties of their nomadic brethren, were predominantly cavalry and showed little appreciation of military art.

In contrast, Russian columns included forces of all three main fighting arms. Infantry, however, was the most essential. Central Asian cavalry could battle regular and Cossack cavalry on even terms or better, but neither native cavalry nor infantry were able to overcome the disciplined fire of European infantry—especially with the advent of the rifle during the 1860s. And when the enemy succeeded in pressing its attack at close range, infantry bayonets proved indispensable. The most useful Russian cavalry in Central Asia was that of the Cossacks due to the superior endurance of the men and their mounts. Though valuable for pursuit and maneuver, cavalry could not be employed in large numbers because of the great demand of the horses for scarce forage and water. Nor could detachments of cavalry long separate from the main column without risk. The native horses of the Kazakhs, inured to the hardships of the steppe, could outlast their better-bred cousins from the north.[43]

Large Russian columns of mixed forces, encumbered by long logistical trains, made little pretense of deceptive maneuver. The establishment of forward supply stations in the steppe also had the disadvantage of warning the enemy of an impending operation and its general direction. The procurement, by rent or purchase, of large numbers of camels and the hiring of drivers similarly alerted the natives. When possible, the Russians selected a line of approach that concealed their final objective, but they seldom preserved operational security for long. Any column moving in daylight could be spotted from great distances, so concealed movement was possible only at night.[44]

Russian advances into the desert frequently culminated in an assault of a fortified town. At first, commanders conducted conventional sieges, but finding most Central Asian fortifications less than impregnable, they soon came to rely on simple bombardments and storming. In 1853, employing standard engineering procedures, a siege took three weeks. In contrast, in 1861, Iany Kurgan fell to the Russians in a single day as did Aulie Ata in 1864. During this period, the Russians learned that the Central Asians lacked the firepower and discipline to keep storming troops away from their city walls. Russia's adoption of rifled artillery in the 1860s was especially noteworthy. Unlike the smoothbore weapons of the past, higher-velocity rifled guns easily battered and penetrated the clay fortifications prevalent in Central Asia.[45]

With the establishment of permanent forts deep in the steppe, the Russians no longer regularly sent detachments ahead to set up temporary supply stations. When on the march, the greatest enemy of the Russian soldier was not the Central Asian he was sent to fight but the ravages of extreme heat or cold, disease, thirst, and exhaustion. Normally, the purpose of reconnaissance and the interrogation of natives was to determine the location of wells. But even with an adequate supply of water, conditions in a train were often grueling and unhealthy. On a large expedition, the sick and wounded required isolation in field hospitals, or if the column was large enough to provide protection, they could travel separately.[46] Fuel was often scarce, and although the native grasses burned well, they did not grow abundantly. The consequent use of animal dung for cooking fires, in turn, necessitated the procurement of pots with lids so that the food would not be tainted by foul odors.[47]

Khan Seid Mahomet-Rakhim, the khan of Khiva

The Khivan Campaign of 1873

Slowly and methodically, the Russians adapted to local conditions and grew bolder in their thinking. The submission of Bukhara in 1868 led Russia almost inevitably to renew its quest to tame an old nemesis, the khan of Khiva, and thereby gain control of the Amu River all the way to the Afghan frontier. In 1870, Miliutin himself suggested that a campaign against Khiva was inevitable.[48] One important step making possible an advance on Khiva from the Caspian shore was the establishment in 1869 of a base at Krasnovodsk. During the next several years, Russian columns from the Caucasus Military District extensively reconnoitered the Trans-caspia region and the periphery of the khanate.[49]

Surrounded by scorching deserts on all sides, the khanate of Khiva made a formidable objective. In addition to the oasis population of over 400,000, the khan claimed sovereignty over neighboring Turkoman nomads, many of whom paid him heed (and taxes) according to the expediency of the moment.[50] Historically, the khan had relied on his geographical position and its harsh environment as his principal defense, but he also maintained an army of variable size, consisting of infantry (mainly Uzbek and armed with antiquated muskets) and cavalry (mainly Turkoman). Though less than a model of efficiency, the khan's army could make life extremely difficult for an adversary worn down by the trials of a desert campaign.

Aware of the perils ahead, Governor General Kaufman was not content to entrust the Khivan expedition to the command of the Caucasus Military District. Command rivalries may have played a role in the decision, but it was equally justified on the basis of past disasters. Thus, Kaufman resolved to launch simultaneous expeditions from the Caucasus (using forces ferried to the eastern shore of the Caspian), Orenburg, and Turkestan—all under his overall command.[51] Notwithstanding security precautions, Khan Seid Mahomet-Rakhim learned of Russia's intentions and did his best to impede Russian preparations. In order to disrupt the formation of an expedition from Krasnovodsk, the khan used his influence among the Kazakhs of the Mangyshlak Peninsula to deny Russia access to their camels. In addition, in 1872, the khan sent an embassy to Krasnovodsk, and then on to the Caucasus, to seek accommodation with Russia. By this time, however, Russia had lost interest in negotiating with the khan, and Kaufman executed his plan.

Kaufman launched his campaign in the spring of 1873 so as to reach Khiva before the advent of the deadly summer heat (see map 7). According to Kaufman's plan, 2 columns would depart the Turkestan District—1 from Tashkent (actually forming in Dzhizak) and the other from Kazalin—and traverse a distance of 600 to 700 miles. They were to link up upon reaching the Amu River (demarcating the end of the desert and the threshold of the

The remains of the old city wall of Khiva (a modern view)

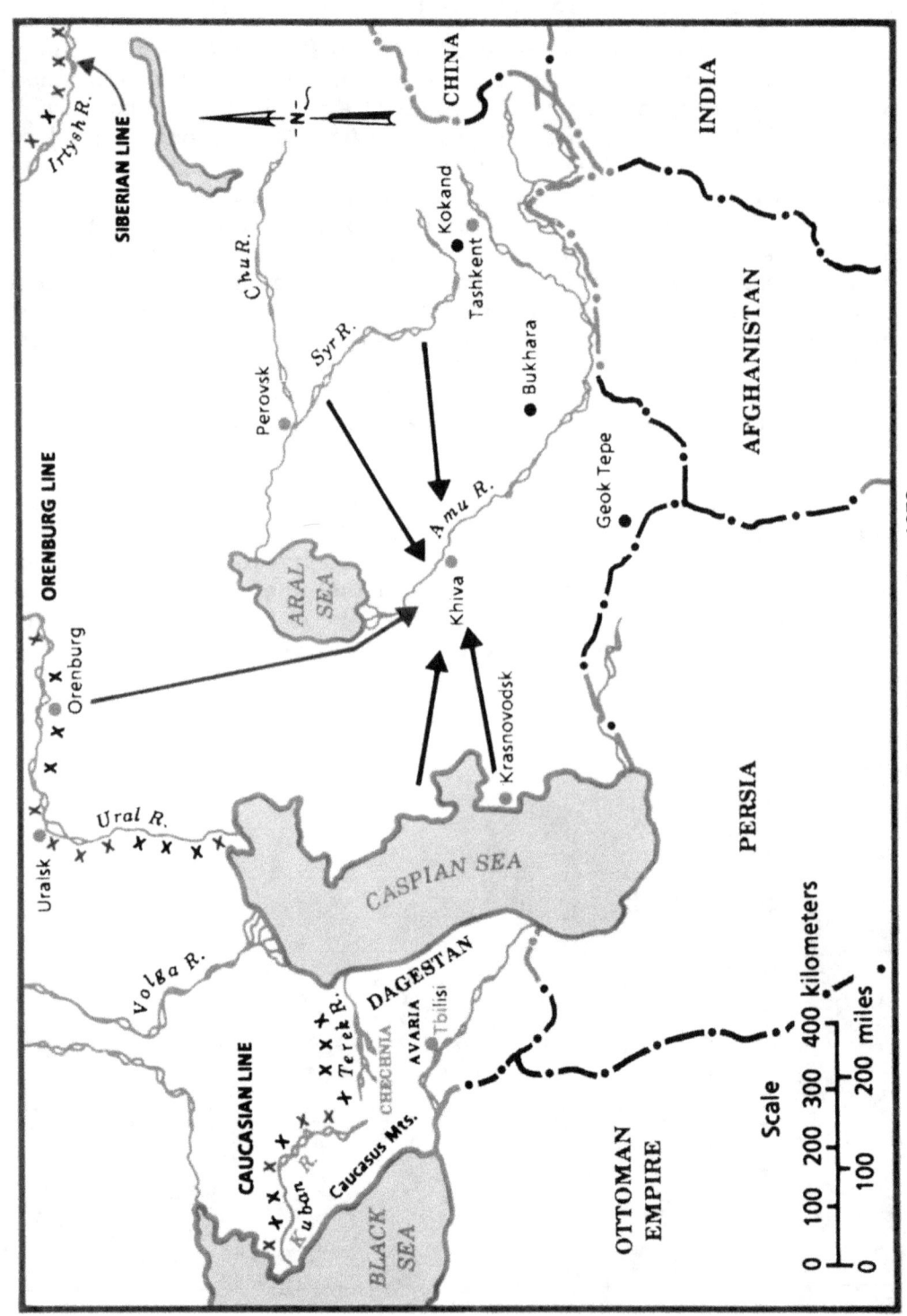

Map 7. The Khivan campaign, 1873

Khivan oasis) and cross together to join up with other advancing forces. The third column, originating in Orenburg, was to travel the greatest distance, almost 1,000 miles. Meanwhile, two additional columns formed by the Caucasus Military District were to move from Mangyshlak and Krasnovodsk, permitting the shortest (perhaps 500 miles) but not the easiest line of approach.[52] The Russians divided the Turkestan and Caucasian forces into separate columns and subdivided the columns into echelons, reflecting the normal Russian concern over the availability of water en route.

Despite lengthy preparation, the Russian columns encountered severe difficulties on the long march. The Dzhizak column, under Kaufman's personal command, departed in March but met terrible heat in April. Several times, Kaufman had to split his column, which in one instance was so badly extended that his lead and rear elements were seven and one-half hours apart on the trail. Eventually, he directed his cavalry to proceed by a separate route and join him at the Amu River. (For the composition of Russian forces in the Khivan campaign, see table 2.)[53]

TABLE 2
Composition of Russian Forces in the Khivan Campaign

	Companies	Squadrons	Guns	Rocket Launchers	Men	Horses	Camels
Dzhizak column	12	5½	14	4	3,400	1,300	7,000
Kazalin column	9	1½	8	4	1,900	350	7,000
Orenburg column	9	9	12	6	3,500	1,800	5,700
Mangyshlak column	12	6	6	3	2,100	650	1,500
Krasnovodsk column	12	4	16	3	2,200	500	2,600

Source: A. I. Maksheev, *Istoricheskii obzor Turkestana* (St. Petersburg: 1890), 313–15.

Kaufman's first concern upon reaching the frontier of the khanate was to establish contact with the other converging columns, from whom he had heard nothing since 30 April, and to explain his presence to the local populace. On 14 May, the general dispatched riders to the other four columns, only two of whom reached their destination. Meanwhile, he sent proclamations to the inhabitants of nearby villages informing them that the emperor was not making war against the "peaceful laborers" of the region but rather against their ruler, who was implacably hostile to Russia and oppressed his subjects. Kaufman promised no harm would come to those who would remain in their villages and carry on their normal affairs. Conversely, those who chose to flee or resist would be considered enemies and forfeit their property. On the whole, the Russians received a satisfactory response and found some natives to be quite helpful as guides or procurement agents.[54]

Poised on the Amu River, Kaufman no longer faced a water shortage but found he had all but exhausted his forage and could no longer rely on his transport animals. Therefore, the Russians availed themselves of native carts over the remaining short distance to Khiva.[55] Kaufman used a modest flotilla of three small iron rowboats, dubbed "Kaufmanki" (or "little Kaufmans"), in exploring the river and supporting the crossing.[56] Meanwhile, Kaufman left three squadrons of cavalry to hold the crossing and advanced with twelve companies of infantry, three "hundreds," and twelve field guns.[57] Having made it this far, he was virtually assured of success.

The Orenburg column, given the long familiarity of its officers and men with the harsh conditions of the steppe, was especially well prepared. Assembling in February, the column marched to the northwest shore of the Aral Sea in mid-April, proceeding in four echelons through deep snow. On 8 May, the Orenburg column approached Kungrad, and on 12 May, lead elements of the Caucasus detachment arrived signaling readiness for the final push toward Khiva.[58]

The Mangyshlak column, perhaps as a consequence of the khan's efforts, was unable to obtain the required number of camels. As a result, its commander, Colonel N. P. Lomakin, had to reduce his infantry by a third, from eighteen companies to twelve. Among his six cavalry squadrons were elements of the Dagestan Irregular Cavalry Regiment, consisting of mountaineers from the very populace so recently conquered in the eastern Caucasus.[59] Even Lomakin's reduced force, which departed Kinderli Bay in April, suffered terribly in the fierce desert conditions and barely reached its supply station at Bish-akt before the men were unfit to continue. The second Caucasian column, the Krasnovodsk detachment, had been unable to complete the journey from Chikishliar across the desert and withdrew to

Khiva and the Hazar-Asp gate

The great square at Khiva

A street in modern Khiva (a restoration of earlier structures)

Courtesy of Dr. Robert F. Baumann

the coast. On 12 May, Lomakin joined forces with the Orenburg column at Kungrad, making a combined detachment of sixteen companies, eight squadrons, and fourteen guns. A large force of Khivans, estimated at 6,000, conducted several attacks against them but withdrew after sustaining heavy losses. The actions cost the Russians only seventeen men.[60]

On 28 May, all forces gathered under Kaufman's command in the environs of Khiva, and the khan, recognizing the inevitable, sent an emissary offering to surrender. By the resultant treaty, Khiva forfeited its lands on the right bank of the Amu River and, like Bukhara before it, granted extensive privileges to Russian merchants.[61] From a military perspective, the campaign of 1873 demonstrated the power of Russia to project its military strength throughout the region. Accumulated experience, meticulous attention to supply and reconnaissance, the establishment of temporary and permanent garrison posts, and tactical superiority made Russian arms all but irresistible in Central Asia. Nature (the climate and topography) had been the Russians' greatest enemy, and it had been overcome.

The Final Phase of Conquest

With the submission of all three khanates, the problems of military administration of the region assumed precedence. Trouble first erupted in Kokand, whose ruler, Khudoiar Khan, was unpopular in his own right—in addition to being an instrument of the tsar. In July 1875, a rebel uprising drove the khan from Kokand into the protection of the Russian Army. Within a short time, the rebels proclaimed support for Khudoiar's son, Nasr-Eddin, and attacked the Russian garrison in Khodzhent, which consisted of one battalion and two companies of infantry, a local militia, a squadron of Cossacks, and an artillery battery. On 9 August, a detachment consisting mainly of 4 infantry companies left the fortress and engaged a horde of rebels estimated at 10,000 and drove them to the outskirts of the town. From Tashkent, Kaufman promptly organized a large expedition to deal with the rebellion.[62]

On 22 August, a Russian column of 16 companies, 9 squadrons, and 20 field guns engaged a huge rebel horde estimated at over 40,000 (probably an inflated figure) near Makhram and was quickly surrounded. Well-directed infantry and artillery fire enabled the Russians to break the encirclement, and an attack in columns followed against enemy positions. A young commander, Colonel M. D. Skobelev, led three squadrons of Cossacks on an attack against the flank of the retreating rebel mob and pursued the scattered remnants for about six miles. Russian casualties in the action totaled six killed and eight wounded.[63] Kaufman followed up his victory with a march on Kokand, from which the rebel leader, Abdurakhman-avtobachi, fled with about 8,000 horsemen. The Russians continued their pursuit to the town of Margelan and beyond. Nasr-Eddin had little choice but to sue for peace and ultimately ceded to Russia all former Kokandian territory on the right bank of the Syr River.[64]

M. D. Skobelev (shown as a general)

What Russia failed to recognize was that Nasr-Eddin had not created the rebellion and that his capitulation did not spell its end. In a pattern foreshadowing the chaotic 1920s, throngs of rebels gathered under the banner of Pulat-bek, a relative of Khudoiar Khan, in the eastern fringes of Kokandian territory, and made a stand at Andizhan. On this occasion, a determined and well-organized defense blunted a Russian assault. The reduction of Andizhan was left to Skobelev, whose recent exploits had brought him rapid elevation to major general. Skobelev attacked Tiura-kurgan and Namangan in succession, carrying the latter by means of heavy bombardment and assault by storm. He then advanced to Andizhan and simply bombarded the defenders into submission. By the end of the year, Russia abandoned its intention to restore Khudoiar to his throne, despite an invitation for his return from the city elders. Instead, Skobelev received orders to occupy the city, and in February 1876, Tsar Alexander II proclaimed the annexation of the entire Kokand region.[65] In order to cement control over the Kirghiz tribes of the remote, mountainous region of southeastern Kokand, Skobelev led a small column officially described as a "scientific expedition"—so as to calm the British—into the Alai Valley in the foothills of the Pamirs. His purpose was to impress upon the inhabitants Russia's ability to project its power to all corners of its new territories.[66]

Yet, as in the Caucasus, the establishment of military superiority was only a part of the equation for effective rule. In 1867, the tsar affirmed the formation of the Turkestan governor generalship, embracing the Syr-Darya and Semireche oblasts (as well as territories to be acquired subsequently, such as Fergana in 1876 under Kaufman). The investment of full military and civil authority (to include foreign relations) in a single individual, Kaufman, streamlined administration. An experienced administrator, Kaufman had served in the Caucasus and knew the pitfalls of treading too heavily on native customs and beliefs.[67] Accordingly, Russia moved patiently and deliberately in the imposition of a new administrative order, showing at least nominal respect for the forms of local social life. To do any less would have been reckless in view of the small numbers of Russians (perhaps 25,000 men) and the dispersal of their forces.

As a practical matter, Kaufman at first found it expedient to rule through native institutions and officials when possible. During the first ten years of his administration, he frequently was diverted from tasks of government by the need to conduct military operations. Still, Kaufman successfully established order in Turkestan. In 1877, in the wake of disorders across Kokand, Kaufman discarded indigenous economic and social institutions in favor of the Russian system of administration. Recruitment of Russian bureaucrats to Central Asian service was a problem, however, as few with any alternative prospects would accept such a purgatorial career.[68] Meanwhile, Russia did not vigorously pursue a policy of settlement in Central Asia as it had elsewhere on the imperial periphery. Colonization was an expensive proposition, and many in St. Petersburg doubted the wisdom of investing in Central Asia.[69]

Following the Russo-Turkish War of 1877—78, the outstanding problem of Russian rule in Central Asia was the stubborn resistance of the Turkoman tribes of the Teke oasis in Transcaspia (modern Turkmenistan). Further, tensions with Britain necessitated a speedy subjugation of the Turkomans.[70] In 1879, General I. D. Lazarev, commander of the First Army of the Caucasus, led a detachment of about 6,000 men (8 1/2 infantry battalions and 10 squadrons of cavalry) into the Teke oasis to subdue the recalcitrant nomads. The campaign began inauspiciously when Lazarev died of an infection on the trail and General N. P. Lomakin assumed charge. Despite supply problems, Lomakin pushed hurriedly on to Geok Tepe near the Iranian frontier, where about 20,000 Turkomans had gathered in a great earthen fortress. The Russians quickly took the outer defensive positions and pounded the fortress with artillery fire. Large numbers of Turkomans, among them many women and children, poured out of the fortress only to be driven back by Russian fire. Believing his enemy in disarray, Lomakin arrogantly elected to storm the fortress and thereby handed the outgunned Turkomans a stunning opportunity. Able to meet the Russians in close, often hand-to-hand combat, the Turkomans repelled the invaders with pikes and sabers, inflicting 453 casualties.[71] Lomakin withdrew in disorder.

A view of the railway station at Geok Tepe, ca. 1890

Teke Turkomans plowing one of their fields, ca. 1890

Subsequent investigation showed that Lomakin's attack had been ill-conceived from the start. Instead of concentrating his assault on a particular portion of the fort, the walls of which were protected by steep ditches, five battalions advanced along a broad front. Lomakin's undoing began with his neglect to coordinate or concentrate artillery fire in support of the attack. Nor did he bother to form special groups of men to surmount the fortress walls.[72] The retreat suffered as well from dismal preparation and a "total lack of unity of control."[73] Furthermore, the eight Red Cross wagons available to transport the wounded had a total capacity of only sixteen men. When the demoralized column completed the eight-mile trek back to its base at Iangi-kala, the men, who had not eaten for two days, were on the brink of exhaustion.[74]

Impatient to expunge any psychological effects of the Russian defeat, Miliutin urged the organization of a new expedition as soon as possible (see map 8).[75] General Adjutant Skobelev, most recently a hero of the Battle of Plevna versus the Turks, took charge of the operation at the tsar's personal direction[76] and, in a style sharply different from that of Lomakin and Lazarev, carried out meticulous preparations. Skobelev conducted extensive reconnaissance of possible routes of approach from Krasnovodsk and Chikishliar and chose Bami as the most suitable position for a supply station from either direction. He further arranged resupply by sea and, with diplomatic support, orchestrated the establishment of a supply point on the Persian side of the frontier opposite Geok Tepe. An enthusiast of gadgetry and technology, Skobelev brought along a water-freshening device as well as the latest military hardware: machine guns, rockets, hand grenades, and several heliographs.[77]

In assembling his force, Skobelev applied the so-called "Turkestan proportions," according to which a 200-man company had sufficient combat power to match 1,000 disorganized Central Asians. Even a company, he believed, if properly commanded was tantamount to a "moving Strasbourg" in the context of Central Asian warfare.[78] Skobelev was not one to rely blindly on his own assumptions, however, and insisted on taking a small expedition of 1,000 men on reconnaissance to the very walls of Geok Tepe. Skobelev even staged a mock assault on the fortress. After firing 120 rounds of artillery at its western face, Skobelev abruptly withdrew his force in perfect order to the accompaniment of music.[79]

In November, Skobelev began the actual expedition to Geok Tepe with a force of about 7,000 men. As in 1879, the Turkomans retreated deep into the Teke oasis and, finally, to Geok Tepe, where perhaps 35,000 men, women, and children congregated.[80] Skobelev first captured the village of Iangi-kala, which controlled the water supply to Geok Tepe.

Before the storming of Iangi-kala on 18 December, Skobelev included in his instructions to his officers a detailed assessment of the fighting qualities of the Turkomans and practical advice for engaging them:

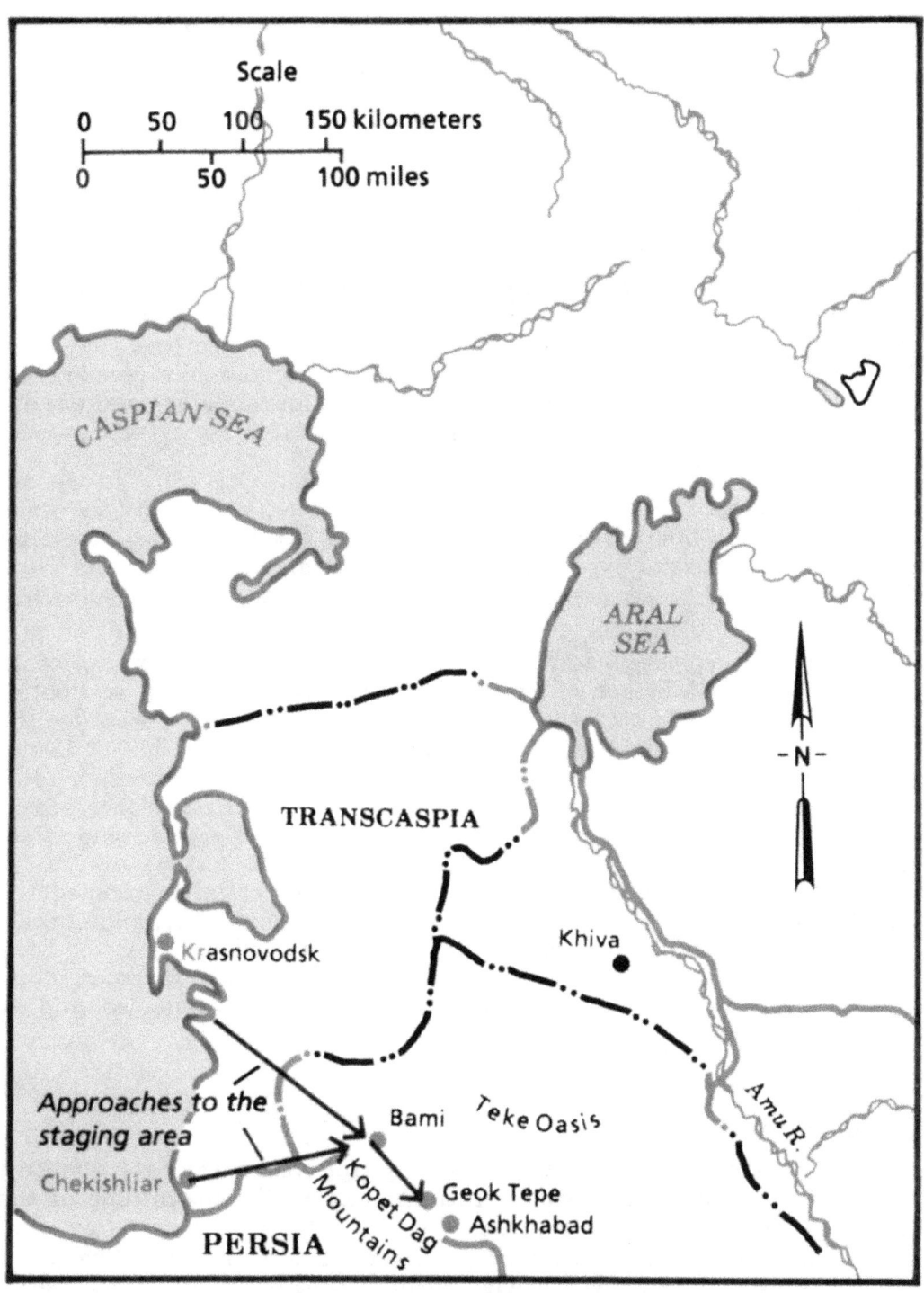

Map 8. The Akhal-Teke campaign, 1880—81

> Obstinate fighting is to be expected for local objects. The enemy is brave, and skillful in single combat; he fires effectively, and is provided with a good sidearm, but he operates in individual extended order, or in detached bodies, but little obedient to the will of their chief, and, therefore, unfit, notwithstanding their overwhelming numbers, for combined action and manoeuvering in masses.[81]

Under no circumstances would Skobelev permit the enemy to dictate the terms of battle.

With the seizure of Iangi-kala, Skobelev methodically opened the siege and assault on Geok Tepe (see map 9). Russian siege lines spread the force dangerously thin, a situation Skobelev himself acknowledged. Fully realizing that the Russians had difficulty manning their established lines, and thus could never hope to impose a full blockade on the two-mile perimeter of Geok Tepe, the Turkomans resolved to await the inevitable general assault in which they hoped to repeat their success of 1879.[82] Skobelev, however, had no intention of repeating Lomakin's errors.

Skobelev's plan called for the detonation of mines underneath the walls and a half-hour bombardment to precede an attack by two storming columns. The Russians expected an intense and prolonged battle for Geok Tepe as evidenced by the issue of a 2-day supply of rations and 200 rounds to each soldier.[83]

The mines exploded according to plan at 1120 on the morning of 12 January, creating a breach of over forty yards in width directly in front of Skobelev's main column on the right flank. As the Russians penetrated the inner fortress, large numbers of Turkomans withdrew to the hill of Dengil Tepe in the northwestern corner of the fortress. A second Russian force broke through a breach on the southern face of the fortress. Once within the walls, the Russians encountered less opposition and greater panic than expected. Thousands of Turkomans streamed out of the fortress toward the north, while fighting continued within. Russian cavalry pursued the fugitives and massacred combatants and noncombatants alike, killing some 8,000 in all. Approximately 6,500 Turkomans perished inside Geok Tepe. Russian losses for the day's action were 59 killed and 254 wounded. Total casualties for the campaign numbered 290 killed and 833 wounded, and an additional 645 men perished from disease.[84]

Conclusions

The Russian victory at Geok Tepe extinguished the last effective resistance to imperial rule in Central Asia, and the magnitude of the slaughter left an indelible impression on the Turkomans as reflected in subsequent recollections of a British observer, who commented: "Five years later, when the railway was opened to Ashkhabad, and in the course of the inaugural ceremonies the Russian military music began to play, the Turkoman women and children raised woeful cries of lamentation, and the men threw themselves on the ground with their foreheads in the dust."[85]

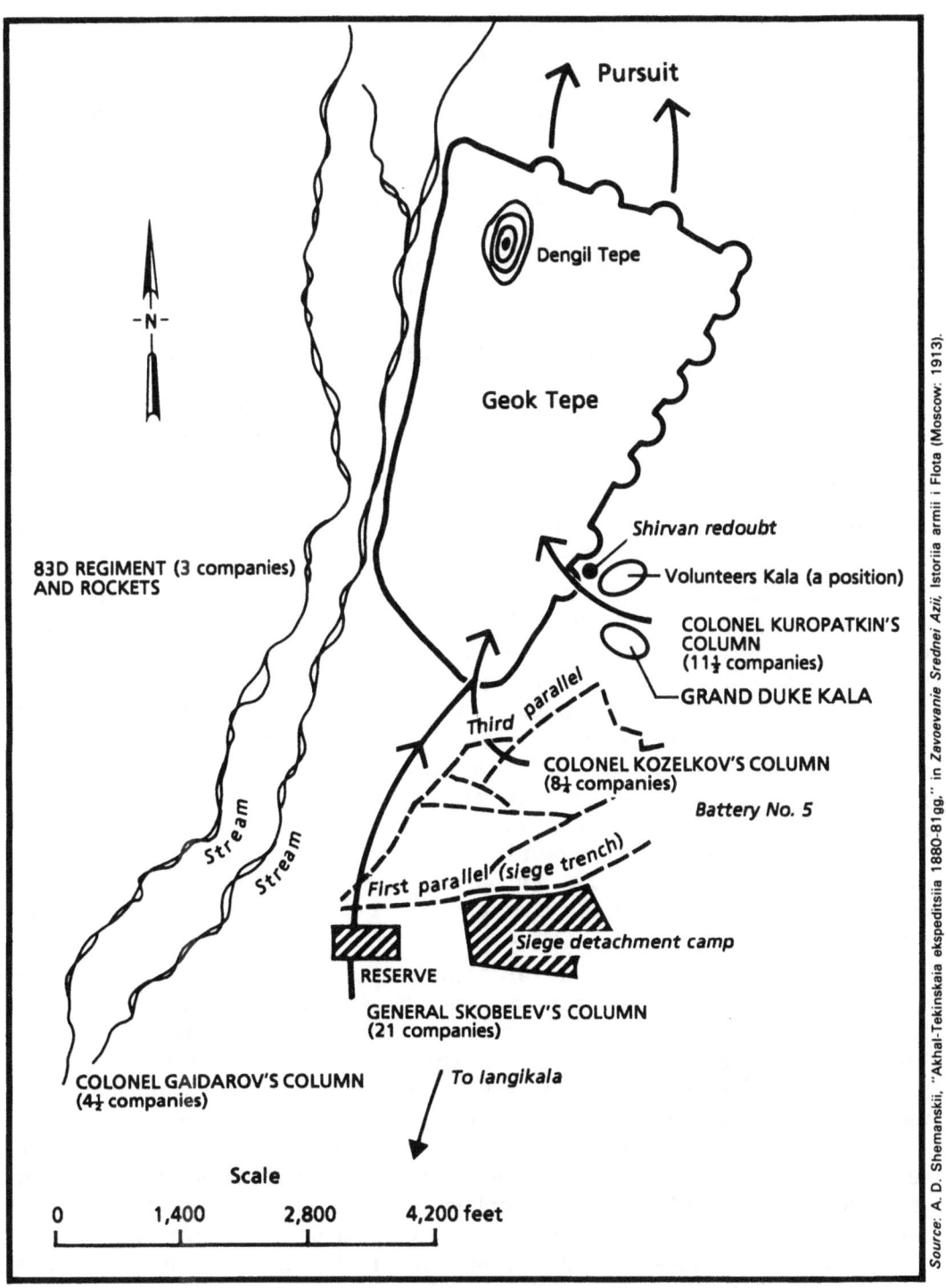

Map 9. The storming of Geok Tepe fortress, 12 January 1881

Such commentaries by British commentators may have been self-serving and even hypocritical, but the psychological impact of events at Geok Tepe was nonetheless profound. The Russians encountered little resistance to their rule in Central Asia and in Turkmenia, in particular, in the decades prior to World War I.

Though similar in many tactical respects, Russia's experience in Central Asia differed in important ways from that in the Caucasus. Resistance in Central Asia was never unified, and at no time did a charismatic leader emerge to guide the disparate rebel efforts in a common direction. Given the modest scale of Russian forces in Central Asia—the total infantry of which never exceeded 31 battalions and the cavalry strength being far less than that—the management of a populace of 5 million people over a vast territory (roughly 3 million square kilometers) would have been extraordinarily difficult had the opposition ever coalesced or had the indigenous population ever engaged in widespread guerrilla warfare. General Skobelev recognized such a potential in the region and argued strenuously that Russia must act decisively and ruthlessly to prevent a prolongation of hostilities. The general never failed to follow his own advice, and Russian rule enjoyed an extended period of stability.[86]

Yet the absence of a genuine resistance movement in Central Asia was due to more than Skobelev's ruthlessness. Conspicuously absent in the Central Asians, in comparison with the Caucasians, was the fusion of a warrior spirit with religious zeal. The nomadic Kazakhs of the steppe and the Turkomans of the Teke oasis were splendid and daring fighters but were motivated almost exclusively by a desire to preserve their traditional way of life. Their numbers were small, and their independent spirit prevented them from massing their strength. Meanwhile, the great settled populace of the khanates, though occasionally volatile, showed little passion for fighting. Their religion, founded on a rich cultural heritage, did not impel them to martyrdom. The ancient commercial centers of Central Asia retained in some measure the cosmopolitan outlook of a more prosperous age.

Russia's absorption of Central Asia was of tremendous import to the empire, both politically and economically, affording Russia complete domination of the Caspian Sea and its markets, strengthening Russia's grip on the affairs of Iran, and granting it new, valuable leverage in its affairs with Britain. The legacy for the army, as in the case of the Caucasus, was modest and short-lived. The sudden death of Skobelev, whose legend had assumed heroic proportions, accounted in part for this fact. Officers who served in Central Asia found no new theater to which they could transfer their experience. Russia became increasingly entangled in European affairs and in the competition for markets and influence in the Far East. Thus, the perspective of Russian officers on the great campaigns of the steppe and desert is perhaps best typified by this view expressed by a Russian officer to an English correspondent, David Ker, of the *Daily Telegraph*:

> Turkestan is to us what Algeria has been to France—a kind of training school for more serious work. A good many of our young officers will learn

> their first lessons from this expedition, and will be all the better for it; but taken altogether, Asiatic warfare is hardly a good school for European soldiers....[87]

Turkestan was, however, a good training ground for unconventional warfare, as the Caucasus had been before it. The unnamed officer's analogy to it and Algeria was more apt than he knew. Just as the French were to learn that unconventional enemies could exhaust the will and resources of a powerful state, so Russia would discover in the twentieth century that unconventional resistance by a highly motivated adversary is extremely difficult to extinguish by conventional military means.

The gulf between cultures on the frontier could not be bombarded away. While failing to close this gulf, Russian administration gradually paved the way for settlement and the intrusion of alien ways. In the aftermath of the Russian Revolution of 1917, accumulated Muslim frustrations would fuel a stubborn resistance movement that would test the collective wits of the Red Army.

As an institution, the Russian Army never codified the lessons learned in decades of campaigning in Central Asia. By World War I, the army of Turkestan lost its distinctive character and became just another European-style formation. The task thus fell to Red Army historical analysts to resurrect the implied doctrine of Central Asian campaigning by combing through military libraries for instructive articles and memoirs, even as combat unfolded in Central Asia during the 1920s.

Notes

Chapter 2

1. "Pis'mo gen. adiut. kn. Bariatinskogo k voennomu ministru, gen. adiut. Sukhozanetu, ot 9-go iiunia 1857 goda," *Akty sobrannye kavkazskoi arkheograficheskoi kommissiei*, vol. 12, pt. 3 (Tiflis, 1893), 196—97. As noted by Jacob Kipp, "Russian Naval Reformers and Imperial Expansion, 1856—1863," in *Soviet Armed Forces Review Annual*, vol. 1 (Gulf Breeze, FL: Academic International Press, 1977), 123, the Naval Ministry also took an active interest in Central Asian expansion.

2. Central State Historical Archive, St. Petersburg, Russia, fund 954 (K. P. von Kaufman), index 1, file 112, sheets 1—8.

3. A. N. Kuropatkin, *Zadachi russkoi armii*, vol. 2 (St. Petersburg, 1910), 96.

4. Elizabeth Bacon, *Central Asians Under Russian Rule: A Study in Culture Change* (Ithaca, NY: Cornell University Press, 1980), 31, 38.

5. N. A. Khalfin, *Prisoedinenie Srednei Azii k Rossii* (Moscow: Nauka, 1965), 52—53.

6. Geoffrey Wheeler, "Russian Conquest and Colonization of Central Asia," in *Russian Imperialism: From Ivan the Great to the Revolution* (New Brunswick, NJ: Rutgers University Press, 1974), 270; and Bacon, *Central Asians Under Russian Rule*, 57—61, 74—75.

7. Mary Holdsworth, *Turkestan in the Nineteenth Century* (London: Central Asian Research Center, 1959), 21—22.

8. V. Potto, "O stepnykh pokhodakh," pt. 2, *Voennyi sbornik*, no. 5 (1873):25.

9. A. Smirnov and N. Ustiugov, eds., *Ocherki po istorii Bashkirskoi ASSR*, vol. 1, pt. 2 (Ufa, Bashkis A.S.S.R.: Akademiia Nauk Bashkirskii Filial, 1959), 36. See also Alton S. Donnelly, *The Russian Conquest of Bashkiria, 1552—1740* (New Haven, CT: Yale University Press, 1968).

10. F. I. Lobysevich, *Postupatel'noe dvizhenie v Sredniuiu Aziiu v torgovom i diplomaticheskovoennom otnoshenniakh (Dopolnitel'nyi material dlia istorii khivinskogo pokhoda 1873 g.)* (St. Petersburg, 1900), 71—72.

11. N. Sereda, "Bunt kirgizskogo sultana Kenisary Kasimova," *Vestnik Evropy*, no. 4 (1871):655—60.

12. E. U., "Stepnaia voina v Turkestanskom krae," *Voennyi sbornik*, no. 7 (1880):71; and Potto, "O stepnykh pokhodakh," 19.

13. Dmitrii Golosov, "Pokhod v Khivu v 1717 godu," *Voennyi sbornik*, no. 10 (1861):364. Golosov provides transcripts of a number of communications by members of the expedition. See also Potto, "O stepnykh pokhodakh," 6—7; and Alton S. Donnelly, "Peter the Great and Central Asia," *Canadian Slavonic Papers*, nos. 2—3 (Summer and Fall 1975):211—12.

14. Lobysevich, *Postupatel'noe dvizhenie v Sredniuiu Aziiu*, 77. See also M. Ivanin, "Zametki po povodu napechatannoi vo 2, 3 nomerakh '*Voennogo sbornika*' nyneshnego goda stat'i

'Pokhod v Khivu 1839 g.,'" *Voennyi sbornik*, no. 4 (1863):484—502. Ivanin offers a different interpretation of the failure of Perovskii's expedition, blaming bungling and intrigues among Perovskii's officers in the administration of supply and transport.

15. Lobysevich, *Postupatel'noe dvizhenie v Sredniuiu Aziiu*, 83—86.

16. *A Narrative of the Russian Military Expedition to Khiva Under General Perofski in 1839* (Calcutta: Foreign Department of the Indian Government, 1867), 67—69. This is apparently a translation of a Russian account, but the original author is not named.

17. Lobysevich, *Postupatel'noe dvizhenie v Sredniuiu Aziiu*, 87a—8.

18. Ibid., 88—89.

19. *A Narrative of the Russian Military Expedition*, 95, 121—122; and "Pokhod v Khivu v 1839 godu: otriada russkikh voisk, pod nachal'stvom general-adiutanta Perovskogo," *Voennyi sbornik*, no. 3 (1863):12.

20. *A Narrative of the Russian Military Expedition*, 112—25; and "Pokhod v Khivu v 1839 godu," 12.

21. *A Narrative of the Russian Military Expedition*, 129—31; and "Pokhod v Khivu v 1839 godu," 4—9.

22. Lobysevich, *Postupatel'noe dvizhenie v Sredniuiu Aziiu*, 90; and *A Narrative of the Russian Military Expedition*, 144.

23. Lobysevich, *Postupatel'noe dvizhenie v Sredniuiu Aziiu*, 92—94.

24. I. F. Babkov, *Vospominaniia o moei sluzhbe v zapadnoi Sibiri 1859—1875 g.* (St. Petersburg, 1912), 11.

25. Central State Military History Archive, Moscow, Russia, fund 483 (Central Asia), index 1, item 21, sheet 244.

26. A. Khasanov, "O prisoedinenii severnykh Kirgizov k Rossii," *Voprosy istorii*, no. 7 (1950):126—28; David MacKenzie, *The Lion of Tashkent: The Career of General M. G. Cherniaev* (Athens: University of Georgia Press, 1974), 29; and Khalfin, *Prisoedinenie Srednei Azii*, 107.

27. M. A. Terentyef [Terent'ev], *Russia and England in Central Asia*, vol. 2, trans. F. C. Daukes (Calcutta: Foreign Department Press, 1876), 78; Khalfin, *Prisoedinenie Srednei Azii*, 157—59; and B. B. Bekmakhanov, *Prisoedinenie Kazakhstana k Rossii* (Moscow: Akademiia Nauk, 1957), 134—35.

28. David Ker, *On the Road to Khiva* (London: Henry S. King & Co., 1874), 74—75.

29. Firuz Kazemzadeh, *Russia and Britain in Persia, 1864—1914* (New Haven, CT: Yale University Press, 1968), 45. Kazemzadeh translated the quoted passage.

30. Ibid.; Terentyef, *Russia and England*, 15; Khalfin, *Prisoedinenie Srednei Azii*, 109. For a good discussion of Russia's nineteenth-century Central Asian policy in a foreign relations context, see Dietrich Geyer, *Russian Imperialism: The Interaction of Domestic and Foreign Policy, 1860—1914* (New Haven, CT: Yale University Press, 1986).

31. Kazemzadeh, *Russia and Britain*, 15. See also D. I. Romanovskii, *Zametki po sredneaziatskomu voprosu* (St. Petersburg, 1868), 30. Romanovskii insists that the declarations of the Russian government, which did not approve Cherniaev's actions, were sincere. On the politics of "bureaucratic absolutism," see Jacob Kipp and W. Bruce Lincoln, "Autocracy and Reform: Bureaucratic Absolutism in Nineteenth Century Russia," *Russian History* 6, no. 1 (1979):1—21.

32. David MacKenzie, "Expansion in Central Asia: St. Petersburg vs. the Turkestan Generals, 1863—1866," *Canadian Slavonic Studies* 3 (Summer 1969):286—311; and N. A. Khalfin, *Politika Rossii v Srednei Azii 1857—1868* (Moscow: Nauka, 1960), 198—99. See also Wheeler, "Russian Conquest," 271.

33. MacKenzie, "Expansion in Central Asia," 300—308.

34. A. G. Serebrennikov, ed. *Turkestanskii krai. Sbornik materialov dlia istorii ego zavoevaniia 1866 god*, pt. 1 (Tashkent, Uzbek S.S.R., 1915), 96—111. Serebrennikov provides a full transcript of the report of the military governor of the Turkestan oblast, D. I. Romanovskii, to the commander of the Orenburg District dated 7 October 1866.

35. Ibid., 121. This is a transcript of Miliutin's note to the Orenburg commander dated 21 October 1866.

36. Potto, "O stepnykh pokhodakh," 18; Seymour Becker, *Russia's Protectorates in Central Asia: Bukhara and Khiva, 1865—1924* (Cambridge, MA: Harvard University Press, 1968), 25; Richard Pierce, *Russian Central Asia, 1867—1917* (Berkeley: University of California Press, 1960), 23; and A. L. Popov, "Iz istorii zavoevaniia Srednei Azii," *Istoricheskie zapiski*, no. 9 (1940):215.

37. Becker, *Russia's Protectorates in Central Asia*, 36—39; Khalfin, *Prisoedinenie Srednei Azii*, 238—39; Popov, "Iz istorii zavoevaniia Srednei Azii," 218; and Pierce, *Russian Central Asia*, 26—27.

38. Wheeler, "Russian Conquest," 272; and Pierce, *Russian Central Asia*, 27.

39. E. U., "Stepnaia voina," 82—83; and "Pokhod v Khivu v 1839 godu," no. 2 (1863):340—41.

40. E. U., "Stepnaia voina," 83—85.

41. Ibid., 83; and M. Veniukov, "Zametki o stepnykh pokhodakh v Srednei Azii," *Voennyi sbornik*, no. 4 (1860):291—92.

42. E. U., "Stepnaia voina," 90; and "Pokhod v Khivu v 1839 godu," pt. 3, 14—15.

43. E. U., "Stepnaia voina," 75; and Potto, "O stepnykh pokhodakh," 19—21.

44. Veniukov, "Zametki o stepnykh pokhodakh," 271—72; and E. U., "Stepnaia voina," 80.

45. E. U., "Stepnaia voina," 91—93; and Potto, "O stepnykh pokhodakh," 22.

46. Potto, "O stepnykh pokhodakh," 26—27.

47. Veniukov, "Zametki o stepnykh pokhodakh," 272.

48. Popov, "Iz istorii zavoevaniia Srednei Azii," 230.

49. N. I. Grodekov, *Khivinskii pokhod 1873 g.* (St. Petersburg, 1888), 4—5; and A. D. Shemanskii, "Zavoevanie Srednei Azii," in *Istoriia russkoi armii i flota*, vol. 12 (Moscow, 1913), 117. See also Becker, *Russia's Protectorates in Central Asia*, 70.

50. Grodekov, *Khivinskii pokhod 1873 g.*, 1—2.

51. See Popov, "Iz istorii zavoevaniia Srednei Azii," 239; Khalfin, *Prisoedinenie Srednei Azii*, 304—6; and A. I. Maksheev, *Istoricheskii obzor Turkestana i nastupatel'nogo dvizheniia v nego russkikh* (St. Petersburg, 1890), 313—15. At the same time, Russia's ambassador to England, Peter Shuvalov, gave assurance that any occupation of Khiva would be temporary.

52. Grodekov, *Khivinskii pokhod 1873 g.*, 1—2.

53. Maksheev, *Istoricheskii obzor Turkestana*, 313—15.

54. V. N. Troitskii, *Opisanie khivinskogo pokhoda 1873 goda* (St. Petersburg, 1890), 181—83.

55. Maksheev, *Istoricheskii obzor Turkestana*, 317.

56. Troitskii, *Opisanie khivinskogo pokhoda*, 176, 180.

57. Maksheev, *Istoricheskii obzor Turkestana*, 318.

58. Ibid., 319—21; and Grodekov, *Khivinskii pokhod 1873 g.*, 219—21. The principal functions of the Aral Flotilla were to explore area waterways, support communications among the forts of the Syr Darya Line, and cooperate with Russian columns moving along waterways. See *Istoricheskoe obozrenie ustroistva upravleniia morskim vedomstvom v Rossii* (St. Petersburg, 1869), 269—70.

59. Troitskii, *Opisanie khivinskogo pokhoda*, 79; and Maksheev, *Istoricheskii obzor Turkestana*, 320.

60. Maksheev, *Istoricheskii obzor Turkestana*, 320—22.

61. Becker, *Russia's Protectorates in Central Asia*, 76; and Khalfin, *Prisoedinenie Srednei Azii*, 308—13.

62. Maksheev, *Istoricheskii obzor Turkestana*, 331—32; and Becker, *Russia's Protectorates in Central Asia*, 89—90. See also Beatrice Forbes Manz, "Central Asian Uprisings in the Nineteenth Century: Fergana Under the Russians," *The Russian Review* 46 (1987):275.

63. Maksheev, *Istoricheskii obzor Turkestana*, 333—34.

64. Pierce, *Russian Central Asia*, 65; and Khalfin, *Prisoedinenie Srednei Azii*, 310—13.

65. Pierce, *Russian Central Asia*, 36—37; Maksheev, *Istoricheskii obzor Turkestana*, 335—44; and Khalfin, *Prisoedinenie Srednei Azii*, 326—27.

66. Khalfin, *Prisoedinenie Srednei Azii*, 325—28.

67. N. S. Kiniapina, "Administrativnaia politika tsarizma na Kavkaze i v Srednei Azii v XIX veke," *Voprosy istorii*, no. 4 (1883):42—43; and David MacKenzie, "Kaufman of Turkestan: An Assessment of His Administration, 1867—1881," *Slavic Review* 26, no. 2 (1967):267—68, 271. MacKenzie points out that although Miliutin believed strongly in the indivisibility of authority in a frontier region, neither the British in India nor the French in Algeria employed such a system.

68. MacKenzie, "Kaufman of Turkestan," 270—73; Khalfin, *Prisoedinenie Srednei Azii*, 225—34; and Pierce, *Russian Central Asia*, 66.

69. The principal exception to this pattern would be the periphery of Kazakhstan along the former borders of the Russian Empire. For an excellent demographic discussion, see George Demko, *The Russian Colonization of Kazakhstan, 1896—1916* (Bloomington: Indiana University Press, 1969). Shemanskii, "Zavoevanie Srednei Azii," 119—21.

70. Central State Military History Archive, fund 483, index 1, file 115, sheets 6—7. The document cited is a situation report filed in 1879 by a colonel of the General Staff on the Transcaspia region. Also, Mehmet Saray, "Russo-Turkmen Relations up to 1874," *Central Asian Survey* 3, no. 4 (1984):15—48.

71. G. Demurov, "Boi s tekintsami pri Dengel-Tepe 28 Avgusta 1879 goda," *Istoricheskii Vestnik* (March 1881):620.

72. Cherniak (Shtabs-kapitan), "Ekspeditsiia v Akhal-Teke v 1879 godu," *Voennyi sbornik*, no. 8 (1887):268; and Shemanskii, "Zavoevanie Srednei Azii," 120. F. Lomakin's report, see A. Solovev, *Rossiia i Turkmeniia v xix veke* (Ashkhabad: Turkmenskoe Gosudarstvennoe izdatel'stvo, 1946), 122—26.

73. P. Bobrovskii, "Akhal-tekinskaia ekspeditsiia 1879 goda," *Voennyi sbornik*, no. 10 (1898):296—97. Bobrovskii cites the official report of Lieutenant General Tergukosov, a participant in the expedition. He also cites Lazarev's report in which the general claimed that the supply plan was adequate but that the column met with unforeseeable difficulties. See pages 268—69.

74. Shemanskii, "Zavoevanie Srednei Azii," 119—21; and Cherniak, "Ekspeditsiia v Akhal-Teke," 265—71.

75. Dmitrii Miliutin, *Dnevnik*, vol. 3 (Moscow: Lenin Library, 1950), 168, 172.

76. Shemanskii, "Zavoevanie Srednei Azii," 121; and N. N. Knorring, *General Mikhail Dmitrievich Skobelev* (Paris, 1939), 159.

77. N. I. Grodekov, *Voina v Turkmenii: Pokhod Skobeleva v 1880—81 gg.*, vol. 2 (St. Petersburg, 1883), 92—93; Shemanskii, "Zavoevanie Srednei Azii," 123—24; and A. Kersnovskii, *Istoriia russkoi armii*, vol. 2 (Belgrade, 1934), 75.

78. Kersnovski, *Istoriia russkoi armii*, 484; and Knorring, *General Mikhail Dmitrievich Skobelev*, 165.

79. Shemanskii, "Zavoevanie Srednei Azii," 131; and Knorring, *General Mikhail Dmitrievich Skobelev*, 165—66.

80. Shemanskii, "Zavoevanie Srednei Azii," 136; and Knorring, *General Mikhail Dmitrievich Skobelev,* 167. See also George Dobson, *Russia's Railway Advance into Central Asia* (London: W. H. Allen & Co., 1890), 1956.

81. M. D. Skobelev, *Siege and Assault of Denghil-Tepe: General Skobelev's Report*, trans. J. Leverson (London, 1881), 10—17, 60; and Shemanskii, "Zavoevanie Srednei Azii," 144.

82. Shemanskii, "Zavoevanie Srednei Azii," 137—38; and A. A. Maier, *Nabroski i ocherki Akhal-tekinskoi ekspeditsii 1880—1881 (iz vospominanii ranennogo)* (Kronshtadt, 1886), 221—22.

83. Muravtsev [Captain], "Turkestanskii otriad v Akhal-tekinskoi ekspeditsii 1880—1881 gg.," *Voennyi sbornik*, no. 1 (1883):149.

84. Skobelev, *Siege and Assault of Denghil-Tepe*, 50—55; and Muravtsev, "Turkestanskii otriad," 291—98.

85. George N. Curzon, *Russia in Central Asia* (London: Longmans, Green & Co., 1899), 84.

86. Central State Historical Archive, fund 954, index 1, file 112, sheet 3; and Charles Marvin, *The Russian Advance Towards India* (London: Sampson, Low, Marston, Searle & Rivington, 1882), 240.

87. Ker, *On the Road to Khiva*, 6.

Bibliography

Chapter 2

Archival Documents

Central State Military History Archive. Moscow, Russia. Fund 483 (Central Asia).

Central State Historical Archive. St. Petersburg, Russia. Fund 954 (K. P. von Kaufman).

Memoirs and Documents

Akty sobrannye kavkazskoi arkheograficheskoi kommissiei. 12 vols. Tiflis, 1893.

Babkov, I. F. *Vospominanii o moei sluzhbe v zapadnoi Sibiri 1859—1875 g.* St. Petersburg, 1912.

Kuropatkin, A. N. *Zadachi russkoi armii.* 2 vols. St. Petersburg, 1910.

Miliutin, Dmitrii. *Dnevnik.* 4 vols. Moscow: Lenin Library, 1947—50.

Serebrennikov, A. G., ed. *Turkestanskii krai. Sbornik materialov dlia istorii ego zavoevaniia.* Tashkent, Uzbek S.S.R., 1915.

Skobelev, M. D. *Siege and Assault of Denghil-Tepe: General Skobelev's Report.* Trans. J. Leverson. London, 1881.

Books

Allworth, Edward, ed. *Central Asia: A Century of Russian Rule.* New York: Columbia University Press, 1967.

Annenepesov, M. *Ukreplenie russko-turkmenskikh vzaimootnoshenii v XVIII-XIX vv.* Ashkhabad, Turkmen S.S.R.: Ylym, 1981.

Bacon, Elizabeth. *Central Asians Under Russian Rule: A Study in Culture Change.* Ithaca, NY: Cornell University Press, 1980.

Becker, Seymour. *Russia's Protectorates in Central Asia: Bukhara and Khiva, 1865—1924.* Cambridge, MA: Harvard University Press, 1968.

Bekmakhanov, B. B. *Prisoedinenie Kazakhstana k Rossii*. Moscow: Akademiia Nauk, 1957.

Curzon, George N. *Russia in Central Asia*. London: Longmans, Green & Co., 1889.

Demko, George. *The Russian Colonization of Kazakhstan, 1896—1916*. Bloomington: Indiana University Press, 1969.

Dobson, George. *Russia's Railway Advance into Central Asia*. London: W. H. Allen & Co., 1890.

Donnelly, Alton S. *The Russian Conquest of Bashkiria, 1552—1740*. New Haven, CT: Yale University Press, 1968.

Dzhamgerchinov, B. *Prisoedinenie Kirgizii k Rossii*. Moscow: Izdatel'stvo sotsial'no-ekonomicheskoi literatury, 1959.

Fuller, William. *Strategy and Power in Russia, 1600—1914*. New York: Macmillan, 1992.

Geyer, Dietrich. *Russian Imperialism: The Interaction of Domestic and Foreign Policy, 1860—1914*. New Haven, CT: Yale University Press, 1986.

Grodekov, N. I. *Khivinskii pokhod 1873 g*. St. Petersburg, 1888.

——— . *Voina v Turkmenii: Pokhod Skobeleva v 1880—1881 gg*. Vol. 2. St. Petersburg, 1883.

Holdsworth, Mary. *Turkestan in the Nineteenth Century*. London: Central Asian Research Center, 1959.

Istoricheskoe obozrenie ustroistva upravleniia morskim vedomstvom v Rossii. St. Petersburg, 1869.

Kazemzadeh, Firuz. *Russia and Britain in Persia, 1864—1914*. New Haven, CT: Yale University Press, 1968.

Ker, David. *On the Road to Khiva*. London: Henry S. King & Co., 1874.

Kersnovskii, A. *Istoriia russkoi armii*. Vol. 2. Belgrade, 1934.

Khalfin, N. A. *Politika Rossii v Srednei Azii 1857—1868*. Moscow: Nauka, 1960.

——— . *Prisoedinenie Srednei Azii k Rossii*. Moscow: Nauka, 1965.

Kiniapina, N. S., M. M. Bliev, and V. V. Degoev. *Kavkaz i Sredniaia Aziia vo vneshnei politike Rossii*. Moscow: Moscow University Press, 1984.

Knorring, N. N. *General Mikhail Dmitrievich Skobelev*. Paris, 1939.

Kostin, B. *Skobelev*. Moscow: Patriot, 1990.

Lobysevich, F. I. *Postupatel'noe dvizhenie v Sredniuiu Aziiu v torgovom i diplomaticheskо-voennom otnosheniiakh (Dopolnitel'nyi material dlia istorii khivinskogo pokhoda 1873 g.)*. St. Petersburg, 1900.

MacGahan, J. A. *Campaigning on the Oxus and the Fall of Khiva*. New York: Harper & Brothers, 1874.

MacKenzie, David. *The Lion of Tashkent: The Career of General M. G. Cherniaev*. Athens: University of Georgia Press, 1974.

Maier, A. A. *Nabroski i ocherki Akhal-tekinskoi ekspeditsii 1880—1881 (iz vospominanii ranennogo)*. Kronshtadt, 1866.

Maksheev, A. I. *Istoricheskii obzor Turkestana i nastupatel'nogo dvizheniia v nego russkikh*. St. Petersburg, 1890.

Marvin, Charles. *The Russian Advance Towards India*. London: Sampson, Low, Marston, Searle & Rivington, 1882.

A Narrative of the Russian Military Expedition to Khiva Under General Perofski in 1839. Calcutta: Foreign Department of the Indian Government, 1867.

Pierce, Richard. *Russian Central Asia, 1867—1917*. Berkeley: University of California Press, 1960.

Romanovskii, D. I. *Zametki po sredne-aziatskomu voprosu*. St. Petersburg, 1868.

Schuyler, Eugene. *Turkistan: Notes of a Journey in Russian Turkistan, Khokand, Bukhara, and Kuldja*. 2 vols. New York: Scribner, Armstrong & Co., 1877.

Smirnov, A., and N. Ustiugov, eds. *Ocherki po istorii Bashkirskoi ASSR*. Vol. 1. Ufa, Bashkis A.S.S.R.: Akademiia Nauk, Bashkirskii Filial, 1959.

Solovev, A. *Rossiia i Turkmeniia v xix veke*. Ashkhabad: Turkmenskoe Gosudarstvennoe izdatel'stvo, 1946.

Spalding, Captain H. *Khiva and Turkestan*. London: Chapman & Hall, 1874.

Stumm, Hugo. *The Russian Campaign Against Khiva in 1873*. Calcutta, 1876.

Terentyef [Terent'ev], M. A. *Russia and England in Central Asia*. Trans. F. C. Daukes. 2 vols. Calcutta: Foreign Department Press, 1876.

Troitskii, V. N. *Opisanie khivinskogo pokhoda 1873 goda*. St. Petersburg, 1890.

Wheeler, Geoffrey. *The Modern History of Soviet Central Asia*. New York: Praeger, 1964.

Selected Articles

Bobrovskii, P. "Akhal-tekinskaia ekspeditsiia 1879 goda." *Voennyi sbornik*, no. 10 (1898):259—97.

Cherniak, (Shtabs-kapitan). "Ekspeditsiia v Akhal-Teke v 1879 godu." *Voennyi sbornik*, no. 8 (1887):134.

Demurov, G. "Boi s tekintsami pri Dengel-Tepe 28 Augusta 1879 goda." *Istoricheskii Vestnik* (March 1881):617—24.

Donnelly, Alton S. "Peter the Great and Central Asia." *Canadian Slavonic Papers*, nos. 2—3, 17 (Summer and Fall 1975):202—17.

E. U. "Stepnaia voina v Turkestanskom krae." *Voennyi sbornik*, no. 7 (1880):69—94.

Golosov, Dmitrii. "Pokhod v Khivu v 1717 godu." *Voennyi sbornik*, no. 10 (1861):303—64.

Ivanin, M. "Zametki po povodu napechetannoi vo 2, 3 numerakh '*Voennogo sbornika*' nyneshnogo goda stati 'Pokhod v Khivu 1839 g.'" *Voennyi sbornik*, no. 4 (1863):484—502.

Khasanov, A. "O prisoedinenii severnykh Kirgizov k Rossii." *Voprosy istorii*, no. 7 (1950):126—30.

Kiniapina, N. S. "Administrativnaia politika tsarizma na Kavkaze i v Srednei Azii v XIX veke." *Voprosy istorii*, no. 4 (1983):36—47.

Kipp, Jacob. "Russian Naval Reformers and Imperial Expansion 1856—1863." In *Soviet Armed Forces Review Annual*. Vol. 1. Gulf Breeze, FL: Academic International Press, 1977, 118—48.

Kipp, Jacob, and W. Bruce Lincoln. "Autocracy and Reform: Bureaucratic Absolutism in Nineteenth Century Russia." *Russian History* 6, no. 1 (1979):1—21.

MacKenzie, David. "Expansion in Central Asia: St. Petersburg vs. the Turkestan Generals, 1863—1866." *Canadian Slavonic Studies* 3 (Summer 1969):286—311.

―――. "Kaufman of Turkestan: An Assessment of His Administration, 1867—1881." *Slavic Review* 26, no. 2 (1967):265—85.

Manz, Beatrice Forbes. "Central Asian Uprisings in the Nineteenth Century: Fergana Under the Russians." *The Russian Review* 46 (1987):267—81.

Muravtsev [Captain]. "Turkestanskii otriad v Akhal-tekinskoi ekspeditsii 1880—1881 gg." *Voennyi sbornik*, no. 1 (1883):149—58; no. 2 (1883):288—331.

Paksoy, H. B. "Muslims in the Russian Empire: Response to Conquest." *Studies in Comparative Communism* 19, no. 3 (1986):247—51.

Pogrebinskii, A. P. "Nalogovaia politika tsarizma v Srednei Azii v 1860—1880 godakh." *Istoricheskie zapiski* (1960):291—300.

"Pokhod v Khivu v 1839 godu: otriada russkikh voisk, pod nachal'stvom general-adiutanta Perovskogo." *Voennyi sbornik*, no. 1 (1863):3—31; no. 2 (1863):309—58; no. 3 (1863):3—71.

Popov, A. L. "Iz istorii zavoevaniia Srednei Azii." *Istoricheskie zapiski*, no. 9 (1940):199—239.

Popov, G. A. "Vospominaniia ob ekspeditsii v Akhal-Teke i shturm kreposti Geok-Tepe 1879—1881 g.g." *Voenno-istoricheskii sbornik*, no. 1 (1915): 177—200.

Potto, V. "O stepnykh pokhodakh." *Voennyi sbornik*, no. 4 (1873):233—64; no. 5 (1873):6—29.

Saray, Mehmet. "Russo-Turkmen Relations up to 1874." *Central Asian Survey* 3, no. 4 (1984):15—48.

Sereda, N. "Bunt kirgizskogo sultana Kenisary Kasimova." *Vestnik Evropy* 4 (1871):655—90.

Shemanskii, A. D. "Zavoevanie Srednei Azii." In *Istoriia russkoi armii i flota*. Vol. 12. Moscow, 1913, 115—67.

Terent'ev, M. A. "Turkestan i Turkestantsy." *Vestnik Evropy*, no. 5 (1872):65—112.

Veniukov, M. "Zametki o stepnykh pokhodakh v Srednei Azii." *Voennyi sbornik*, no. 4 (1860):270—96.

Wheeler, Geoffrey. "Russian Conquest and Colonization of Central Asia." In *Russian Imperialism: From Ivan the Great to the Revolution*. New Brunswick, NJ: Rutgers University Press, 1974.

The Liquidation of the Basmachi Resistance, 1918—1933

Bolshevik Russia's war against the Basmachis (the Central Asian resistance) constituted a complex military, social, and political struggle that in important ways foreshadowed the multidimensional nature of modern conflicts involving developed powers in regions of the Third World. Lasting roughly from 1918 to 1933, the conflict reflected both continuities and significant departures in the history of Russia's Central Asian relations. The roots of the conflict can be traced to Russia's conquest of the region. Between the Russian conquest and the outbreak of World War I, the rapid expansion of cotton cultivation and associated industries, extensive Russian settlement, and repeated episodes of inept or corrupt administration disrupted traditional native living patterns and stirred bitter resentment. Festering social tensions helped ignite the conflict and gave impetus to incipient Pan-Islamic and Pan-Turkic tendencies.[1]

The imposition of Red rule in Central Asia also marked a historic first attempt by the Bolsheviks to extend their revolutionary order beyond the cultural frontiers of Europe into Muslim Asia. Central Asians little understood the October 1917 Revolution in Russia, though most applauded the collapse of imperial power. Nonetheless, Bolshevism held an appeal for Westernized members of the native intelligentsia of Central Asia by virtue of its proclaimed respect for self-determination and equality among all subject nationalities of the former empire. That such respect was based upon the naive belief that the oppressed peoples would gladly join their fate to that of Red Russia soon resulted in the disillusionment of Bolsheviks and Central Asians alike. Another inevitable issue of contention between the Bolsheviks and Central Asians was the ideological hostility of the former to the religion and traditional patterns of social organization in Central Asia. Accordingly, the Bolsheviks found that in order to prosecute the war against the Basmachis successfully, it was necessary to mute or modify much of their political program.

The Basmachis, on their part, generally lacked a coherent organization or clear program. However, by positioning themselves to varying degrees as the defenders of local self-rule, traditional society, Pan-Turkism, and the Islamic faith, they assembled a dangerous, if fragmented, resistance movement. For significant periods between 1918 and 1933, they denied the Red Army control of much of rural Central Asia. Furthermore, they severely tested the ability of Red Army commanders to adapt to irregular warfare in an alien cultural and geographical setting.

Overall, the Basmachi War posed several challenging problems for the Bolsheviks. First, the Red Army, through 1921, was concurrently engaged in a war against White counterrevolutionary forces and Poland. And physically isolated by White forces from the Central Asian theater until mid-1919, the Red Army leadership could neither direct the struggle against the Basmachis in its early stages nor contribute significant resources to the defense of Central Asia. Second, the geography of the Central Asian theater posed extraordinary and unfamiliar difficulties, requiring important Russian adaptations in tactics and logistics. Third, the cultural setting demanded that the Bolsheviks correctly assess the political, ethnic, and religious dimensions of the conflict and adapt their programs accordingly.

The Basmachi War in Perspective

Following the conquest of Central Asia, Russian imperial administration did not aggressively Russify the native populace, although it did endeavor to develop the regional economy. Rather, Russian immigrants congregated in a few major towns where industrial jobs awaited them and formed largely separate communities. The natives, in turn, lived according to their traditions, although modest numbers took jobs in new enterprises or even received a Russian education. Meanwhile, Russian institutions had only a slight influence on the local culture. A typical case in point was the Russian Army. Fearful that the natives would violently resent conscription, the War Ministry (with the exception of a few irregular cavalry formations) preserved a blanket exemption for Central Asians from military service.

Yet the immigration of Russians and other nonnatives into Central Asia presaged important demographic shifts. According to the imperial census of 1911, over 1.5 million Russians and other nonnatives had taken residence in the Kazakh steppe, where they constituted 41.5 percent of the population. A further 407,000 resided in Turkestan, to the south, where, although they made up only 6.4 percent of the population, their impact on urban development was noteworthy. Least affected were the lands of Bukhara, where immigrants made up only 1 percent of the 2.5 million inhabitants, and Khiva.[2] Natives and immigrants coexisted uneasily in cities, where factories began to transform the landscape. A bloody uprising in the city of Andizhan in 1898 evidenced mounting disgruntlement among the indigenous population.[3]

In the midst of World War I, when the slaughter on the Eastern Front created a critical shortage in Russian manpower, the government decided to draft Central Asians into labor battalions. A violent uprising subsequently ensued in Kazakhstan and spread like a brushfire into the Dzhiak district of Samarkand and the Fergana Valley in Uzbekistan. By October

Governor General A. N. Kuropatkin served under Skobelev in Central Asia. He was war minister from 1898 to 1904 and governor general of Turkestan from 1916 to 1917.

1916, the total number of rebels approached 50,000, leading Aleksei N. Kuropatkin, the governor general of Turkestan (and Skobelev's former chief of staff), to plan a punitive expedition and the resettlement of rebellious tribes eastward into Kirghizia. Word of his intentions triggered a panic flight of Kazakhs and Kirghiz across the frontier into northwest China.[4]

The February 1917 Revolution interceded before Kuropatkin could implement his scheme, and a provisional government assumed power in St. Petersburg. A committee headquartered in Tashkent assumed authority in Turkestan at the behest of the new regime, but the momentum of events was already beyond control. Revolutionary upheaval gripped St. Petersburg, crippling the ability of the central government, whatever its makeup, to control events on the periphery of the empire. In Central Asia, the emerging political map devolved into a mosaic of autonomous factions and centers. In May 1917, inspired by a small, politically conscious elite, a congress of Muslim nationalities convened and issued a demand for the formation of an autonomous republic of Turkestan in federation with Russia. Many of these Muslim nationalists viewed socialism as the most likely path to autonomous national development and were not, at first, adversely disposed toward the Bolsheviks and other Russian socialists.[5] Independent political groups arose among the Russian population in Central Asia as well, and a Soviet (council) of Workers' and Soldiers' Deputies dominated by Mensheviks and Socialist Revolutionaries (rivals of the Bolsheviks), formed in Tashkent.

The unstable political situation in Central Asia degenerated further after the October Bolshevik Revolution. Local Bolsheviks, disgruntled both with

The Registan complex in Samarkand, as restored during Soviet rule

their Russian socialist rivals and the Muslim congress, proclaimed their own Tashkent Soviet loyal to Lenin's regime in Moscow. In November, the Bolshevik Tashkent Soviet became the Council (Soviet) of Peoples' Commissars. Meanwhile, Muslim regimes formed in Bukhara and Khiva. Neither recognized Lenin's revolutionary government, whose influence would scarcely be felt in Central Asia before 1920. Similarly, a short-lived Islamic government formed in Kokand, calling for autonomy within a federated Russia.[6]

During the first half of the civil war against the White armies, Lenin's Bolshevik state was in constant peril, fighting an assortment of enemies on multiple fronts. Consequently, it had little hold over the former imperial borderlands of Central Asia, where the local Bolsheviks were geographically cut off from Moscow by White counterrevolutionary forces operating in the southern steppe and Siberia. Acting on their own, the Tashkent Bolsheviks clung to the absurd vision of creating a proletarian order in a region almost devoid of proletarian elements. Predominantly Russian in makeup and outlook, they promoted a revolutionary agenda scripted in code words rooted in the ideas of radical nineteenth-century European social theorists. Their efforts to realize their ideas could hardly fail to antagonize most of Central Asian society.

Yet because they were better armed and organized than other factions, the Tashkent Council of Peoples' Commissars gathered support among the Russian population and moved to liquidate its enemies. Red forces crushed the Muslim nationalist government in Kokand in January 1918. However, they lacked the resources to overpower the new regimes in Bukhara and Khiva, and partisan warfare soon spread from the Fergana Valley and engulfed the Central Asian countryside.[7]

A 15 July telegram from the chairman of the Council of Peoples' Commissars representing the self-proclaimed Turkestan Autonomous Soviet Socialist Republic reflected the emerging crisis: "The Army is without ammunition and guns... the situation is catastrophic. In Ashkabad, the uprising has assumed grand proportions. Stores have been seized, government institutions have lost communications with Vernoe. Tashkent is cut off."[8] In August, the new government established the Revolutionary Military Council of the Turkestan Army to direct the war but faced a shortage of manpower. Red garrisons outside Tashkent were small and scattered (see table 3).[9] Still, by frantically raising local forces of all descriptions, the Tashkent Bolsheviks managed to establish a tenuous hold over a number of major cities and towns in Turkestan. In the countryside, Basmachi bands exploited the power vacuum to create centers of resistance.

TABLE 3
Composition of Russian Garrisons Outside Tashkent

Garrison	Troops	Red Guards	Artillery	Machine Guns
Skobelev	290		6 guns	4
Kokand	126	400	3 guns	4
Namangan	134		2 guns	4
Andizhan	168		2 guns	4
Osh	70			1

Source: Kh. Sh. Inoiatov, *Narody Srednei Azii v borbe protiv interventov i vnutrennei kontrrevoliutsii* (Moscow: Mysl, 1984), 31.

Ironically, some of the first Basmachis actually were outlaws loosely fitting the characterization applied in Red propaganda and later by Soviet historians. Two of the most prominent Basmachi leaders, Irgash and Madamin Bek, had been exiled by the imperial regime in 1913.[10] Still, at the root of the widespread resistance lay social dislocation and ethnic and religious tensions. The durability of the resistance was especially remarkable since the Basmachi bands possessed no common program and minimal political or military organization. Indeed, historian Richard Pipes describes the movement as "essentially a number of unconnected tribal revolts...."[11] Mustafa Chokaev, briefly president of a provisional government in Kokand, recalled that the lack of a means of mass propaganda or a literate, politically conscious populace hampered efforts to organize the people.[12] In the end, the diverse and autonomous groups under the umbrella of the *Basmachestvo* shared little but a deep resentment of Russian domination and a fierce determination not to submit.

As a rule, the Basmachis were poorly armed. They carried a variety of mostly outdated side arms, among them many Berdan rifles of Russo-Turkish War (1877—78) vintage, and possessed a modest number of equally antiquated artillery pieces. The Reds believed the Basmachis also received weapons from foreign (especially Britain) sources through Afghanistan, but there is little evidence that such assistance assumed significant proportions.[13] Indeed, the motley collection of weapons that the Basmachis actually employed in the field argues to the contrary.

If the quality of Basmachi arms was poor, the tactical coordination among their large groups was worse—a condition appallingly evident when they confronted Red units in the open field. As a result, even at the apex of their power, the Basmachis tended to rely on hit-and-run raids against factories or isolated Red garrisons. They generally withdrew in the face of superior force. Operating in small groups, they were tough and elusive and exploited three advantages associated with successful guerrilla operations: intimate knowledge of the terrain, superior mobility away from roads and towns, and active or passive support of the populace (which both shielded them and provided recruits). One Russian military observer, recording an impression that might as easily have come from the field in Algeria, Vietnam, or Afghanistan, said, "Without anything distinguishing them [the Basmachis] on the outside, clothed in the same way as the peasant population, they were all around our units, not hesitating to infiltrate, and unrecognizable and elusive, they devoted themselves to espionage that has no equal, whose network extends from the Afghan frontier to Tashkent."[14] The consequences manifested themselves in many ways. In one recorded instance, an armored train en route from Aidyn to Belak stopped at a prearranged signal and turned fifty boxes of ammunition over to the Basmachis.[15] On another occasion, a saboteur drugged the food of a small, besieged Red garrison, leaving only nine conscious defenders to hold the fort until relief came.[16]

The Central Asian Theater, 1919—22

Full-blown war in Turkestan did not begin until late 1919, after the Red Army broke the Whites' grip on Western Siberia, at which time, the physical isolation of Central Asia from Moscow ended. Anxious to take stock of the situation, Lenin's government in Moscow dispatched a six-member Turkestan Commission—including Fourth Army Commander Mikhail Frunze and Fourth Army Political Commissar V. V. Kuibyshev—to assume authority in Tashkent in November. The commission noted in its official assessment that existing party organizations lacked credibility with the masses, who little understood the Communist program.[17] The official newspaper of the Commissariat of Nationalities, *Zhizn' natsional'nostei*, grimly acknowledged in March 1920 that overzealous local cadres had committed serious policy errors. The paper also unequivocally declared the Communist stake in Central Asia, saying: "Turkestan is the center of the dissemination of our ideas in the East. Turkestan is the flower garden from which the bees of surrounding countries of the East must receive their nourishment."[18]

At about the same time, Moscow recognized the need to bolster its military presence in Central Asia. On 24 March, Frunze informed Lenin by telegram that the units of the recently organized (August 1919) Turkestan Front presented a "most wretched picture," and the troops were an "indescribable rabble." Red units were numerically weak, soldiers lacked uniforms, and (in the Fergana Valley) many had no shoes. Fully one-quarter of them carried old Berdan rifles, and another one-quarter used English weapons sent to Russia during World War I. A mere 4,500 infantrymen and 700 cavalrymen, some of whom would have been deemed too old or unfit for duty on other fronts, held the extensive First Army region from Termez (on the Afghan frontier) to Krasnovodsk.[19] Red units in Turkestan consisted of diverse elements, including so-called international regiments, organized from foreign prisoners taken during World War I, volunteer Muslim formations, and territorial Red Guards. Units arrived from Russia in random fashion, and in 1919, the staff of the Fergana Front had been unable to ascertain its own order of battle.[20] Aside from reorganization of the forces in the theater, Frunze found that his most pressing task was to raise proficient cavalry units capable of interdicting and pursuing Basmachi bands.

The Turkestan Front comprised two entire armies and elements of a third. The Fourth Army consisted of 3 rifle divisions (equipped with 203 machine guns) and reserves totaling 21,650 men. The First Army consisted of 3 rifle divisions and a Tatar Brigade, for a published strength of 32,129 men, 515 machine guns, and 99 field guns. Elements of the Eleventh Army based in Astrakhan contributed 17,236 men to the cause. In addition, during 1920—21, units of the Cheka (the original Soviet security forces) served under the Turkestan Front as well.[21] The actual strength of Red Army units varied from time to time and unit to unit. Frunze found, for example, upon reviewing the 2d Turkestan Division in 1920 that cavalry regiments ranged from 130 to 220 men and infantry regiments from 200 to 400.[22]

Red military initiatives against Khiva and Bukhara in 1920 were successful but did much to inflame existing ethnic and religious antagonisms. Khiva fell in February 1920. The Reds elevated the radical Young Khivans to power and proclaimed the Peoples Republic of Khorezm. A similar scenario unfolded in Bukhara. In August 1920, the Young Bukharans staged an uprising in Bukhara (city) and, according to a prearranged signal, called upon the Red Army for assistance to depose the emir.[23] In November, a treaty of cooperation cemented Bukhara's relationship to Soviet Russia.

Notwithstanding military gains, Frunze determined that basic policy changes were essential to success in Central Asia. Lenin himself directed a series of conciliatory measures: the reopening of bazaars, equalization of food distribution, and recruitment of native party members. The Red Army dispatched the Tatar Brigade, raised among the Muslim Tatars of the central Volga region, to Turkestan, and Frunze raised "Soviet Basmachi" detachments, consisting in part of converted (or so he assumed) Basmachis.[24] In August 1920, the party central committee of Turkestan ordered the mobilization of 500 Muslim Communists in the Syr Darya, Samarkand, Fergana, and Transcaspia oblasts for assignment to companies and squadrons of the Red Army.[25]

Red organizational successes proved more illusory than real, however. The proclamation of the Bukharan People's Soviet Republic, a secular state, sparked discontent throughout Bukhara. A motley array of resistance forces soon assembled around former Emir Said Alim Khan and Uzbek strongman Ibragim Bek.[26] Trouble erupted in Khiva once again in March 1921, when the Turkestan Commission directed the overthrow of the Khorezm Republic and proclaimed the Soviet Socialist Republic of Khorezm. Much of the deposed Young Khivan leadership joined the resistance.

Just as tensions heightened in Turkestan, events elsewhere threatened the entire edifice of Bolshevik power in Russia. Concurrently engaged in a desperate war with Poland and liquidating remnants of the White forces in the Crimea, the Red Army was in dire need of additional manpower. To cope with the crisis, Moscow imposed conscription on Central Asian Muslims in the summer of 1920. Though aware of native reaction to the draft of 1916, the Red leadership, nonetheless, embarked on that risky course. Publicly, the Bolsheviks maintained that they had alleviated the oppressive conditions that had made military service unacceptable to the native populace in the past. Once again, heady optimism based on facile social analysis proved unfounded.

On 7 May, Frunze signed the directive to conscript 35,000 Central Asians. By August, approximately 25,000 native conscripts had entered the ranks. Local Soviets assumed full responsibility not only for conscript enrollment but for the moral and political reliability of every recruit. Frunze categorically refused the demands of Muslim Communists that distinct Muslim units be formed. To do so, Frunze asserted, would establish a harmful precedent encouraging separate units for every faith. Yet Frunze did not object to the creation of national units (which happened to be Muslim) of Uzbeks, Kirghiz, Turkomans, Tajiks, and so forth.[27] Frunze probably believed that the establishment of such national units, though seemingly risky in itself, would inhibit the spread of dangerous Pan-Islamic or Pan-Turkic tendencies. The recruitment campaign was so successful that national formations soon accounted for one-third of the Red Army's published strength in Turkestan.[28] However, the rapid infusion of Central Asians into the army entailed serious difficulties. On 10 October, *Zhizn' natsional'nostei* acknowledged great cultural and linguistic obstacles in the adaptation of Central Asians to military life and reported that reliable cadres must be placed among the *inorodtsy* (aliens) to ensure a successful transition.[29] Consistent with this position, the Red Army made some practical concessions to local customs and intensified its recruitment of native officers. In fact, a Central Muslim Military College had operated in Moscow and subsequently Kazan since January 1918 for the purpose of training Muslim officers, at first chiefly Tatars and Bashkirs. Political and military education received equal attention in the program. Commissions also became attainable through a Muslim Cavalry and Infantry Course which opened in Kazan in September 1919.[30]

Such palliative measures were scarcely sufficient, however, to make conscription a tolerable burden to peoples thoroughly unaccustomed either

Turkomans drinking tea in front of a dwelling, ca. 1890

with the concept of a service obligation or military regimentation. The result was predictable. Turmoil in Bukhara forced a postponement of the local draft until 1921.[31] Many Muslim draftees fled to the Basmachis, and the Bolsheviks were forced to disarm the 1st Uzbek Cavalry Brigade, once considered a model native unit.[32] Native political cadres were in short supply. Frunze, in a telegram of 29 May, attributed an unspecified unfortunate incident in the 11th Tatar Regiment to the diversion of political workers from field units to civic work with the populace.[33] Evidence of mounting mistrust between Russians and native Central Asians abounded. In October, 640 men of the Muslim Kazan Regiment defected to the Basmachis.[34] In turn, in 1920, the Russian 27th Rifle Regiment mutinied in Vernoe, and demanded the disarming of Muslim units of the Red Army.[35]

The chief result of the conscription decree, aside from its failure, was to swell the ranks of the resistance to 30,000 strong during the summer of 1920.[36] The Basmachi movement also received a boost in political support. The Bashkir nationalist, Zeki Validov, former president of the short-lived Bashkir Autonomous Republic in the southern Urals region, cast his lot with the resistance after Moscow disbanded his government. Even more important, Enver Pasha, invited by the Soviet government to visit Bukhara in 1921, decided to support his ethnic and religious brethren in Central Asia by joining the resistance. A former minister of war of the Ottoman Empire and only forty years old, Enver Pasha had served as chief of the General Staff in Turkey during the Second Balkan War of 1913 and brought a wealth of tactical and organizational knowledge, as well as a handful of Turkish officers, to the cause. His first political gesture was to proclaim a holy war against the Bolsheviks and name himself commander of the armies of Turkestan, Bukhara, and Khiva. At the peak of his success in the spring of 1922, Enver held virtually all of western Bukhara and much of the east.[37]

Just what Enver might have achieved had he survived beyond 1922 (when he died in battle) is a subject of scholarly disagreement. Although one scholar of the Basmachis, Martha Olcott, contends that Enver "could have upset the Bolshevik plans for a Soviet Turkestan," another, Glenda Fraser, points out that Enver himself probably doubted the probability of his success.[38]

Even as Enver's fortunes reached their zenith, powerful forces gathered to oppose him.[39] By late 1922, the Red Army in Turkestan numbered from 100,000 to 150,000 men, including a mixture of regular and irregular forces.[40] No longer forced to concentrate manpower in other theaters, the Bolsheviks turned the military tide irreversibly in their favor. Moreover, the death of leaders such as Enver Pasha and continued overtures by the Bolsheviks to independent tribal chieftains wore down the resolve of the resistance. Though weakened, the Basmachis proved a resilient and dangerous foe. By the account (perhaps inflated) of the emir of Bukhara, there remained 60,000 Basmachis in Turkestan, among them 21,000 in Bukhara and 26,000 in the Fergana Valley.[41] Fighting would continue sporadically in many localities in the decade to come, but Bukhara and the Fergana Valley would constitute the most enduring pockets of resistance.

The Evolution of Red Army Tactics and Strategy

Due in large measure to confused lines of authority and political fragmentation, the struggle to establish Soviet power in Central Asia had a most inauspicious beginning. Indeed, in January 1918, the People's Commissar for Military Affairs, Osipov, himself led an uprising against the Red regime in Turkestan. This calamity triggered a military reorganization resulting in a clearer division of functions. Organization and administration fell to the Military Commissariat, while the Supreme Operational Staff (headed by a party member) assumed charge of field operations.[42]

Through careful study of their combat operations during the period 1920—22, Red Army analysts concluded that the character of the war in Central Asia diverged significantly from that in other theaters. As D. Zuev observed in 1922, although Western warfare was characterized by mechanized infantry, in view of "the roadless mountains and deserts of the Central Asian theaters, and the backwards and disorganized enemy in Turkestan, the old principle—the training of a steadfast and calm individual soldier— has not outlived its usefulness." While official guidance for commanders in Central Asia advised adherence to the general principles established in the official regulations of the Workers and Peasants Red Army, it also reminded commanders that the regulations did not prescribe stereotypical solutions to all tactical situations. Zuev cautioned readers of the official military periodical, *Voennyi rabotnik Turkestana*, to bear in mind the lessons of imperial Russian campaigns in the deserts of Central Asia and, in particular, the importance of wells and sources of fuel.⁴³

The topic of mountain warfare also drew special attention. Analyst V. Lavrenev warned that no matter how able a commander may have been in other theaters, he "will be entirely unprepared here [the mountainous zones of Central Asia] and in most instances will begin with a series of blunders." Lavrenev placed emphasis on flank security operating in parallel movement with main units and the role of advance and rear patrols. He also noted the value of strong, hardy soldiers and native units in the demanding mountain environment. Because supply trains would often be unable to follow units, soldiers would have to carry their own packs and equipment. Furthermore, the decentralized character of mountain combat mandated "the broadest initiative" by ordinary soldiers. Perhaps most important, attacks depended upon expert fire control due to the inevitable dispersal of troops in broken terrain and difficulties of orientation. Thus, advised Lavrenev, commanders should personally direct machine-gun fire.⁴⁴

In 1923, Sergei Kamenev, the commander in chief of the armed forces from 1919 to 1924, penned what was probably the most coherent and comprehensive general prescription for victory. Following an inspection tour in May and June, Kamenev summarized his conclusions in a secret document titled "System for the Struggle with the Basmachis." In accord with a well-established pattern of conduct, he called first for the military occupation of important population centers, the defense of key railroad lines, communications, and industry and also strikes against known Basmachi lairs. As a given area came under government control, responsibility would be shifted from the military to appropriate political officials.⁴⁵

In principle, Red Army units aimed to isolate and destroy hostile bands or, if this proved impossible, to curtail their flight to remote sanctuaries or across the frontier into Afghanistan. To execute this policy, military units in the field had to be as flexible and mobile as circumstances allowed. As explained by Kamenev, because elusive Basmachi bands operated as raiding parties, the Reds formed light irregular cavalry formations known as "flying detachments" (*letuchie otriady*) for the purpose of maintaining communications lines among garrisons and attacking Basmachi bases. Such forces varied in size from a platoon to a division (in theory up to about 2,000 men, though probably fewer in practice) and became the "main active force" in combating Basmachi bands. To enhance the opportunity for surprise, flying detachments seldom remained in one place for long and they usually operated in concert with other forces. Supporting the flying detachments were "raiding detachments" (*istrebitel'nye otriady*), local formations of a more partisan character. Their mission included reconnaissance and harassment of the enemy. Red forces regularly conducted sweeps to flush out Basmachis in hiding.⁴⁶

As a rule, based on Frunze's advice, the Reds managed to avoid spreading their forces too thin. Frunze insisted that only concentrated forces would be capable of carrying out the pursuit and destruction of Basmachi bands.

In contrast, small outposts in every trading village would be too weak either to defend or attack. At the same time, steam locomotives, pulling wagons of soldiers and firing platforms armored with pressed cotton bales, patrolled the railroad net.[47]

Though not central elements in the anti-Basmachi campaigns, aerial and naval assets played a significant supporting role. Red Army airplanes performed an invaluable service in a reconnaissance role and, occasionally, in combat. Although strafing and bombing seldom resulted in great physical harm to the enemy, their psychological effects were considerable. Late in the war, the Soviets were the first to employ airlift in combat.[48] In addition, naval forces provided transport across the Aral Sea. Since traffic on the Amu River was insecure as long as the Basmachis held Bukhara and Khiva, Frunze maintained a combat fleet on the Amu River consisting of nine steamers, two vessels powered by internal combustion, and a cutter.[49]

As in the imperial campaigns in Central Asia during the nineteenth century, the support of units in the field was a paramount concern. Initially, Red supply trains carried not only ammunition and provisions for the soldiers but often their belongings and even their families. In general, units were reluctant to operate at any significant distance from their sources of supply. Only gradually did troops become accustomed to traveling in relatively light, mobile columns. Because of requirements for animals and forage, supply trains were large and cumbersome. Four-wheeled wagons could scarcely move at all in the mountains. The mundane but crucial art of loading camels had been forgotten.[50]

Resupply in the field required meticulous preparation and reliable communications. The heliograph, virtually a forgotten technology by World War I, proved extremely useful across an expansive territory possessed of minimal railroad and telegraph networks (and these vulnerable to interdiction). Contemporary radios were extremely bulky and did not bear up well during difficult mountain marches. In contrast, the heliograph, particularly lighter models designed for field use, was easily transported by two donkeys and reliable under most conditions.[51] A miniature version used by cavalry required a mirror only three inches in diameter, yet permitted a small unit to remain in contact with its parent force up to a distance of fifteen miles.[52]

The greatest impediment to rapid movement in the mountains and desert was artillery. Heavy guns and even modest stocks of ammunition could virtually paralyze a force advancing over difficult terrain. As early as 1921, Red Army analysts reviewed the experience of the Russian Imperial Army in Central Asia and advised the use of portable mountain guns which, unlike field guns, could achieve a steep enough angle of fire to hit elevated targets. In addition, the sharp trajectory of descent of the projectiles magnified their effects upon impact.[53] Perhaps the principal role of machine guns and artillery in the mountains was to provide covering fire to support the advance of infantry into dead ground as they closed on the enemy.[54]

Mobility and the application of combat power in Central Asia naturally depended upon solid intelligence for their effective employment against the

Basmachis. In 1925, analyst P. Antonov wrote an article in *Krasnaia zvezda* titled, "Tactics of the Struggle with the Basmachis," in which he faulted Soviet understanding of local conditions. He stressed the value of intensive interrogations of prisoners and soldier interviews to assist in the identification and location of Basmachi bands. Further, he cautioned, if permitted to retreat in peace, defeated Basmachi bands would regroup and return. Only unremitting military pressure could ensure their submission. Similarly, the simple disbanding of surrendering Basmachi groups offered insufficient guarantee of their future conduct. Antonov called for their assignment to specific locales for supervision. In other words, victories in the field alone constituted a mere prelude to solving the root problem of population control.[55]

Frunze maintained that the central problem was not to defeat the Basmachis militarily, a painstaking but relatively certain endeavor (if other conditions were met), but to convince the population that the Basmachis were the enemy—or at least that they could not be victorious.[56] In June 1920, at Kuibyshev's initiative, the first Congress of Political Workers of Turkestan met to determine the best means of propagandizing among Muslims in Red Army units. The congress resolved that political work must reflect the cultural and religious preferences of the native population and strive to eliminate all manifestations of national chauvinism among the colonists. To implement this plan, the party established party schools in every oblast (district) of Turkestan. Schools opened under the auspices of the political sections of every Red Army front, army, and division. The Turkestan Front's political section alone operated party schools for Russians, Muslims, Magyars, and Germans.[57] Political action in the Red Army sometimes entailed the dissolution and reorganization of whole units and the creation of others. Kuibyshev, for example, oversaw the disarming and disbanding of the Soviet 4th Regiment for the commission of crimes against the native populace.[58]

Inside and outside the army, the most sensitive propaganda objective of Red political workers was to neutralize Islam as a source of resistance strength. Aware that early attempts at antireligious agitation had proved clumsy and counterproductive, the Soviets elected to proceed patiently and curtail frontal attacks on Islamic institutions. The revised approach emphasized economic development and secular public education to promote the training of native cadres. Native religious institutions, such as courts and schools, would for a time continue to function. The Reds also found to their dismay that the members of the indigenous cultures in the area were intolerant of efforts to broaden the range of social roles for women. For example, members of the Military Revolutionary Council for the Turkestan Front conceded in reports in 1926 that attempts to declare women of any age fit for employment in accord with Soviet law proved futile in the face of local custom.[59]

Overall, the Reds invested considerable resources in education and propaganda. They pioneered the staging of mass political spectacles. Kuibyshev mobilized two so-called agitation trains, the "Rosa Luxumberg" and "Red

East," to make whistle-stop tours on behalf of the revolution.[60] By 1925, the Turkestan authorities staged political rallies before crowds as large as 60,000.[61] More pragmatic measures included tax assistance for peasants in Uzbekistan and Tajikistan, delivery of seed to farmers, extension of offers of amnesty, and temporary concessions such as the restoration of Muslim schools and property in December 1921.[62]

Economic conditions were of no small significance, and Lenin's New Economic Policy brought much-needed relief from state requisitions of agricultural goods and draconian restrictions on the conduct of commerce. In 1922, Moscow increased its direct control of the regional party apparatus and purged, for example, approximately 1,000 of 16,000 members of the Bukharan Communist Party. In March 1923, the newly formed Soviet republics of Turkestan, Bukhara, and Khorezm agreed to a joint economic plan to stabilize conditions throughout the region.[63] Though by no means a total success, the political effort played a vital role in reducing native antagonism toward the regime.

Case One: The Fergana Resistance

Throughout the course of the struggle in Central Asia, the largest and most persistent center of resistance was the populous Fergana Valley, scene of prolonged fighting during Russia's conquest of the region a half century earlier. The local topography was well suited to the Basmachi style of warfare. Steep mountains gouged by deep ravines surrounded the valley, which was crossed by numerous irrigation canals.

The resistance in Fergana consisted of many small, independent factions organized along clan lines—a fact reflected in the conduct of battle, which took place in isolated valleys and mountain pockets rather than along a coherent front. The resistance dispersed its efforts and seldom undertook concerted actions. Although there was little coordination among the Basmachi groups, each maintained strong internal discipline. The Fergana Basmachis generally lacked late-model weapons but typically were good horsemen whose most successful tactics were the ambush and small raid. A Red Army account depicts a classic instance of a Basmachi ambush in November 1920. A band of 400 Basmachis struck a 95-man column of the Turkestan Rifle Regiment from the flanks and rear a short distance from Kokand. The Red infantrymen were unable to form a defense quickly enough to repel the assault, and a small, mounted rear guard disintegrated. Then, the attackers captured the unit supply train and a machine gun, vanishing as suddenly as they struck.[64] This solitary incident, of course, meant little, but multiplied many times over, it suggests the character of the conflict and the staying power of the Basmachis.

The Fergana Basmachis often labored as peasants by day and operated secretly by night. Some, especially during the hard winter of 1921–22, became "seasonal Bolsheviks," accepting provisions from the government and biding their time until spring.[65] A Red Army estimate of 1920 identified

12 separate Basmachi bands with a total of 5,650 armed fighters. Red strength in the valley was roughly 4,000 to 5,000 regulars, supplemented by a few Communist Party members and local militias. Red military actions, hampered by the lack of a clear command relationship between garrisons and a capable administrative apparatus, accomplished little.[66]

The most visible resistance leader to emerge in Fergana was Madamin Bek, a former Soviet militia commander in the town of Margelan. Madamin sought allies wherever he could find them, embracing Bashkir and Tatar intellectuals as well as renegade White forces. The most significant among the latter was the self-proclaimed Russian Peasant Army, under a one-time Red officer, Konstantin Monstrov, which formed in opposition to government grain requisitions. By September 1919, Madamin had established his own rudimentary administration and in October reached agreement with other major Basmachi leaders, including Irgash, Kurshirmat, and Khalkhodzha, to establish regions of command. Local commanders, called *kurbashi*, combined civil and military powers. Madamin then proclaimed the Fergana Provisional Government with himself at its head and Monstrov as his deputy. Another Russian served as his military chief of staff.[67] The British War Office credited Madamin with a force of 4,000 men armed with Berdan and Turkish rifles. Irgash commanded about 1,500 men and Khalkhodzha about 1,000. An Indian Office report claimed the Basmachis possessed machine guns but no artillery.[68]

The combined forces of Madamin and Monstrov captured Jalalabad and laid siege to the Red garrison at Andizhan in September. However, weak discipline and poor coordination rendered the siege ineffective, and the 500-man garrison under V. N. Sidorov exploited tactical opportunities to break the encirclement. As Monstrov's forces began to disintegrate, Madamin's Basmachis retreated under the pressure of Red counterattacks, and some individual bands surrendered.[69]

Born of a common enemy rather than any fundamental shared purpose, this inherently unstable coalition unraveled within a year. Madamin's call for a holy war, for example, could hardly fail to antagonize his Russian allies. Still, the central cause of the rebel collapse was the end of the military isolation of Turkestan. The arrival of Red reinforcements and the Turkestan Commission drastically altered military and political conditions. The success of new policies in Fergana corresponded closely to the degree of class differentiation in any given local populace. Urban areas, which were more economically developed, proved more receptive than remote areas such as the Lokai Valley or the Kara Kum desert, where life was virtually unchanged from a century before.

By March 1920, Madamin was in irreversible retreat. Elements of his defeated forces were soon reorganized by the Reds into the Russian 1st Uzbek Cavalry Brigade—a potentially potent example of Muslims allying themselves with the Red Army (as, in fact, thousands of Volga Tatars and Bashkirs had during the defeat of the White armies in the Southern Urals and Siberia).[70]

Such attempts at mass conversion, however, were seldom lasting. Many surrendering Basmachis sooner or later returned to the resistance. One such group, under the command of Rakhmankul, defected back to the Basmachis after a month and a half.[71] The incidence of disciplinary problems and defections led local military authorities to abandon the policy of preserving entire Basmachi bands intact and to the intensification of political indoctrination of recent converts.

Madamin himself became a Red emissary to other Basmachi chieftains but was murdered by a former ally. This episode steeled Frunze's resolve to press the attack even more. He strengthened Red garrisons, ceased all negotiations, and announced that anyone entering the service of the Basmachis would be summarily shot. The centralization of military and civil authority followed in the summer of 1920 with the creation of a military council in every district. In the Fergana region, for example, the Military Council of the 2d Turkestan Division received full dictatorial powers.[72]

Unified authority made administration more effective, and subsequent success was as much the result of political as military acumen. Frunze was keenly appreciative of the political, ethnic, and social origins of the conflict and understood that defeat of the native resistance depended heavily upon alleviating outstanding grievances and mistrust. Accordingly, in 1920, Frunze called for a maximum political effort among the Fergana population, beginning with land and water reform. In addition, during March 1920, the party conducted seventy-eight meetings, staged eighteen lectures and twenty-one discussions, circulated copies of its reports in Uzbek as well as Russian, and began to establish public schools.[73]

Although the effects of such programs defy precise measurement, policy reform and propaganda apparently exerted a calming influence on popular opinion. Yet, as happened throughout Central Asia, the native reaction to conscription in the summer of 1920 infused new life into the Fergana resistance, where Kurshirmat gathered about 6,000 fighters to renew the struggle. Many Muslims drafted by the Soviet government fled to join the resistance, and the Bolsheviks found it necessary to disarm the 1st Uzbek Cavalry Brigade.[74] Benefiting from local support and good intelligence, the resistance again dominated the countryside.

The Red Army responded aggressively but found itself embroiled in a protracted conflict. Although Red units could prevail in any conventional tactical encounter, resistance remained widespread throughout 1921, especially in the eastern Fergana region (modern Tajikistan). The business of hunting down elusive guerrilla bands across great distances and into remote mountainous defiles proved risky and arduous.[75] Yet relentless pressure by Red forces gradually bore fruit. By one estimate, from February to October 1922, Red forces eliminated 119 of approximately 200 Basmachi groups, killing over 4,000 men in the process. The following year, the Fergana Revolutionary Military Soviet organized mobile detachments operating from garrisons in all the key administrative centers. Further, it established parallel local administration for Russian and native quarters in mixed cities.[76] By the end of the year, Kurshirmat fled to Afghanistan, and not more than 2,000 Basmachis remained in the valley.⁷⁷

Thus, in 1923, Fergana lost its designation as a front, although sporadic fighting persisted. In the summer of 1925, Ibragim Bek attempted to revive the resistance but was unable to organize tribal leaders—most of whom still operated over small territories with full autonomy—into an effective coalition. As a result, lacking secure bases and permanent forage, resistance bands receded into the most distant corners of the Fergana Valley.⁷⁸

Case Two: The Resistance in Bukhara

As of the summer of 1920, no clearer impediment to the establishment of Red rule could be found than Bukhara, where events in Fergana sparked a sympathetic explosion. Kuibyshev contended that the strength of the Basmachi movement in Central Asia depended above all upon the political posture of Bukhara and Afghanistan, which had been drawing nearer one another politically. Basmachi control of Bukhara, which lay across major lines of communication in Turkestan, was a threat to Soviet power in the region. In turn, the disposition of Afghanistan, a potential sanctuary as well as a conduit of support for Muslim resistance, might well hinge on events in Bukhara.⁷⁹ Thus, possession of Bukhara was crucial. Under the emir, Bukhara could serve as a rallying point for opposition to Soviet power; in Red hands, it could become a staging area of revolution in Asia.

Bolstered by the strong support of the Muslim clergy, Bukharan Emir Alim Khan moved to consolidate his power. He conducted an unprecedented mobilization to raise an army that, according to Red estimates (probably inflated), consisted of 8,275 infantry, 7,580 cavalry, and up to 27,000 irregulars.⁸⁰ With the aid of a motley assortment of fugitive Whites, Turks, and a few Afghans, the emir levied young Bukharans into his army and established garrisons in Bukhara, Khatyrchi-Kermine and Kitab-Shakhrisiabe.

Given its political and military significance, as well as its complexity, the Red Army's Bukharan operation stands as an instructive case study for analysis of the war with the Basmachis. At the start of the operation, Frunze's Turkestan Front had responsibility for an expanse of 2,000 kilometers from east to west, across which it was concurrently suppressing a peasant uprising in Semireche, fighting Basmachis in the Fergana Valley, lending military support to the newly established Khorezm Peoples Republic, and fomenting a revolt against the emir in Bukhara. His resources stretched to the utmost, Frunze depended upon achieving complete surprise in his assault on Bukhara, a result accomplished in part by a Soviet emissary to the emir, who carried on negotiations up to the eve of the Red offensive.⁸¹

For his operation against Bukhara, Frunze had at his disposal from 6,000 to 7,000 infantry, 2,300 cavalry, 35 light and 5 heavy guns, 8 armored cars, 5 armored trains, and 11 aircraft. In addition, Red units expected to benefit from planned uprisings by radical elements in Kata-Kurgan, Samarkand, and Novyi Chardzhui. Frunze's requests for additional Red Army

Bukhara, as it appeared around 1890

units went unanswered because of the demands of concurrent Russian operations against the White and Polish armies. As a result, he resorted to the formation of national units, beginning with the 1st Muslim Regiment and including armed political and railroad workers.[82]

Frunze's plan emerged in two orders and hinged on a simultaneous strike executed by four independent operational groups. To ensure absolute secrecy, nothing was written down or communicated by phone. The first order, promulgated on 12 August, designated assembly areas for units assigned to each group, and the second, issued on 25 August, described their coordinated movements.[83] The Kagan Group, consisting of the 4th Cavalry Regiment, the 1st Eastern Muslim Regiment, and militia from several local garrisons, was to advance northward on the main axis of attack from Kagan to Old Bukhara and Star-Makhassa. Its aim was to destroy the emir's main field force and, above all, deny the emir and his government any chance of escape. The commander, one Comrade Belov, was to await word of a successful uprising in Chardzhui as the cue to attack.

A second, independent column was to support the Red-instigated uprising in Chardzhui, after which Red Army and Bukharan cavalry forces would sweep north to take Kara-Kul and hold the railroad line at Iakka-tut to prevent the emir's flight in that direction. At the same time, other cavalry elements would seize the crossings of the Amu River and Burdalyk and cut the railroad line from Old Bukhara to Termez. The Chardzhui Group consisted of a rifle regiment, a rifle battalion, a cavalry squadron, and a detachment of Bukharans.

Two additional groups, assembled at Katta-Kurgan and Samarkand, were to operate to the east of Old Bukhara. The first group, including a cavalry regiment and squadron and a detachment of Red Bukharans, was to occupy Khatyrchi, Ziaetdin, and Kermine along the road from Samarkand to Old Bukhara. The second group, consisting of a rifle regiment, a cavalry division, an independent cavalry brigade, and an engineer company, was charged with the defeat of the emir's forces along the Shakhrisiabe-Kitab axis and seizure of the Kushka River territory.[84]

The Bukharan operation began as planned with the seizure of Old Chardzhui on the night of 28—29 August by a force designated the 8th Bukharan Revolutionary Detachment (see map 10). Cavalry elements from Chardzhui assumed covering positions on the right bank of the Amu River at Marazym and Burdalyk on 30—31 August, while a special detachment, including subunits of the 5th Rifle Regiment, advanced north to Kara-Kul. From the east, Red forces marched westward from Katta-Kurgan as far as Kizil Tepe and from Samarkand southward beyond Kitab and along the Kushka River. Farther south and west, the Amu flotilla patrolled the Amu River along the Afghan frontier to seal off possible escape routes.

Meanwhile, on 29 August, the Kagan Group pressed north to Old Bukhara in two columns. The right column, made up of the 10th and 12th Rifle Regiments, the 1st Cavalry Regiment, and an armored car detachment, moved along the main highway and parallel to the railroad to within sight of the city's Karshin gates. The left column, comprised of the 1st Eastern Muslim Rifle Regiment, a cavalry detachment, and a special forces regiment (*polk osobogo naznacheniia*), advanced and then halted before the Kara-Kul gates. Neither column encountered serious resistance en route, and both reached the city environs by evening.

Operations bogged down against Bukhara's old but massive walls, which were comprised of 130 defensive towers and 11 gates.[85] On 31 August and 1 September, the 25th, 26th, and 43d Aviation Reconnaissance Detachments harassed the defenders with a light aerial bombardment. Nevertheless, penetration of the city walls, roughly ten meters high and five meters thick, depended first upon fire from 122-mm and 152-mm artillery pieces, some of which were mounted on an armored train. The Reds concentrated artillery fire on the city gates, which were less formidable than the walls. In this instance, however, the misapplication of force exposed the inexperience of Red officers. Although no effective defensive counterfire impeded their closing to virtually point-blank range, the Reds were content to commit their artillery fire from a distance of five to six kilometers, with a corresponding diminu-

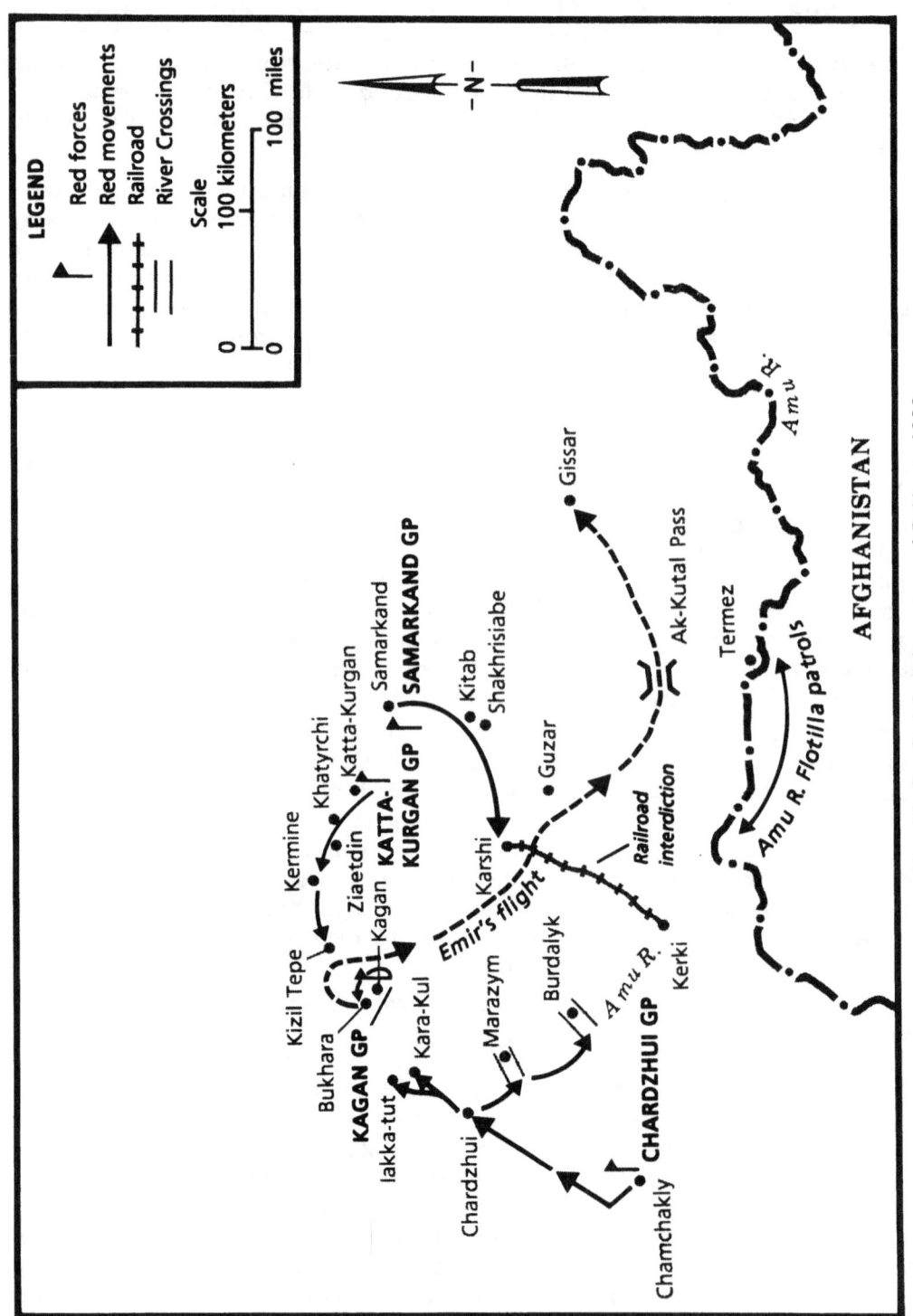

Map 10. The Red Army's capture of Bukhara, 1920

tion of effect. Led by the 1st Eastern Muslim Regiment, the Reds made their first attempt to storm the city on 31 August but failed to carry the outer fortifications after a brief penetration. Poor use of artillery, uncoordinated employment of a small tank force, and vaguely framed objectives vitiated the effort. An exasperated Frunze lamented after learning of the attack: "If the operation will be conducted this unskillfully, the city will never be taken."[86]

On 31 August, G. V. Zinoviev arrived with elements of the First Army to assume overall command. After regrouping, Red forces staged an attack on 1 September against the eastern Karshin and Samarkand gates. Heavy street fighting followed a breakthrough of the outer fortifications. On 2 September, Red Army sappers blew a breach in the inner fortress wall, and a dawn artillery and aerial bombardment followed. Having held firmly as long as their defensive perimeter remained secure, the defenders wavered and then scattered before a Red assault by three rifle brigades, a regiment of cadets, and the 1st Muslim Regiment (formed by Bukharan Communists in Samarkand). The 4th Cavalry cleared the city in street-to-street fighting but, amidst the chaos and looting, failed to cover escape routes to the north and northeast. Taking advantage of poor Red Army intelligence and the dissolution of attacking forces inside the city, the emir, who by his own account was in his private residence outside the city when the attack began, managed to escape with about 500 mounted fighters. A Red aviation detachment subsequently reported the emir's movement northward. A cavalry unit picked up the trail but was detained by the emir's rear guard. Slipping deftly past a Red patrol near Kizil Tepe, the emir turned abruptly southward, hurried through the Ak Kutal Pass, and then rushed eastward to the fortress at Gissar. His escape would cost the Red Army dearly in the future but could not prevent the proclamation on 14 September of the Bukharan Peoples Republic.[87] In November, Kuibyshev proclaimed the Bukharan revolution the world's first peasant revolution against medieval, feudal exploitation.

Bolstered by military success, party activists frantically organized a political offensive. The Bukharan Union of Youth (BUY) formed in October 1920 and immediately began creating local chapters. There being no room in its ranks for passive members, the BUY conducted an intensive three-week training course in political agitation for new recruits. Yet zeal could not overcome all obstacles. Of the original nine members of the BUY Central Committee, four, all native Central Asians, were shortly expelled for dereliction of their responsibilities. To revitalize BUY, the party dispatched a small group of experienced Muslim organizers to Bukhara.[88]

The Bukharan Communist Party (BKP) experienced similar growing pains but, by its Third Congress in 1923, felt secure enough to purge its membership (1,560 full members and 167 candidates) of hostile class elements: merchants, landowners, mullahs, and former government bureaucrats. Reliance on proletarians created problems in recruitment, however, and many entering members possessed no formal education. Party figures indicated that 40 percent of the membership was illiterate and another 50 percent was only partially literate, a fact that hampered the dissemination of printed propaganda. As evidence of further accommodation to local conditions, the membership was 70 percent Muslim. And despite its public commitment to women's equality, the BKP included only one native female.[89]

Meanwhile, under the guidance of the party, the Bukharan Red Army transformed itself in 1921 from a volunteer force to an army of two-year conscripts. The initial draft included 1,000 party members and 1,000 nonmembers.[90] The Bukharan Nazirat or Commissariat of Public Enlightenment assumed responsibility for predraft education of youths from age eight through sixteen. The program entailed both political indoctrination and physical training.[91]

Despite such organizational progress, however, liquidation of the resistance in the field remained incomplete. In 1921, the emir retained about 15,000 armed followers in the Bukhara region. The principal group of Basmachis withdrew under pressure to the fortress of Gissar in eastern Bukhara, which covered the approaches to the village of Kok-Tash where Ibragim Bek maintained a residence. Pursuit by Red forces, including the 1st Turkestan Cavalry Division, 1st Turkestan Cavalry Brigade, and 5th and 12th Rifle Regiments, continued beyond the Surkhan River. From there, Red units rampaged unchecked, occupying Dushanbe and other towns and driving the emir into refuge in Afghanistan.[92] Yet Soviet forces were unable to transform tactical success into strategic victory.

In defiance of the apparent logic of the battlefield, Basmachi uprisings erupted in the rear of Red Army units, sometimes in response to alleged Red outrages against the populace. The emir subsequently charged that Red soldiers executed 50,000 persons in the district of Ferez alone.[93] Remarkably, Basmachi strength in remote eastern Bukhara approached its peak in early 1922. Scattered Red units retreated in January, and in February, fighting returned to the Bukhara city environs.[94]

Just as the Basmachi movement drew upon heretofore unseen reserves of energy, Enver Pasha appeared on the scene in the spring of 1922 to infuse the resistance with a sense of political purpose and overarching military strategy. More than any other leader to serve the cause, Enver possessed the intellectual gifts and grasp of politics to form a coherent movement. Russian Central Asia, however, was scarcely more fertile soil on which to sustain a national (Pan-Turkic) movement than it was to nurture Bolshevik socialism. Tribal politics and a warlord mentality among its chieftains left the *Basmachestvo* weaker than the sum of its parts. Ibragim, on his part, continued to vie for leadership and operated independently. At the apex of his strength, Enver commanded up to 3,000 of the estimated 16,000 Basmachis in Bukhara and achieved, even in the assessment of Soviet scholar K. Vasilievskii, a broad-based popular support (*obshchenarodnyi*). In February, Enver's force occupied Dushanbe and briefly held much of Bukhara. Yet his strength was always limited by disunity and shortages of weapons, especially artillery and ammunition.[95]

In response to Enver's challenge, Red Army Commander S. S. Kamenev created the Bukharan Forces Group (under the control of the Turkestan

Front), which included 2 cavalry brigades, 2 cavalry squadrons, and 1 rifle division—7,530 men in all. The Reds pursued Enver in two columns, one to seal the Afghan frontier and the other to envelop him from the north and expel him from the fertile Gissar Valley. Over the course of a two-month campaign in eastern Bukhara, the Reds kept Enver on the run, recapturing Dushanbe in July and denying him any opportunity to assume the initiative or regather his strength. The final battle occurred east of Dushanbe, between Baldzhuvon and Khovaling, and ended in a Red triumph. Enver's influence came to a sudden end with his death in combat on 4 August 1922.[96]

Absent Enver's leadership, the Basmachi strength faded. Bands that had recently numbered from 500 to 1,000 subsequently diminished to as few as 25 or 30. As of January 1923, the Turkestan Front estimated Basmachi strength in the Bukharan Republic at 25 bands with a combined strength of 2,495 men. An additional 2,290 Basmachis continued to operate in eastern Bukhara.[97]

Turkestan Front Commander A. I. Kork continued to prosecute the war aggressively. The 3d Cavalry Brigade chased Selim-Pasha, Enver's deputy, deep into the mountains, conducted an encircling maneuver over a distance of 175 kilometers, and cornered his Basmachis in the geographical triangle of Koludar, Guzar, and Tengi-Khoram. On 13 March, the Reds achieved yet another tactical triumph but could not cut off the fleeing remnants of Selim's force, which maneuvered rapidly to the remote Lokai Valley in western Bukhara. At Lokai, among the last bastions of Basmachi strength, Selim linked up with Ibragim Bek to face the Red Army. Executing a swift flanking maneuver to strike the Basmachi rear, Red units delivered a devastating blow. Upon absorbing crippling losses, the Basmachis dispersed.[98]

Basmachi bands surfaced in western Bukhara again in 1924 and captured several towns only miles from Old Bukhara before the Red cavalry intervened. But such guerrilla attacks no longer galvanized a war-weary populace, and strikes against villages reconciled to Soviet rule proved counterproductive.[99] In all, the cumulative effect of military successes, skillful propaganda reinforced by pragmatic social policies, and infinitely superior organization enabled the Soviets to prevail.

Conclusion of the Basmachi Campaigns

In the autumn of 1924, the Soviet government reorganized most of Central Asia into the Uzbek and Turkoman Soviet Socialist Republics and the Tajik Autonomous Republic. (Kirghizia would achieve autonomous status in 1926 and become a union republic in 1936.) Though symbolic of increasing Soviet control, political reorganization did not spell the end of conflict in remote rural areas.

The final pacification of Khiva continued for nearly a decade. Traditional strongman Dzhunaid Khan exploited political blunders by the fledgling (and soon to be absorbed by the Uzbek SSR) Khorezm Soviet Socialist Republic to seize the republican capital in Khiva in early 1924. He was particularly aided by two decisions. First, the Khorezm leadership proclaimed the nationalization of religious lands and denied clergy the right to vote. Second, Red military units disarmed unreliable detachments of the Turkoman volunteers and executed their leaders. Moscow subsequently disbanded the Khorezm Republic and rushed military assistance to the region, but Dzhunaid carried on the struggle until his flight to Iran in 1927. Ibragim Bek launched a new offensive in the Lokai Valley region in 1926 only to be chased into Afghanistan. Further Afghan support of the Basmachi movement ended, however, with the signing of a treaty with the USSR in 1926.[100]

Soviet social policy reignited the resistance in 1928. Stalin's decision to collectivize agriculture stirred peasant resistance and precipitated famine in many parts of the Soviet Union, including Central Asia.[101] Ibragim reappeared yet again in Tajikistan in 1930—31, forcing the Soviet government to send the 83d Division of the OGPU (security forces) to help the Red Army restore order. Similarly, Dzhunaid Khan returned to Turkmenistan in 1931 and captured the Caspian Sea fort of Krasnovodsk before elements of the OGPU's 63d Division drove him back across the Iranian frontier. Even then, the establishment of Soviet power remained incomplete. Nomads in outlying areas of modern Turkmenistan and elsewhere continued to range across deserts and steppes beyond the reach of Soviet institutions.[102]

The Soviet defeat of the Basmachis stands apart in two fundamental respects from prior Russian experiences in fighting the Muslim tribal resistance in Central Asia and the Caucasus. First, by 1917, major towns and cities in Central Asia harbored a substantial Slavic and European population. Although the growing presence of immigrants alienated the natives, it also proved a pillar of moral and material support for the revolution. Second, unlike their imperial Russian predecessors, the Bolsheviks sought the full integration of Central Asia into the new order. Consequently, they had to cultivate greater sensitivity to the political and cultural nuances of their policies. Although Marxism-Leninism provided no clear blueprint for victory in Central Asia, it predisposed the Bolsheviks to undertake a social analysis of the theater of conflict. Above all, the Bolsheviks were aware of the significance of "political consciousness," whether more or less developed, in determining the will of a people to resist or seek accommodation.

This does not, of course, mean that the Bolsheviks—especially local cadres in Central Asia—were not guilty of serious errors in political judgment. They treaded heavily on native traditions (especially where the social roles of women and clergy were concerned), prematurely imposed conscription, and at times engaged in wanton destruction and atrocities. Furthermore, fulfillment of Kamenev's 1923 strategic vision proved difficult in reality. But they also possessed the ability to ameliorate the consequences of their mistakes. The Bolsheviks committed themselves to a major propaganda effort and repeatedly reversed or deferred unpopular decisions. Though bound to an ideological framework in their thinking, they—at least key figures such as Lenin, Stalin, Kuibyshev, Kamenev, and Frunze—exhibited a pragmatic instinct that served them well in crucial situations.

Thus tempered, ideology permitted the Bolsheviks to understand that the outcome in Central Asia must ultimately transcend events on the battlefield, that the military and political aspects of the war were thoroughly interwoven. What is perhaps the most remarkable evidence of this fact is the extent to which the Red Army was also an instrument of the political war. During crucial periods of the conflict, Red Army commanders exercised civil and military powers and, for the most part, did so effectively. Moreover, the Soviets made economic concessions and moderated their stance on religion. The creation of national units officered by natives—notwithstanding significant defections—was symbolically important. So, too, was the use of native Communists as political officers. Still, despite their success, it would be a mistake to conclude that Russian Bolsheviks in Central Asia had rid themselves of traditional ethnic chauvinism or a colonizer's mentality.[103] Nor, as would remain true until the dissolution of the USSR, had they won over the large rural populace to the Soviet order.

On the battlefield, the Reds successfully exploited the disunity of the resistance. Superior organization, tactics, and equipment eventually neutralized the natural advantages of the Basmachis. Once confined to the farthest reaches of the Soviet Union or reduced to raiding from across the border, the Basmachis no longer had access to the population and thus posed no great threat.

The success of the Red conquest of Central Asia is attributable to three general causes. First, with the exception of the brief period of Enver Pasha's command, the Basmachi resistance lacked even a semblance of cohesion. Second, the Reds overcame initial political errors and effectively adapted economic and social policies to local conditions, even at the cost of ideological concessions (which could later be reversed). And, third, the Red Army learned from its own experience, as well as from its study of imperial campaigns, how best to operate against an unconventional foe in the rugged deserts and mountains of Central Asia.

Notes

Chapter 3

1. The Red Army campaigns against the Basmachestvo have not been widely studied in the West. Although the political contours of the struggle are generally known, the exploits of the Red Army have received comparatively little scholarly examination. While Soviet scholars have produced many monographs on the upheavals in Central Asia, they have dealt only obliquely with the sharp cultural and religious cleavages between the Russian and Central Asian peoples that engendered political antagonism and resistance. Eden Naby, "The Concept of Jihad in Opposition to Communist Rule," *Central Asian Survey* 19, no. 3—4 (1986), points out that it was the Russians themselves who introduced concepts of ethnicity and national self-determination to Central Asia to encourage "the dismemberment of the Soviet area into five union republics..." The intent was to resist Pan-Islamic or Pan-Turkic tendencies.

   A handful of recent Western scholarly studies have done much to improve the state of research on the Basmachis. See, in particular, Martha Olcott, "The Basmachi or Freemen's Revolt in Turkestan, 1918—24," *Soviet Studies* 33 (July 1981):352—69; Glenda Fraser, "Basmachi," *Central Asian Survey* 6, no. 1 (1987):1—74; no. 2 (1987):7—42; and Marie Broxup, "The Basmachi," *Central Asian Survey* 2, no. 1 (1983):57—82. Broxup provides a useful selected bibliography. Valuable general works on Central Asia include Alexandre Bennigsen and S. Enders Wimbush, *Muslim National Communism in the Soviet Union* (Chicago, IL: University of Chicago, 1979); Seymour Becker, *Russia's Protectorates in Central Asia: Bukhara and Khiva, 1865—1924* (Cambridge, MA: Harvard University Press, 1968); Michael Rywkin, *Moscow's Muslim Challenge* (Armonk, NY, 1982); Serge Zenkovsky, *Pan-Turkism and Islam in Russia* (Cambridge, MA: Harvard University Press, 1960); and Teresa Rakowska-Harmstone, *Russia and Nationalism in Central Asia: The Case of Tadzhikistan* (Baltimore, MD: Johns Hopkins University, 1970). Many Soviet scholars, especially after 1978, identified scholarship on the Basmachi movement as a field of ideological struggle. See, in particular, A. I. Zevelev, Iu. A. Poliakov, and L. V. Shishkina, *Basmachestvo: Pravda istorii i vymysel fal'sifikatorov* (Moscow: Mysl', 1986).

2. Rywkin, *Moscow's Muslim Challenge*, 59. Rywkin cites data from *Aziatskaia Rossiia*, vol. 1 (St. Petersburg: Glavnoe pereselenskoe upravlenie, 1921); and V. Denisev, "Bukhara," *Voennyi rabotnik Turkestana*, no. 2 (April 1922):93. Also, for an excellent analysis of migration patterns into Kazakhstan, see George Demko, *The Russian Colonization of Kazakhstan, 1896—1916* (Bloomington: Indiana University Press, 1969).

3. On the uprising of 1898, see Ann Sheehy, "The Andizhan Uprising of 1898 in Soviet Historiography," *Central Asian Review* 14, no. 2 (1966):139—50.

4. Ibid.; Rywkin, *Moscow's Muslim Challenge*, 17—19; and S. D. Asfandiarov, *Natsional'no-osvoboditel'noe vosstanie 1916 g. v Kazakhstane* (Alma-Ata, Kazakh S.S.R., 1936), 100—105.

5. Bennigsen and Wimbush, *Muslim National Communism*, 39—40.

6. Rywkin, *Moscow's Muslim Challenge*, 21—22; and Ann Shukman, "Soviet Central Asia: The Turkestan Commission, 1919—20," *Central Asian Review* 12, no. 1 (1964):5—15; and N. Berezin, "Istoriia krasnoi armii v Turkestane: Basmachestvo v Bukhare. Istoriia ego vozniknoveniia," *Voennyi rabotnik Turkestana*, no. 7 (September 1922):40. Stalin, the first commissar of nationalities, knew better but subsequently dismissed native nationalism on the ground that it was not the expression of the will of self-conscious proletarians. See also Fraser, "Basmachi," no. 1, 5—6.

7. Richard Pipes, *The Formation of the Soviet Union* (New York: Atheneum, 1974), 178—79. This is a superb study of the Basmachi movement in the broader context of Soviet national politics throughout the old empire.

8. Kh. Sh. Inoiatov, *Narody Srednei Azii v bor'be protiv interventov i vnutrennei kontrrevoliutsii* (Moscow: Mysl', 1984), 31.

9. Ibid., 74.

10. Iu. Poliakov and A. I. Chugunov, *Konets Basmachestva* (Moscow: Nauka, 1976), 35.

11. Pipes, *The Formation of the Soviet Union*, 178.

12. Mustafa Chokaev, "The Basmachi Movement in Turkestan," *Asiatic Review* 24 (1928): 280—83, as cited in Fraser, "Basmachi," no. 1, 5.

13. *M. V. Frunze na frontakh grazhdanskoi voiny*, sbornik dokumentov (Moscow: Voennoe izdatel'stvo, 1941), 275, telegram, Frunze to Lenin, 24 March 1920. This work is a compilation of documents, especially orders and telegrams from Frunze's service on various fronts of the civil war. Various Soviet sources make extravagant claims concerning the extent of outside, notably British, support for the Basmachis. Inoiatov, *Narody Srednei Azii*, 9, explicitly compares the situation in Turkmenia to the funneling of American aid to Afghanistan after 1979. On page 70, Inoiatov claims the Whites provided 25,000 rifles to the Fergana Basmachis. Although assertions that the Basmachis received assistance are plausible, the motley assortment they employed in the field suggests that outside support could not have been extensive. An early Soviet source, Berezin, "Istoriia krasnoi armii," 39, notes that intercepted letters of Enver Pasha include complaints of insufficient outside support.

14. D. Lavrenev, "Gornaia voina," *Voennyi rabotnik Turkestana*, no. 1 (March 1922), as quoted in Helene Aymen de Lageard, "The Revolt of the Basmachi According to Red Army Journals, 1920—1922," *Central Asian Survey* 6, no. 3 (1987):23. De Lageard surveys several military publications during a two-year period and provides their most salient observations on the war in translation.

15. B. Usmankhodzhaev, "Boevye dela Revkoma," in *V boiakh za sovetskuiu vlast' v ferganskoi doline* (Tashkent, Uzbek S.S.R., 1957), 22—23.

16. Iu. Baitmatov, "Epizody iz geroicheskikh boev sovetskikh voisk," in *V boiakh za sovetskuiu vlast'*, 44—49.

17. Pipes, *The Formation of the Soviet Union*, 182; and G. Safarov, *Kolonial'naia revoliutsiia, opyt Turkestana* (Moscow, 1921), 133.

18. "Nasha politika v Turkestane," *Zhizn' natsional'nostei*, 21 March 1920.

19. *M. V. Frunze na frontakh*, 274, telegram, Frunze to Lenin, 24 March 1920; and E. Kozlovskii, *Krasnaia armiia v Srednei Azii* (Tashkent, 1928), 37, as cited in Fraser, "Basmachi" 6, no. 1 (1987):40.

20. Aleksandrov, "Organizatsiia vysshego upravleniia krasnoi armiei turkestanskoi respubliki v 1919 g.," *Voennyi rabotnik Turkestana*, no. 2 (March 1922):71.

21. Broxup, "The Basmachi," 68; and A. Iur'ev, "Boevoi put' vozhd'ia," *Krasnaia zvezda*, 3 November 1925.

22. *M. V. Frunze na frontakh*, 280, telegram, 23 May 1920. Frunze also complained about the exclusion of the Transcaspia District (Turkmenia) from the control of the Turkestan Front.

23. Pipes, *The Formation of the Soviet Union*, 184.

24. Ibid., 183; and "The Basmachis: The Central Asian Resistance Movement, 1918—1924," *Central Asian Review* 7, no. 3 (1959):239.

25. *M. V. Frunze na frontakh*, 289, telegram, 27 August 1920.

26. Olcott, "The Basmachi," 358.

27. *M. V. Frunze na frontakh*, 278—79 (directive to the Turkestan Front, 7 May 1920); Mi. I. Vladimirov, et al., *M. V. Frunze: Voennaia i politicheskaia deiatel'nost'* (Moscow: Voennoe izdatel'stvo, 1984), 125; and Shukman, "Soviet Central Asia," 10.

28. Inoiatov, *Narody srednei azii*, 222; and *Istoriia grazhdanskoi voiny v Uzbekistane*, vol. 2 (Tashkent, Uzbek S.S.R.: FAN, 1970), 279.

29. D. Liianov, "K voprosu o prizyve inorodtsev v Krasnuiu Armiiu," *Zhizn' natsional'nostei*, 10 October 1920; and N. Lykoshkin, "Lokot' k loktiu," *Voennaia mysl'* (May—July 1921):27, as cited in de Lageard, "The Revolt of the Basmachi," 12.

30. "Obiavlenie: Vsem musul'manskim organizatsii R.K.P. . . . natsional' nykh men'shestvu," *Zhizn' natsional'nostei*, 14 September 1919; Zvers, introductory note to archival index, fund 17 (Central Muslim Military College), Central State Archive of the Soviet Army.

31. O. Khudoverdiev, "Bukharskaia Krasnaia Armiia," *Voenno-istoricheskii zhurnal*, no. 9 (1981), as translated in JPRS (Joint Publications Research Service) 79812, 7 January 1982, USSR Report MA 1643, 113—14; and "Doklad soveta narodnykh nazirov BNSR ob obuchenii voennomu iskusstvu i o fizicheskom vospitanii detei i iunoshei, 21 July 1921," in *Istoriia Bukharskoi Narodnoi Respubliki* (1920—1924 gg., sbornik dokumentov) (Tashkent, Uzbek S.S.R.: Izdatel'stvo FAN, 1926), 244—45.

32. Rywkin, *Moscow's Muslim Challenge*, 36; and A. Kokanbaev, *Bor'ba s basmachestvom i uprochenie sovetskoi v Fergane* (Tashkent, Uzbek S.S.R.: Gosudarstvennoe izdatel'stvo Uzbekskoi S.S.R., 1958), 74—75.

33. *M. V. Frunze na frontakh*, 283, telegram, 27 May 1920.

34. Fraser, "Basmachi," no. 1, 35.

35. *M. V. Frunze na frontakh*, 296—97, telegram Frunze to Lenin, 12 June 1920; and Dm. Furman, untitled article from *Pravda*, 4 July 1920, as printed in *Inostrannaia voennaia interventsiia i grazhdanskaia voina v Srednei Azii i Kazakhstane*, vol. 1 (Alma Ata, Kazakh S.S.R.: Izdatel'stvo Akademii Nauk Kazakhskoi SSR, 1963), 376—78.

36. Poliakov and Chugunov, *Konets basmachestva*, 44.

37. Broxup, "The Basmachi," 60; and Olcott, "The Basmachi," 359.

38. Olcott, "The Basmachi," 359; and Fraser, "Basmachi," no. 1, 8.

39. Olcott, "The Basmachi," 350; and Broxup, "The Basmachi," 61.

40. Ibid.

41. Fraser, "Basmachi," no. 2, 7—8. Fraser cites a document of the India Office, 1922.

42. Aleksandrov, "Organizatsiia vysshego upravleniia," 71—72; and D. Zuev, "K kraevoi partinnoi konferentsii k soveshchaniiu voennykh delegatov kraevoi partkonferentsii," *Voennyi rabotnik Turkestana*, no. 7 (September 1922):31.

43. D. Zuev, "Primenenie norm polevogo ustava k osobennostiam sredne-aziatskikh teatrov voennykh deistvii," *Voennyi rabotnik Turkestana*, no. 1 (March 1922):25—31.

44. Lavrenev, "Gornaia voina," as quoted in de Lageard, 16—20.

45. Central State Archive of the Soviet Army, fund 110 (Turkestan Front), index 3, item 1402, sheets 1—18.

46. Ibid., sheets 5—9; Broxup, "The Basmachi," 69; *M. V. Frunze na frontakh*, 314—15, Order to the Fergana Front, 28 May 1920; M. M. Kozlov, "Vklad M. V. Frunze v razvitii strategii

47. i operativnogo iskusstva," *Voenno-istoricheskii zhurnal*, no. 3 (1985):31—34; and *Inostrannaia voennaia interventsiia*, 434—36.

47. *Istoriia grazhdanskoi voiny*, 117, 126—27.

48. A. A. Kotenev, "O razgrome basmacheskikh band v Srednei Azii," *Voenno-istoricheskii zhurnal*, no. 2 (1987):61—63; Kozlov, "Vklad M. V. Frunze," 33; and A. Tasin, "Obzor raboty vozdushnogo flota v Turkestana za 1920," *Voennaia mysl'* (May—July 1921):191, as cited in de Lageard, "The Revolt of the Basmachi," 191.

49. Ibid.; and *M. V. Frunze na frontakh*, 276—78, telegram, 10 April 1920.

50. D. Zuev, "Osobennosti oboznogo dela v Turkestane," *Voennyi rabotnik Turkestana*, no. 2 (April 1922):52—60.

51. N. Siniavskii, "Geliosviaz'," *Voennoe delo v Srednei Azii*, no. 1 (September 1922):54—56; N. Liapin, "Chimganskii pokhod," *Krasnaia zvezda*, 15 October 1925.

52. Stabs-kapitan Maksimovich, "Geliosviaz' i geliografnaia komanda v Akhal-tekinskoi ekspeditsii 1880—1881 gg.," *Voennyi sbornik*, no. 8 (1881):289—90.

53. V. Ionov, "V gorakh—gornaia artilleriia," *Voennoe delo v Srednei Azii*, no. 1 (September 1922):40—50.

54. Liapin, "Chimganskii pokhod."

55. P. Antonov, "Taktika bor'by s basmachestvom," *Krasnaia zvezda*, 8 December 1925.

56. Vladimirov, *M. V. Frunze*, 126; and A. A. Epishev, "Voenno-politicheskaia deiatel'nost' M. V. Frunze," *Voenno-istoricheskii zhurnal*, no. 3 (1985):25.

57. *Valerian Vladimirovich Kuibyshev: Biografiia* (Moscow: Izdatel'stvo politicheskoi literatury, 1988), 131—32.

58. Ibid.

59. G. Markov, "Antireligioznaia propaganda sredi narodov vostoka," *Voennyi rabotnik Turkestana*, no. 2 (April 1922):39—40; Central State Archive of the Soviet Army, Moscow, Russia, fund 25895 (Central Asian Military District), index 1, item 11, sheets 2—6.

60. Inoiatov, *Narody Srednei Azii*, 220.

61. "Polozhenie basmachestva (Beseda s komanduiushchim voiskami Turkfronta tov. Levandovskim)," *Krasnaia zvezda*, 10 September 1925.

62. Ibid.; and Vasilevskii, "Fazy basmacheskogo dvizheniia v srednei Azii," *Novyi vostok* 29 (1930):135.

63. "The Basmachis," 246; and M. Irkaev, *Istoriia grazhdanskoi voiny v Tadzhikistane* (Dushanbe: Irfan, 1971), 386—87. See also William Ritter, "Revolt in the Mountains: Fuzail Maksum and the Occupation of Garm," *Journal of Contemporary History* 35 (1990):547—80.

64. "Operativnaia svodka shtata ferganskoi armeiskoi gruppy o boevykh deistviiakh protiv Basmacheskikh shaek," 7 November 1920, in *Inostrannaia voennaia interventsiia*, 470—71.

65. Broxup, "The Basmachi," 63—64; Olcott, "The Basmachi," 363; and A. Castagne, *Les Basmachis* (Paris, 1925), 52.

66. Kokanbaev, *Bor'ba s basmachestvom*, 54—57; and "Svodka shtaba ferganskogo fronta o chislennosti i raspolozhenii otriadov Basmachei," 8 October 1920, in *Inostrannaia voennaia interventsiia*, 462—63.

67. "The Basmachis," 237; *Istoriia grazhdanskoi voiny*, 53; Inoiatov, *Narody Srednei Azii*, 72; and S. B. Ginzburg, "Basmachestvo v Fergane," *Novyi vostok* 10—11 (1925):185—89.

68. Fraser, "Basmachi," no. 1, 30.

69. Kokanbaev, *Bor'ba s basmachestvom*, 57—58.

70. Ibid., 68—70; *Istoriia grazhdanskoi voiny*, 56—57; R. Madaminov, "Kokandskie sobytiia," in *V boiakh za sovetskuiu vlast'*, 11; "The Basmachis," 239; and Rywkin, *Moscow's Muslim*

Challenge, 35. It is worth noting that thousands of Volga Tatars and Bashkirs had served in the Red Army during the struggle against the Whites in the South Urals and Western Siberia. Bashkir cavalry also figured in the final Red offensive against Poland.

71. Kokanbaev, *Bor'ba s basmachestvom*, 67.
72. *Istoriia grazhdanskoi voiny*, 116—17, 128.
73. Kokanbaev, *Bor'ba s basmachestvom*, 76—77; and Inoiatov, *Narody Srednei Azii*, 291.
74. Rywkin, *Moscow's Muslim Challenge*, 36; and Kokanbaev, *Bor'ba s basmachestvom*, 74—75.
75. I. Kas'kov, I. Ulianov, K. Iachmenov, et al. *Boevoi put' voisk turkestanskogo voennogo okruga* (Moscow: Voenizdat', 1959), 122—24, 148—49.
76. Kotenev, "O razgrome basmacheskikh band," 60; Fraser, "Basmachi," no. 2. Fraser uses papers from the British Foreign Office.
77. Vasilevskii, "Fazy," 135.
78. Arkadii Borisov, "Basmachestvo v Tadzhikistane," *Krasnaia zvezda*, 13 November 1925.
79. *Istoriia grazhdanskoi voiny*, 62; Becker, *Russia's Protectorates*, 204, 290; and Iakubov, "Bukharskaia operatsiia," *Voina i revoliutsiia*, no. 8 (1931):90.
80. Iakubov, "Bukharskaia operatsiia," 90—91; and Ia. A. Mel'kumov, *Turkestantsy* (Moscow: Voennoe izdatel'stvo, 1960), 10—11. Mel'kumov was a brigade commander in the 1st Cavalry Division. Some Soviet sources assert that Frunze operated against a force of 40,000 in Bukhara, but it is improbable. Moreover, even had such a force existed, it could not have concentrated in a single effort.
81. Iakubov, "Bukharskaia operatsiia," 92; and Fraser, "Basmachi," no. 1, 48. Fraser quotes directly from the emir's own account of the action (as recorded in the India Office), which is no less biased than Soviet accounts but does contain some noteworthy details.
82. Iakubov, "Bukharskaia operatsiia," 93; and Mel'kumov, *Turkestantsy*, 10—12.
83. Mel'kumov, *Turkestantsy*, 12; Iakubov, "Bukharskaia operatsiia," 93—94; and *M. V. Frunze na frontakh*, 320—25 (directive to the Turkestan Front, 12 August 1920).
84. Iakubov, "Bukharskaia operatsiia," 94—95; and *M. V. Frunze na frontakh*, 323—25 (directive to the Turkestan Front, 25 August 1920).
85. Mel'kumov, *Turkestantsy*, 24.
86. Iakubov, "Bukharskaia operatsiia," 96—98; Mel'kumov, *Turkestantsy*, 24—25; and Kaskov, *Boevoi put'*, 134—35.
87. Kas'kov, *Boevoi put'*, 134—35, 146—48; Iakubov, "Bukharskaia operatsiia," 99—101; Mel'kumov, *Turkestantsy*, 25—26; Fraser, "Basmachi," no. 1, 48; and *Valerian Vladimirovich Kuibyshev*, 144.
88. "Doklad TsK Bukharskogo Soiuza Molodezh'ob organizatsii i deiatel'nosti komandskikh organizatsii v Bukhare," 25 October 1980, in *Istoriia Bukharskoi Narodnoi Respubliki*, 80—83.
89. "Iz informatsionnoi svodki Sredazbiuro TsK RKP o politicheskom i ekonomicheskom polozhenii Bukharskoi Respubliki o sovetskom stroitel'stve i sostoianii partii," 15 January 1924, in *Istoriia Bukharskoi Narodnoi Respubliki*, 131—38.
90. Khudoberdiev, "Bukharskaia Krasnaia Armiia," 113—14.
91. "Dekret soveta narodnykh nazirov BNSR," in *Istoriia Bukharskoi Narodnoi Respubliki*, 244—45.
92. Kas'kov, *Boevoi put'*, 146; and Vasilevskii, "Fazy," 133.
93. Fraser, "Basmachi," no. 1, 52.
94. Vasilevskii, "Fazy," 133.
95. Ibid., 134; Becker, *Russia's Protectorates*, 304; and Fraser, "Basmachi," no. 1, 60.

96. Kas'kov, *Boevoi put'*, 159—63. Kotenev, "O razgrome basmacheskikh band," 61, identifies the units as the 1st and 2d Independent Turkestan Cavalry Brigades, the 3d Turkestan Rifle Division, and 2 cavalry squadrons for a total of 4,500 infantry, 3,030 cavalry, and 20 field guns. D. Zuev, *Turkestanskaia Pravda*, no. 22 (1922), as reprinted in *Istoriia Bukharskoi Narodnoi Respubliki*, 260—63.

97. "Doklad TsK BKP v Sredazbiuro TsK RKP ob itogakh raboty TsK za period s ianvaria po oktiabr' 1922 g.," 22 October 1922, in *Istoriia Bukharskoi Narodnoi Respubliki*, 119; and Irkaev, *Istoriia grazhdanskoi voiny v Tadzhikistane*, 383—84.

98. Ibid.

99. A. Zler, "Musul'manskie otriady," *Krasnaia zvezda*, 3 September 1925; and A. Borisov, "Basmachestvo v Tadzhikistane."

100. Iu. Ibragimov, "Krasnyi Turkestan, Khiva," *Zhizn' natsional'nostei*, 20 April 1919; and Olcott, "The Basmachi," 360—63. See also Ritter, "Revolt in the Mountains."

101. Central State Archive of the Soviet Army, Moscow, fund 25895 (Central Asian Military District), index 1, item 62, sheets 12—13. A 1931 "top secret" situation report by the Military Revolutionary Council of the Central Asian Military District obliquely referred to the role of disruptive economic policies in stirring opposition.

102. Ibid., sheet 22. This document is a "top secret" report by a member of the Central Asian Military District on the latest Basmachi incursions.

103. Mustafa Chokay, *Turkestan pod vlast'iu sovetov* (Paris: Iash Turkestan, 1935; reprint, Society for Central Asian Studies), 89.

Bibliography

Chapter 3

Archival Documents

Central State Archive of the Soviet Army. Moscow, Russia. Fund 110 (Turkestan Front).

Central State Archive of the Soviet Army. Moscow, Russia. Fund 25895 (Central Asia Military District).

Memoirs and Documents

"Beseda s komanduiushchim voiskami Turkfronta tov. Levandovskim." *Krasnaia zvezda*, 12 September 1925.

M. V. Frunze na frontakh grazhdanskoi voiny. Moscow, 1941.

Istoriia Bukharskoi Narodnoi Respubliki (1920—1924 gg., sbornik dokumentov). Tashkent, Uzbek S.S.R.: Izdatel'stvo FAN, 1926.

"Obiavlenie: Vsem musul'manskim organizatsii R.K.P., musul'manskim pod otdelom gubernskikh i uezdnykh otdelov natsional'nostei, musul'manskim sektsiiam politotdelov armii Vosfronta, musul'manskim podotdelam gubernskikh i uezdnykh otdelov prosveshcheniia natsional'nykh men' shestv." *Zhizn' natsional'nostei*, 14 September 1919.

"Polozhenie basmachestva (Beseda s komanduiushchim voiskami Turkfronta tov. Levandovskim)." *Krasnaia zvezda*, 10 September 1925.

Shcherbakov, N. M. *Takim bylo nachalo . . . (Vospominaniia o boevom pokhode amudar'inskoi gruppy voisk v 1919—1920 g.g.)*. Tashkent, Uzbek S.S.R., 1964.

V boiakh za sovetskuiu vlast' v ferganskoi doline. Tashkent, Uzbek S.S.R., 1957.

Books

Asfandiarov, S. D. *Natsional'no-osvoboditel'noe vosstanie 1916 g. v Kazakhstane*. Alma-Ata, Kazakh S.S.R., 1936.

Becker, Seymour. *Russia's Protectorates in Central Asia: Bukhara and Khiva, 1865—1924*. Cambridge, MA: Harvard University Press, 1968.

Bennigsen, Alexandre, and S. Enders Wimbush. *Muslim National Communism in the Soviet Union*. Chicago, IL: University of Chicago, 1979.

Castagne, A. *Les Basmachis*. Paris, 1925.

Chokay, Mustafa. *Turkestan pod vlast'iu sovetov*. Paris: Iash Turkestan, 1935. Reprint. Society for Central Asian Studies.

Demko, George. *The Russian Colonization of Kazakhstan, 1896—1916*. Bloomington: Indiana University Press, 1969.

Dzhenchuraev, D. *Po sledam Basmachei*. Frunze: Izdatel'stvo Kyrgyzstan, 1966.

Golinkov, D. L. *Krushenie antisovetskogo podpol'ia v SSSR*. Moscow: Izdatel'stvo politicheskoi literatury, 1908.

Inoiatov, Kh. Sh. *Narody Srednei Azii v bor'be protiv interventov i vnutrennei kontrrevoliutsii*. Moscow: Mysl', 1984.

Inostrannaia voennaia interventsiia i grazhdanskaia voina v Srednei Azii i Kazakhstane. 2 Vols. Alma Ata, Kazakh S.S.R.: Izdatel'stvo Akademii Nauk Kazakhskoi SSR, 1963.

Irkaev, M. *Istoriia grazhdanskoi voiny v Tadzhikistane*. Dushanbe: Irfan, 1971.

Istoriia grazhdanskoi voiny v Uzbekistane. 2 Vols. Tashkent, Uzbek S.S.R.: Izdatel'stvo FAN, 1970.

Kas'kov, I., I. Ulianov, K. Iachmenov, et al. *Boevoi put' voisk turkestanskogo voennogo okruga*. Moscow: Voenizdat', 1959.

Kokanbaev, A. *Bor'ba s basmachestvom i uprochenie sovetskoi vlasti v Fergane*. Tashkent, Uzbek S.S.R.: Gosudarstvennoe izdatel'stvo Uzbekskoi SSR, 1958.

Mel'kumov, Ia. A. *Turkestantsy*. Moscow: Voennoe izdatel'svto, 1960.

Pipes, Richard. *The Formation of the Soviet Union*. New York: Atheneum, 1974.

Pogorel'skii, I. V. *Istoriia khivinskoi revoliutsii i Khorezmskoi Narodnoi Sovetskoi Respubliki*. Leningrad: Leningrad State University, 1984.

Poliakov, Iu. A., and A. I. Chugunov. *Konets basmachestva*. Moscow: Nauka, 1976.

Rakoska-Harmstone, Teresa. *Russia and Nationalism in Central Asia: The Case of Tadzhikistan*. Baltimore: Johns Hopkins University, 1970.

Rywkin, Michael. *Moscow's Muslim Challenge*. Armonk, New York, 1982.

Safarov, G. *Kolonial'naia revoliutsiia, opyt Turkestana*. Moscow, 1921.

Valerian Vladimirovich Kuibyshev: Biografiia. Moscow: Izdatel'stvo politicheskoi literatury, 1988.

Vladimirov, Mi. I., et al. *M. V. Frunze: Voennaia i politicheskaia deiatel'nost'*. Moscow: Voennoe izdatel'stvo, 1984.

Zenkovsky, Serge. *Pan-Turkism and Islam in Russia*. Cambridge, MA: Harvard University Press, 1960.

Zevelev, A. I., Iu. A. Poliakov, and L. V. Shishkina. *Basmachestvo: Pravda istorii i vymysel fal'sifikatorov*. Moscow: Mysl', 1986.

Selected Articles

A Correspondent. "The Revolt in Transcaspia 1918—1919." *Central Asian Review* 7, no. 2 (1959):117—30.

Adignov, A. "Pravda o bashkirakh." *Zhizn' natsional'nostei*, 13 July 1919.

Aleksandrov. "Organizatsiia vysshego upravleniia krasnoi armii turkestanskoi respubliki v 1919 g." *Voennyi rabotnik Turkestana*, no. 2 (March 1922).

Antonov, P. "Taktika bor'by s basmachestvom." *Krasnaia zvezda*, 8 December 1925.

"The Basmachis: The Central Asian Resistance Movement, 1918—1924." *Central Asian Review* 7, no. 3 (1959):236—50.

"Basmachestvo i ferganskaia problema." *Zhizn' natsional'nostei*, 16 September 1921.

Bennigsen, Alexandre. "Muslim Guerilla Warfare in the Caucasus." *Central Asian Survey* 2, no. 1 (July 1983):45—56.

Berezin, N. "Istoriia krasnoi armii v Turkestane: Basmachestvo v Bukhare. Istoriia ego vozniknoveniia." *Voennyi rabotnik Turkestana*, no. 7 (September 1922):38—44.

Borisov, Akardii. "Basmachestvo v Tadzhikistane." *Krasnaia zvezda*, 13 November 1925.

Broxup, Marie. "The Basmachi." *Central Asian Survey* 2, no. 1 (1983): 57—82.

d'Enccausse, Héleñe Carrère. "Civil War and New Governments." I *Central Asia, A Century of Russian Rule*, ed. E. Allworth, New York: Columbia University, 1967:224—53.

De Lageard, Helene Aymen. "The Revolt of the Basmachi According to Red Army Journals, 1920—1922." *Central Asian Survey* 6, no. 3 (1987): 1—35.

Denisov. "Bukhara." *Voennyi rabotnik Turkestana*, no. 2 (April 1922).

Dickson, Keith. "The Basmachi and the Mujahideen: Soviet Responses to Insurgency Movements," *Military Review* (February 1985):29—44.

Epishev, A. A. "Voenno-politicheskaia deiatel'nost' M. V. Frunze." *Voenno-istoricheskii zhurnal*, no. 3 (1985):25—30.

Fraser, Glenda. "Basmachi." *Central Asian Survey* 6, no. 1 (1987):1—74; no. 2 (1987):7—42.

Ginzburg, S. B. "Basmachestvo v Fergane." *Novyi vostok* 10—11 (1925): 175—202.

Iakubov. "Bukharskaia operatsiia." *Voina i revoliutsiia*, no. 8 (1931): 88—103.

Ibragimov, Iu. "Krasnyi Turkestan, Khiva." *Zhizn' natsional'nostei*, 20 April 1919.

Ionov, V. "V gorakh—gornaia artilleriia." *Voennoe delo v Srednei Azii*, no. 1 (September 1922):40—50.

Iur'ev, A. "Boevoi put' vozhdia." *Krasnaia zvezda*, 3 November 1925.

Khudoberdiev, O. "Bukharskaia Krasnaia Armiia." *Voenno-istoricheskii zhurnal*, no. 9 (1981):94.

Kotenev, A. A. "O razgrome basmacheskikh band v Srednei Azii." *Voenno-istoricheskii zhurnal*, no. 2 (1987):60—64.

Kozlov, M. M. "Vklad M. V. Frunze v razvitii strategii i operativnogo iskusstva." *Voenno-istoricheskii zhurnal*, no. 3 (1985):31—34.

Lavrenev, D. "Gornaia voina." *Voennyi rabotnik Turkestana*, no. 1 (March 1922).

Liapin, N. "Chimganskii pokhod." *Krasnaia zvezda*, 15 October 1925.

Liianov, D. "K voprosu o prizyve inorodtsev v Krasnuiu Armiiu." *Zhizn' natsional'nostei*, 10 October 1920.

Maksimovich, Shtabs-kapitan. "Geliosviaz' i geliografnaia komanda v Akhal-tekinskoi ekspeditsii 1880—1881 gg." *Voennyi sbornik* 8 (1881):288—315.

Markov, G. "Antireligioznaia propaganda sredi narodov vostoka." *Voennyi rabotnik Turkestana*, no. 2 (April 1922).

Naby, Eden. "The Concept of Jihad in Opposition to Communist Rule." *Central Asian Survey* 19, no. 3—4 (1986):287—300.

"Nasha politika v Turkestane." *Zhizn' natsional'nostei*, 21 March 1920.

"Neskol'ko slov o deiatel'nosti registrantsionno-verbovochnogo otdela tsentral'noi musul'manskoi voennoi kollegii." *Zhizn' natsional'nostei*, 18 April 1920.

Olcott, Martha. "The Basmachi or Freemen's Revolt in Turkestan, 1918—24." *Soviet Studies* 33 (July 1981):352—69.

Pestkovskii, S. "Natsional'naia kul'tura." *Zhizn' natsional'nostei*, 8 June 1919.

Polozhenie basmachestva (Beseda s komanduiushchim voiskami Turkfronta tov. Levandovskim." *Krasnaia zvezda*, 10 September 1925.

Ritter, William. "Revolt in the Mountains: Fuzail Maksum and the Occupation of Garm." *Journal of Contemporary History* 35 (1990):547—80.

Sheehy, Ann. "The Andizhan Uprising of 1898 in Soviet Historiography." *Central Asian Review* 14, no. 2 (1966):139—50.

Shkliar, M. "Musul'manskaia bednota i Krasnaia Armiia." *Zhizn' natsional'nostei*, 17 October 1920.

Shukman, Ann. "Soviet Central Asia: The Turkestan Commission, 1919—20." *Central Asian Review* 12, no. 1 (1964):5—15.

Siniavskii, N. "Geliosviaz'." *Voennoe delo v Srednei Azii*, no. 1 (September 1922):54—63.

Usmankhodzhaev, B. "Boevye dela Revkoma." *V boiakh za sovetskuiu vlast' v ferganskoi doline*. Tashkent, Uzbek S.S.R., 1957.

Vasilevskii. "Fazy basmacheskogo dvizheniia v srednei Azii." *Novy vostak* 29 (1930):121—46.

Zler, A. "Musul'manskie otriady." *Krasnaia zvezda*, 3 September 1925.

Zuev, D. "K kraevoi partinnoi konferentsii k soveshchaniiu voennykh delegatov kraevoi partkonferentsii." *Voennyi rabotnik Turkestana*, no. 7 (September 1922):30—31.

———. "Primenenie norm polevogo ustava k osobennostiam sredne-aziatskikh teatrov voennykh deistvii." *Voennyi rabotnik Turkestana*, no. 1 (March 1922):25—31.

———. "Osobennosti oboznogo dela v Turkestane." *Voennyi rabotnik Turkestana*, no. 2 (April 1922):52—60.

The Soviet-Afghan War

Although Soviet involvement in Afghanistan predates the formal creation of the Soviet Union in 1922, most of the world took little notice of Soviet activities in the area until their lightning military intervention in Kabul in December 1979 (see map 11). From that time until the spring of 1988 when the withdrawal of Soviet military units began, the Soviet Union waged a protracted and difficult war against a determined resistance movement. The war in Afghanistan marked the first time in several decades that Soviet forces had fought an unconventional war—one in which engagements were limited and the enemy did not fight or maneuver as a conventional army but instead relied on guerrilla-style tactics characteristically associated with insurgencies or partisan resistance movements.

An analysis of the war in Afghanistan and the extraction of its lessons pose a considerable problem for historians, mainly because insufficient time has elapsed to provide historical perspective and the available documentary record of the struggle remains fragmentary at best. Throughout the conflict, the Soviet Union made scant information available, and several years elapsed before the Soviet press even acknowledged that their soldiers were routinely involved in combat. Nevertheless, a general glimpse of the Afghan War emerged in Soviet military periodicals, which offered insightful commentary of a theoretical nature. During the course of the war, articles on troop and unit training, though sometimes containing no explicit reference to Afghanistan, reflected a sharply increased emphasis on tactical scenarios typical of mountainous or desert terrain and were obviously intended to educate their readers on the lessons of combat in Afghanistan.[1] Through the use of such analyses, it is possible to identify in broad terms those problems that the Soviet command believed warranted the most urgent attention and thus learn something of the nature of the fighting. By 1984, the Soviet press began to provide glimpses of specific military actions or the exploits of individual soldiers. Progressively more revealing and critical descriptions appeared in print with the emergence of Mikhail Gorbachev's policy of *glasnost*.

From the perspective of the Afghan resistance, first- and second-hand accounts were always plentiful but varied widely in objectivity. Furthermore, like Soviet accounts, they were often tailored to serve political purposes.

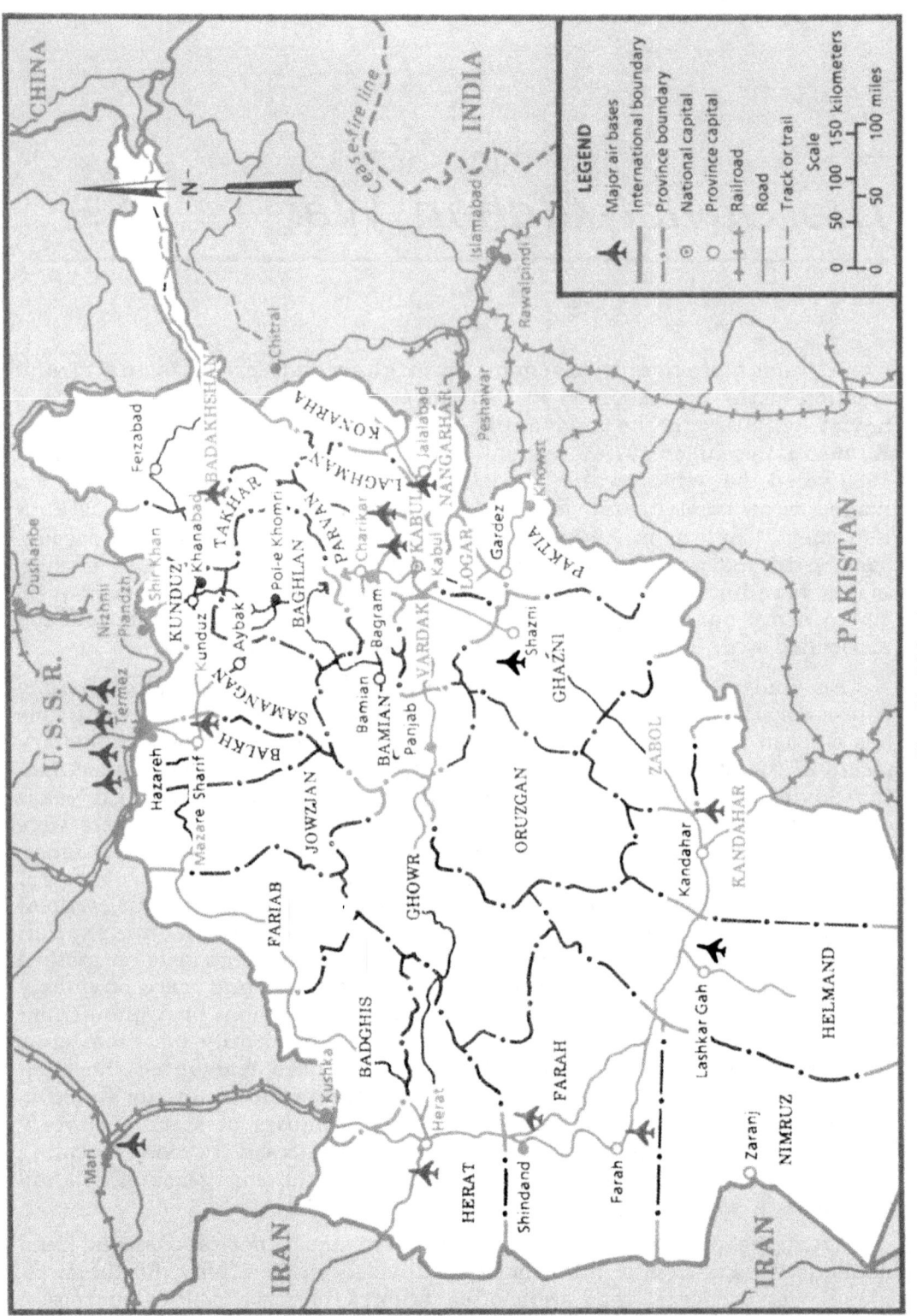

Map 11. Afghanistan

Consequently, when trying to gain a more accurate and integrated picture of the war, descriptions by Western correspondents and independent observers (who entered Afghanistan secretly with the cooperation of the resistance) are often helpful.

The Afghan War in Perspective

Russia's historic interest in Afghanistan dates back to Peter I, but recent Soviet involvement traces its origins to specific circumstances of modern Soviet-Afghan relations. After World War II, the Soviet Union made a concerted effort to win influence in Afghanistan, in competition at times with one or more Western powers. As of 1946, the Afghan regime could be characterized as a limited democracy headed by a monarch but governed under a parliamentary structure.[2] Emerging nationalist and reform movements played a prominent role in establishing the direction of the young state. Lieutenant General Mohammed Daoud Khan assumed the office of prime minister in 1953 and undertook not only to modernize Afghanistan internally but to broaden its international economic ties by making overtures to the Soviet Union. Closer relations by Afghanistan with the COMECON* nations followed, along with the beginnings of Soviet military assistance. In 1956, a landmark year in Afghan-Soviet relations, an accord provided for the reequipping of the Afghan Army by the USSR, a step that necessitated, in turn, the extensive training of the Afghan Army by Soviet specialists. In 1961, Afghanistan began sending large numbers of cadets and officers to the Soviet Union for advanced schooling, and by 1963, Soviet officers were highly visible as military instructors in Afghanistan.

The Soviets also built the country's major highway linking Kabul and other key cities as well as the Salang tunnel on the road to Termez on the Soviet border.[3] In total, counting economic projects, school construction, and other material support, the Soviet Union proffered aid to Afghanistan in excess of a billion dollars in value by the mid-1970s.[4]

In 1973, Daoud staged a successful coup against the Afghan monarchy that resulted in little apparent change in the country's relationship with the USSR. Indeed, a number of his cabinet advisers belonged to or had ties with the pro-Soviet Peoples Democratic Party of Afghanistan (PDPA). Nevertheless, when Daoud visited Moscow in April 1977, Soviet General Secretary Leonid Brezhnev conveyed dissatisfaction with the measure of Daoud's fealty.[5]

Afghanistan's 1978 "April Revolution," as it was hailed by the Soviets and the PDPA, ushered in a more open and concrete political relationship between the USSR and the proclaimed Democratic Republic of Afghanistan (DRA). Even before his ouster, Daoud had gradually distanced himself from the Parcham faction of the PDPA (based among the more urbane and

---

*An economic association of Communist countries established in 1949 to facilitate trade and development.

educated elements of the population) and purged several Parcham ministers from his cabinet in 1976.[6] However, a subsequent corresponding rise in the influence of the Khalq faction, which had many well-placed cadres in the Afghan military, probably made Daoud's overthrow more likely. The Soviet Union, India, and various Eastern bloc states promptly recognized the new regime under the PDPA, and a series of hasty political and aid agreements ensued. In December 1978, DRA Prime Minister Nur Mohammed Taraki visited Moscow, signed a friendship pact, and agreed, in a joint communiqué, to pursue long-term cooperation with the USSR.[7]

In the meantime, years of political wrangling in Kabul had estranged the Parcham and Khalq factions both from one another and the population at large. Following the PDPA takeover, Afghanistan plunged into a descending spiral of chaos and recrimination. Taraki tried and failed to do away with his rival, Hafizullah Amin, who in turn seized power in September and saw to Taraki's liquidation in October 1979.[8] Notwithstanding conciliatory gestures toward the Soviet Union, such as an address to the General Assembly of the United Nations in Russian, Amin did not gain the trust of the Soviet government. In a confidential report dated 15 September 1979, Soviet Foreign Minister Andrei Gromyko cautiously advised that Moscow continue to deal with Amin's government but give no support to "repressive actions" against his political rivals.[9] As the political situation in Afghanistan deteriorated, competence may have surpassed trust as the central Soviet concern. Amin perpetuated a policy of rapid modernization along socialist principles, thereby further antagonizing many people who remained devoted to the traditional Muslim mode of life.

In practical terms, the war in Afghanistan had begun by late 1978, over a year before the large-scale insertion of Soviet forces.[10] At that time, high-level Soviet military delegations, headed by General Ivan Pavlovskii, deputy minister of defense and commander in chief of the ground forces, and General Alexei Epishev, a key participant in the intervention in Czechoslovakia in 1968, arrived from Moscow to evaluate the situation and convey Soviet concerns to Taraki. There was ever more to be concerned about. In March 1979, mobs in Herat broke into open rebellion, and a number of Russians, principally technical advisers, were brutally murdered in the streets. The Soviets responded by rushing in additional military equipment, including Mi-24 helicopters, which had proven their effectiveness against the Eritrean rebels in Ethiopia, and expanded their corps of military advisers to about 3,000.[11] By autumn, the northeastern portion of the country was completely beyond Kabul's control.[12] With the seizure of power by Amin, the Soviets may well have concluded that direct intervention was essential to prevent the collapse of the state apparatus.

The motives for a large-scale Soviet military intervention were the subject of exhaustive comment and speculation. Observers tending toward an "expansionist" view held that Soviet advances in Afghanistan itself were not the ultimate Red objective but were merely initial steps presaging a future Soviet move to capture Iran's petroleum, warm-water ports, and a strategic position on the Persian Gulf. Subsequent Soviet actions, however, offered little to substantiate such an interpretation. A second or "reactive" view postulated, on the contrary, that the Soviet Union acted preemptively out of defensive concerns over the spread of Islamic fundamentalism and the possible formation of a hostile state on their sensitive Central Asian border. If, however, the Soviets were genuinely worried about the ideological contamination of Central Asia in 1979, they provided scant evidence to that effect in their official press. In fact, official concerns over the negative influence of Islam on Central Asia or incipient nationalist tendencies were far more in evidence eight years later, on the eve of the Soviet withdrawal. A third and more satisfying explanation of the Soviet decision is that Moscow acted to rescue a neighboring client regime on which it had lavished considerable resources and attention.[13] Viewed in light of the Soviet use of force in Czechoslovakia, as justified by the so-called Brezhnev Doctrine (which asserted the right of the collective socialist states of Europe to intervene in the affairs of a single member for the preservation of socialism), Soviet behavior appeared consistent. Especially given the volatile situation in Poland in 1979, a Soviet decision to let events in Afghanistan run their apparent course might have set an unfortunate precedent. Poor intelligence and analysis probably contributed to the Soviets' unreasonable conclusions concerning conditions in Afghanistan and encouraged their decision to intervene.

The Soviet government maintained from the beginning that its "assistance" had been requested by the government of Afghanistan—an assertion that has never been reconciled with the overthrow and execution of Amin, the head of that government. Following the start of the Soviet withdrawal in 1988, a number of Soviet journalists, as well as prominent military and governmental figures, joined in a debate over both the motives of Soviet intervention and the responsibility for the decision. A partial release of diplomatic documents indicates that the Soviets' initial reluctance to insert large combat forces gave way as the position of the DRA deteriorated. Taraki and Amin made at least sixteen formal requests for Soviet troops between 14 April and 17 December 1979. According to an account in *Komsomol'skaia pravda* in 1990, the first indication of a policy shift occurred on 1 August 1979, when three key Soviet officials in Kabul, Ambassador Alexander Puzanov, Lieutenant General (KGB) B. S. Ivanov, and Lieutenant General L. N. Gorelov (chief Soviet military adviser), filed this recommendation: "... in view of possible stepped-up activity by the rebel formations in August and September ... it is essential to respond affirmatively to the request from the Afghan friends and to send a special brigade to Kabul in the immediate future."[14]

Gorelov described his own role differently, however, in a 1989 interview with *Krasnaia zvezda*. Recalling his participation in an August 1979 meeting with KGB Chief Iurii Andropov, Defense Minister Dmitrii Ustinov, Foreign Minister Andrei Gromyko, and Chief of the General Staff Nikolai Ogarkov, Gorelov allegedly termed it "inexpedient to strengthen our military presence in Afghanistan ... and even more to send our troops there."[15]

Perhaps as a result of this belief, Gorelov was replaced as the head of Soviet advisers in November.

Details of the final decision to intervene remain obscure. According to a Supreme Soviet review committee report published on 27 December 1989, the decision rested with Brezhnev and a small circle of his closest aides, including Ustinov, Andropov, and Gromyko. The review committee continued to hope that its military, political, and economic efforts in Afghanistan would yield success. During the early stages of the war, the Soviet press repeatedly emphasized that the aim of the USSR was to help the Afghan people preserve their "revolution" against mercenary bandits and their foreign sponsors—notable among them the United States, China, and several Islamic states. By 1987, however, the Soviets emphasized the alleged security imperative of preventing Afghanistan from becoming a base for hostile American actions similar to Iran's role under the shah. One Soviet military observer in 1989 even claimed that the northeastern region of Afghanistan was preparing to secede and join with hostile Pakistan.[16] Perhaps, by stressing security objectives as their purpose in Afghanistan, the Soviets hoped to establish a political basis for their claims of at least partial success in the war.

Theater Overview

An oversimplified geography of Afghanistan would roughly divide it into five regions. The eastern fringe of the country is predominantly mountainous, especially in the extreme northeast where the protruding Wakhan corridor joins the Pamirs. Elevations frequently exceed 10,000 feet, and forests often appear at medium elevations. The central mountain region, the Hindu Kush, forms an imposing barrier to travel across the heart of the country. Two major communications links wind through the area. The Salang road, made possible by Soviet construction of the Salang tunnel in the late 1960s, runs north from Kabul to the Soviet frontier. The Shibar road, west of Kabul, was the first route to cross the Hindu Kush upon its establishment in the 1930s. The Turkoman plain, characterized by sandy desert and scattered scrub grasses, dominates the northern edge of Afghanistan. The Herat-Farah lowlands in the west are part of the Iranian plateau and feature some areas suitable for cultivation. Southwestern Afghanistan consists overwhelmingly of sandy desert. The ethnic makeup of Afghanistan is equally diverse. The Pushtuns, with a population of about 6 million, inhabit southeastern and south-central Afghanistan and constituted the dominant ethnic group prior to the war. Along the northern Afghan frontier reside the ethnic cousins of the Soviet Central Asians, the most numerous being the Tajiks, with a population of about 3.5 million. Less numerous are the Uzbeks and Turkomans. Other prominent groups include the Hazara in central Afghanistan and the Baluchis in the west and southwest.[17] Beyond ethnic differentiation, Afghanistan's population of about 15 million is strongly divided along local and clan lines, a fact that has long perpetuated political disunity. Virtually the entire populace is Muslim, the vast majority are Sunni, although a notable Shiite minority resides in the west.

In assessing Afghanistan as a potential theater of operations, the Soviets might well have drawn conclusions similar to those contained in a 1941 Soviet General Staff study of Iran. Aside from the identification of operational axes, strategic cities and junctions, airfields, and so on, the study reflected a detailed examination of ethnic and social factors and indeed any considerations influencing national strength. Theater analysis of Iran indicated that terrain posed an overriding consideration, constituting "a natural obstacle in nearly all direction[s]" and providing many favorable defensive positions. Movement at higher elevations was difficult, particularly for motorized units and heavy artillery. In addition, the limited availability of vital provisions, such as food, water, and fuel, would necessitate constant logistical support. Moreover, soldiers would have to overcome climatic extremes from the mountains to the deserts. In all, Iran appeared to be a most demanding theater, notwithstanding the apparent weakness of the country's fighting forces.[18]

Elements of Soviet Strategy in Afghanistan

The overriding element in Soviet strategy from December 1979 was the determination to limit the level of its military commitment. With the forces at hand, no plan of conquest and occupation was feasible, and there is no indication that such was ever contemplated. Rather, Soviet strategy was predicated from the beginning upon the resuscitation of the Democratic Republic of Afghanistan's army. The Soviet military mission was to hammer the resistance until Red forces were no longer needed. At first, the Soviets no doubt believed that they faced a limited insurgency in Afghanistan, but they grew to realize that the alienation among the populace was so great that it dwarfed the DRA's capacity and resources to respond effectively. Ironically, the Soviets' arrival may have intensified the struggle by providing a terribly fragmented and inchoate resistance with a common enemy and focus.

To be sure, no common program emerged among the Mujahideen; nor could it, given historic tribal divisions. The reaction throughout the country could not be described as nationalistic. Rather, it was founded on a historically conditioned, instinctive opposition to foreign intrusions, reinforced by a deep resentment against interference by outsiders in local village and religious affairs. It is noteworthy that a significant component of the population of northern Afghanistan is Uzbek or Tajik, including the descendents of many who fled southward in the wake of the Russian conquest of Central Asia during the nineteenth century and the liquidation of the Basmachis in the twentieth century.[19] As a result, despite the inability of the ten major resistance groups to create a unified military command, or even to put a stop to fratricidal attacks on one another, the DRA could not succeed militarily or politically since it lacked a constituency outside the PDPA and represented only a narrow slice of the urban populace. Soviet military assistance was incapable of filling this void. While the Russians historically had reduced such regions by subjecting them to gigantic envelopments and reductions, in Afghanistan, it was the DRA itself that was besieged. Furthermore, the very Soviet support that sustained the regime, in turn, denied it the credibility necessary for its own self-sufficiency.

Under these circumstances, Soviet strategy necessarily concentrated on five major objectives, only three of which were military. First, the Soviets recognized the imperative to secure Kabul and the highways linking the capital to Kandahar and Herat in the south and, via the Salang Pass, Termez on the border of the USSR. At least 60 percent of the Soviet forces in Afghanistan, primarily motor-rifle units, were committed to these tasks.[20] Kabul became a fortified city, wrapped in an elaborate three-layer security belt ten to twenty miles deep entailing a network of bunkers, gun emplacements, and mines. The Soviet Army positioned outposts along all major roads and was especially active in pacifying the northern provinces between Kabul and Termez. Even so, the Kabul regime faced enormous difficulties in ensuring the personal security of its own officials, who were often subject to attacks within the capital itself. The resistance network in Kabul repeatedly carried out shootings, bombings, and assassinations. The newspaper, *Sovetskii sport*, recounted in 1987 the story of an Afghan wrestler who participated in the 1980 Moscow Olympiad despite warnings from the resistance not to do so. After the competition, he was forced to live as a fugitive in Kabul, staying secretly with friends and moving frequently. All the same, he was murdered in 1982.[21]

The Soviets carried the war to the resistance, conducting repeated operations into rebel-controlled areas. Aerial bombing, sometimes massive, typically accompanied such campaigns and contributed to a population exodus on such a scale that Afghanistan scholar Louis Dupree coined the term "migratory genocide" to describe it.[22] By 1986, 5 million Afghans had taken refuge in Pakistan or Iran. By 1987, according to a Western study, approximately 9 percent of the Afghan populace had been killed. Survey data gathered among refugees further indicated that 45.8 percent of all casualties were the result of bombings. Bullets accounted for an additional 33 percent, artillery 12 percent, and mines 3 percent.[23] Like the United States in Vietnam, the Soviets targeted suspected resistance pockets, destroying villages, crops, and anything else that might sustain guerrilla activity. Thus, although the Mujahideen may have exercised control over a majority of the country a majority of the time, their authority was less than enduring. As a practical matter, neither the resistance nor the government could maintain control in much of Afghanistan. By keeping the Mujahideen busy and driving the population that supported them into exile, the Soviets hoped at best to cripple the resistance and at least to hold the military initiative.

Third, the Soviets sought to close the Pakistan frontier to rebel caravans bringing fighters and weapons back into Afghanistan. They had

Far from the nearest doctors and medicine, the freedom fighters tend to their own wounds

no more success in this endeavor than the United States enjoyed in its attempt to close the Ho Chi Minh Trail from the north in Vietnam. As a result, large amounts of foreign aid helped sustain the resistance. Through 1987, U.S. support alone exceeded $2.5 billion in value.[24]

The two principal nonmilitary elements of Soviet strategy were no less vital to the cause, and it was failure in these areas, above all, that prevented success. First, the Soviets recognized the urgency of rebuilding the infrastructure of the Afghan government and army, both torn by dissension and plummeting morale. Thus, much effort was devoted to educating new cadres, and thousands of young Afghans were dispatched to the USSR for extended periods. The Soviet Army struggled to mold a competent officer corps in the aftermath of a severe hemorrhaging of Afghan Army (the DRA Army) ranks. Only enormous diligence in the effort made possible the modest achievements of eight years.

Second, the Soviets had to acknowledge the unpopularity of their client regime and organize a plan of civic and political action to win adherents. At Soviet insistence, the regime undertook all manner of campaigns to galvanize the public on its behalf, but again, large investments yielded modest returns. The resistance specifically targeted government workers and projects for attack. The DRA claimed, for example, that in 1983 the *dushmany* (outlaws) destroyed 1,812 schools and killed 152 teachers across the country. Furthermore, Soviet-DRA combat operations often compromised political programs by antagonizing the populace.[25]

The Course of Soviet Military Involvement

Contrary to Soviet policy calculations, the injection of Soviet forces into the turmoil of Afghanistan triggered greater uprisings and chaos across the country. Yet the Afghan War began on a deceptively auspicious note for the Soviet Army. In the days immediately preceding Christmas 1979, Soviet units made their way to Kabul by land and air. On 26—27 December, a combined force of about 15,000 men began a series of well-timed maneuvers to paralyze Kabul. Soviet forces locked up the garrison of the Afghan 7th and 14th Divisions, seized the airfield at Bagram, disarmed loyal units of the Ministry of Interior, and stormed Amin's Darulaman Palace.[16] Meanwhile, during the preceding two months, the Soviet Fortieth Army had been organizing in the Turkestan Military District (TMD). Colonel General Iu. V. Tukharinov, former first deputy commander of the TMD and commander of the Fortieth Army, received the operational plans for entering Afghanistan on 12 or 13 December. The plan called for Soviet forces to garrison the major centers along the two major routes, which would serve as lines of communications throughout the war: Termez—Khairaton—Pul-e-khumri—Kabul and Kushka—Herat—Shindand—Kandahar. Because the Friendship Bridge over the Amu River had not yet been constructed at Termez, the first division across employed pontoon bridges. Before deployment, Tukharinov received a change of orders to direct the first division from Termez to Kunduz—not to Kabul. His new mission probably reflected the importance of security on the Salang highway. In any case, other troops were proceeding to Kabul by airlift. River crossings began on 25 December, and by the 27th, airborne troops had secured the Salang Pass, while advanced units pushed on to Kabul.[27] Following the

The Salang Pass

well-executed Kabul takeover in December 1979, the Soviets conducted their first major offensive of the war in the Kunar Valley in February—March 1980, employing a force of approximately 5,000 men with modern armor and generous air support. The guerrillas found themselves virtually powerless to stem the Soviet drive, and large numbers of the shell-shocked populace, 150,000 at the start of the war, abandoned their devastated villages. Helicopters deployed small forces on strategic ridges and the tops of buildings to secure the path of advance but did not block the withdrawal of the Mujahideen. Thus, although the Soviets proved that they could go wherever they wanted, they were unable to hunt down and rout the resistance, which melted away into the mountains and lateral ravines. The offensive achieved little lasting impact. When Soviet forces withdrew, the guerrillas returned. After a 700-mile trek through the mountains in 1981, *Christian Science Monitor* correspondent Edward Girardet wrote that he saw few indications of the Soviet presence.[28]

According to a postwar analysis by Soviet historian V. G. Safronov, both sides made early tactical adjustments. The Mujahideen found that large armed groups of 1,000 or more presented lucrative targets for a powerful conventional army and soon operated primarily in partisan detachments of 20 to 200 men. The Soviets, in turn, discovered that "attempts of the command to organize an offensive and pursuit against 'dushman' formations employing large military formations by the rules of classical war were without effect."[29]

Afghan villagers carefully examine an unexploded bomb dropped by the Soviets

Large-scale Soviet operations in 1981 focused on the Panjshir Valley, a guerrilla stronghold only forty miles northeast of Kabul and within easy reach of the vital Salang highway linking Kabul to the USSR. The result was indecisive, and subsequent Soviet attempts in 1982 brought no greater

Rebel commander Ahmad Shah Masoud inspecting a captured Russian AKS-74 with an underbarrel 40-mm BG-15 grenade launcher.

success. The fifth and sixth offensives into the Panjshir Valley in April, May, and August reflected Soviet determination to batter the resistance and cripple the power of rebel commander, Ahmad Shah Masoud (a Tajik), who early proved to be among the most capable resistance organizers. The May campaign, involving roughly 15,000 Soviet and Afghan soldiers and 150 Mi-24 gunships, was the largest of the war to date.[30] Combat in the Panjshir continued for about 6 weeks, during which time, Soviet and DRA forces suffered up to 3,000 casualties. A further 1,000 Afghan regulars were reported to have defected to the resistance. Girardet, a witness to the battle, estimated that the Soviets lost fifty vehicles and thirty-five helicopters in the first ten-day span of heavy fighting. Prior to the drive into the Panjshir, Soviet aircraft bombed suspected rebel positions, including towns and villages, for over a week. Three days before the column arrived, heli-borne forces were placed at key points along the valley rim. The guerrillas did not open fire on the Soviet armored column until it had stretched well into the valley, at which time they unleashed fire from mortars and RPG-7 rocket launchers. Curiously, the column was stationary at night, and only after receiving fire in their tents did Soviet soldiers begin digging trenches

An assembly of Afghans amid their mountainous terrain

for protection. In late June, having inflicted only light damage on the resistance, the Soviets withdrew to the valley entrance.[31]

Soviet forces also carried out a drive into the Paghman area in June and July. Soviet claims of success there were belied by a second offensive into the same area the following autumn. By this time, a persistent pattern, quite congruent with past Russian experience, was already emerging: Soviet command of an area lasted only so long as its forces remained in physical occupation of the ground. As soon as Soviet forces departed, control reverted to the resistance.

In response, the Soviets gradually relied more on battalion-size maneuvers supported by heliborne assault.[32] Girardet likens Soviet tactics in 1982 to American-style search-and-destroy missions in Vietnam, which also did not succeed in eliminating or cowing a less well-equipped foe. Others compare Soviet tactics to a "scorched earth" policy, citing the Soviets' systematic destruction of villages, crops, irrigation systems, and livestock to deny use of the area to guerrillas. Such tactics had proved effective in the Caucasus over a century before, but other, less sanguine, comparisons emerge as well. Soviet columns often extended themselves on the march and became progressively more vulnerable to sudden counter-attacks in narrow defiles and when isolated from friendly forces or supply lines. The Soviets, in many instances, lacked the means to finish their enemy, which fired on the Soviets from inaccessible points and took full advantage of the extremely rugged and defensible terrain. Equally ominous for the Soviets was the skillful and charismatic leadership of commanders like Masoud, whose repeated successes enhanced his reputation and attracted support from guerrillas in neighboring provinces—a striking occurrence in such a tribally fragmented society.[33]

On a nationwide scale, 1982 saw the Soviets assert their strength in Farah province (April), Gorband Valley (May), Paghman (June—October), and the Logar Valley (June) in order to reopen the highway south of Kabul and the Laghman Valley east of Kabul. In each instance, rebel forces rushed to fill the vacuum left by the Soviets' and government forces' departure.[34] Later in the year, the resistance staged numerous attacks inside Kabul itself. The Soviet Union continued to invest in the political and economic infrastructure of Afghanistan, completing a road and railroad bridge across the Amu River linking the large transshipment complex at Khairaton with the Soviet city of Termez. It also assisted in the organization of the First National Congress of the PDPA, in which delegates from all government-controlled areas participated. In the meantime, however, millions of Afghans had already fled the country, and the resistance showed no signs of abating.

Against the backdrop of United Nations-sponsored talks in Geneva (in which resistance leaders did not participate), the government achieved a six-month truce in the Panjshir Valley with Masoud in 1983. Hardly indicative of a substantive change of position on either side, the accord gave the government an opportunity to focus its attention elsewhere, while Masoud received a much needed breathing spell during which to prepare for battles to come. Combat, again, occurred in a number of provinces but focused for a time on urban centers such as Herat and Kandahar, which suffered enormously destructive bombings. Unfortunately, neither side provided coherent accounts of such urban combat. Meanwhile, the strategic picture remained unchanged, as most of the countryside—80 percent by one estimate—remained outside effective government control.[35]

By 1984, despite vast political efforts, civic works projects, the dispatch of large numbers of Afghans to the Soviet Union for education and indoctrination, relentless government attempts to penetrate and subvert the resistance, and ceaseless military pressure that contributed to a mass exodus of the populace in the countryside (either outside the borders of Afghanistan or into the comparative sanctuary of government-controlled cities), the war gave little evidence of progress. Moreover, members of the Afghan regime were subject to attack, the rate of desertion in the army remained debilitating, and the resistance continued to conduct raids in the vicinity of Kabul—the very heart of DRA power. Busily engaged in protecting Kabul, key provincial centers, and lines of communication, Soviet and DRA forces took the offensive selectively, and small operations by highly trained units received increased emphasis.

The seventh Panjshir campaign of April and May, launched upon the expiration of the year-long truce with Masoud, encountered familiar diffi-

The villagers near Herat clear away debris after a Soviet aerial attack

culties. From high altitude, Tu-16 Badgers executed some of the heaviest air strikes of the war, while Su-24 Fencers attacked from close range. But the results were indecisive. Meanwhile, Masoud's forces harassed Soviet convoys on both sides of the crucial Salang Pass and once again eluded destruction. Invasion forces did succeed in laying waste to much of the economic base of the valley—crops, livestock, and irrigation canals—and official Kabul radio proclaimed government control of the area. Buoyed by the strength of an entire motorized rifle division with approximately 250 tanks and 150 armored personnel carriers, complemented by helicopter gunships, the Soviets remained in strength until September to attempt one more push. But then, again, they pulled back to the valley entrance. Press reports, citing Western intelligence sources, contend that Soviet forces carried the burden of the fighting, leaving DRA units to occupy captured areas and defend lines of communication. Masoud's force, variably estimated at from 5,000 to 10,000 men, simply retreated into the mountains leaving the Soviets the extremely difficult choice of further pursuit, indefinitely prolonged occupation of the ground, or eventual withdrawal.[36]

In 1985, the Soviets visibly increased their employment of heliborne and special forces for strikes on remote resistance strongpoints. The most noteworthy actions of the year were a large-scale push into the Kunar Valley to cut rebel lines of communication to Pakistan, which entailed an attempt to rescue a beleaguered government garrison at the isolated outpost of Barikot and a Soviet summer campaign into Paktia. Early in the year, a Soviet armored column failed to break through to the besieged garrison at Barikot, but a second attempt succeeded. Employing air strikes and heliborne assaults on ridgelines, a force of about 10,000 fought its way up the valley in two weeks to relieve the garrison and then pulled back. Meanwhile, the fall of Peshgor, the first capture of a significant government base by the resistance, and the capture of 700 government soldiers in June triggered a Soviet drive to recapture the base using a division-size force. Masoud withdrew from Peshgor before the Soviet-DRA forces arrived. Next, the resistance mounted its largest coordinated attack of the war, employing about 5,000 men against the government garrison at Khowst, but was unable to take it. Guerrillas also engaged in fierce street fighting in Kandahar and seized much of the city, thereby provoking Soviet bombings. In general, the Soviets enjoyed limited success in interdicting resistance supply lines by air, a development that may have reflected the growing effectiveness of the village intelligence network founded by the Afghan security force, the KHAD.[37]

Although the level of combat diminished slightly into 1986, the military trends of the previous year continued. A political event, the replacement of DRA leader Babrak Karmal on 3 May by Dr. Najibullah Admadzi, head of the KHAD, overshadowed developments on the battlefield and signaled a watershed in the Soviet approach to the war. By this time, Karmal had probably become a political liability because of his compromising association with the Soviet-inspired takeover of 1979 and his failure to prosecute the war successfully. In 1989, General V. I. Varennikov justified the change on the ground that Karmal "did not earn the trust of his comrades in arms, the people or advisers."[38] Above all, his removal paved the way for more fruitful pursuit of the National Reconciliation Campaign, by which the regime pledged to open itself to participation by all political factions in Afghanistan.[39]

Still, the new policy in no way signified an end to military pressure, and the fighting was as brutal as during any period of the war. The Soviet Army held the initiative, and the resistance confined its actions to scattered strikes and ambushes. Operations conducted in the first months of 1986 focused on the eastern border provinces of Nangarhar and Paktia for the purpose of curbing the movement of rebel fighters and supplies from Pakistan. In fact, according to a United Nations' report authored by Professor Felix Ermacoul of the University of Vienna, the DRA even considered a scheme to depopulate the eastern border region by resettling 350,000

Babrak Karmal, leader of the Parcham faction of the PDPA and president of the DRA after the Soviet intervention in December 1979

Afghans from the provinces of Kandahar, Laghman, and Paktia to western provinces adjoining Iran.[40] Meanwhile, the caravan trails from Pakistan remained so secure (from the Mujahideen point of view) that *The Washington Post* correspondent William Branigan recorded encountering a number of teahouses along the way, and Fredericke Kempe of *The Wall Street Journal* noted supply garages dug into mountainsides.[41]

Challenged to interdict a well-entrenched supply system operating over unimproved trails snaking across mountains and ravines, the Soviets employed a variety of methods, including air strikes, interception by airborne units, mining of trails, and the establishment of fortified positions at important junctures. They also solicited the cooperation of Pushtun tribes along the frontier, sometimes by the outright purchase of support or by the infiltration of government security personnel. At the same time, the Soviets were beginning to prepare Afghanistan for their own withdrawal. Particularly symbolic was an offensive during April and May 1986 into Zhawar employing approximately 12,000 to 15,000 DRA soldiers backed up by 1,200 to 2,000 Soviets. The aim was not only to capture a major resistance stronghold but to demonstrate the viability of the Afghan Army (much in the manner that forces of the Republic of Vietnam executed major operations with American assistance late in the Vietnam War). The combined effort resulted in the seizure of a mile-long underground bunker and repair complex near the frontier with Pakistan and featured dawn assaults by heliborne forces. TASS described the encampment as a command center, complete with radios, British-made Javelin missiles, antiaircraft guns, machine tools, an assembly line for producing copies of Enfield 303 rifles (a weapon used extensively by the allies in World War I but possessing greater range than modern, automatic weapons), an automotive repair garage, 18,000 mines, and other assorted stocks. In addition, the Soviets claimed to have killed 2,000 rebels in the action.[42]

In 1987, Soviet and DRA forces executed Operation *Magistral* (Mainline), the largest combined action of the war, to deliver supplies from

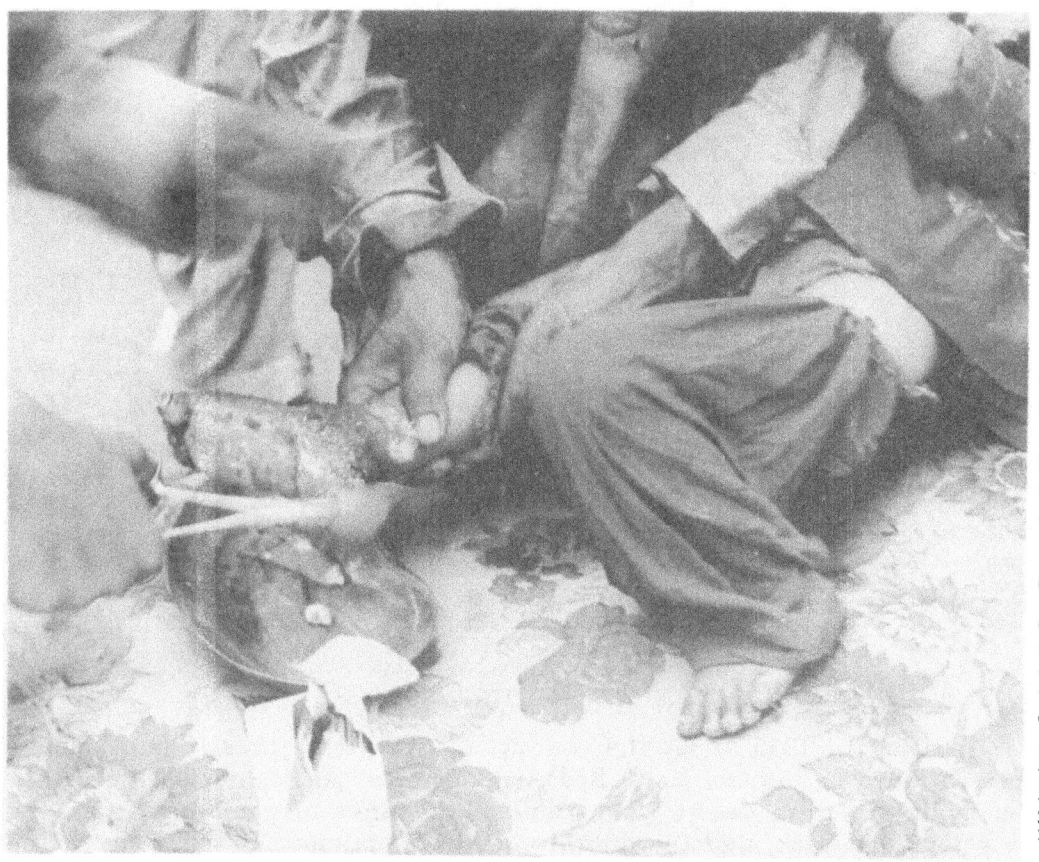

An Afghan child injured by one of the mines planted by the Soviets along the roads and trails of Afghanistan

Gardez and break through to Khowst in Paktia province. Gromov, the Fortieth Army commander, recalled that his most crucial concerns were to secure the Satekundau Pass and preserve operational security. To obtain this result, the Soviets dropped a dummy air assault force directly on the pass to trigger rebel defenses and permit air and artillery fire on heavy weapons positions.[43] Hard fighting, particularly around Khowst and Kandahar, continued into 1987, as the Soviet Union sought to hold the initiative and drive home the point that any prospective withdrawal should not be construed as a defeat. A Soviet journalist, A. Prokhanov, expressed this viewpoint succinctly in a statement for foreign consumption shortly before the start of the Soviet pullout in May 1988: "The departure of our troops is not a defeat. The army is in excellent fighting form. The morale of officers and men is high. It is an organized departure from a country that we did not intend to occupy, did not intend to destroy and subjugate. The troops are leaving as the vector of politics changes into reverse, and the army follows that vector."[44] Such a tortured formulation was not entirely facile—Soviet soldiers were not driven from Afghan soil—but the pronouncement could scarcely conceal a serious policy reversal. (For Soviet losses in Afghanistan, see table 4.) As Soviet forces left, the DRA retained a tenuous grip on political power and groped for a means of accommodation with at least some of Afghanistan's tribal factions.

TABLE 4
Soviet Losses in Afghanistan, 1979–89

Year	Total Losses	Officer Losses	Total KIA	Officers KIA
1979	86	10	70	9
1980	1,484	199	1,229	170
1981	1,298	189	1,033	155
1982	1,948	238	1,623	215
1983	1,446	210	1,057	179
1984	2,343	305	2,060	285
1985	1,868	273	1,552	240
1986	1,333	216	1,068	198
1987	1,215	212	1,004	189
1988	759	117	639	106
1989	53	10	46	9

Source: Colonel V. Izgarshev, "Afganskaia bol," *Pravda*, 17 August 1989.

The Nature of Combat in Afghanistan

Writing in 1933 about the conduct of operations in an "undeveloped theatre" such as Central Asia, Red Army analyst G. Pochter observed that the mountains and desert would dictate the lines of communication, the directions of attack, and the lateral maneuver options and extend both the attack columns and rear area. Under such conditions, the role of conventional infantry would be reduced largely to garrison duty. Nature would always limit the scale of forces, and a division in Central Asia would possess the operational significance of an army in the European theater. Technology, Pochter speculated, might eventually provide an answer to some of these difficulties. Horse cavalry raids supported by air power would offer the optimal combination of mobility and firepower. Chemicals dispersed from the air would block enemy movement or escape through the sealing of passes and ravines. Pochter also forecast a central role for the helicopter, then in its infancy, in a mountainous environment.[45]

Soviet experience in Afghanistan validated much of Pochter's analysis. Terrain and the absence of a well-developed transportation infrastructure in large measure determined the terms of combat. Aside from a single major highway connecting the main cities and the route to the Soviet frontier, there was scarcely any road network. As a result, movement by modern mechanized and motorized forces through the rugged mountains in the northern and central regions of the country proved exceedingly slow and subject to interdiction by small armed bands or mines. Of course, throughout its history, Afghanistan has proved inhospitable to invaders. In particular, the British campaigns of 1842, 1878—79, and 1919 exemplified the enormous risks of trying to sustain conventional forces over great distances. The British were repeatedly unable either to secure their lines of communication or to supply their forces adequately in the field. The Afghans generally chose the time and place of combat and never offered their forces to massed British firepower for general destruction. As a result, British columns were harassed into surrender or extinction.

For most of the latest Afghan War, Soviet troop strength stood between 80,000 and 115,000 men, organized into six military zones, and supplemented by from 30,000 to 50,000 troops based in the Turkestan Military District. DRA units brought the effective combat strength in Afghanistan to about 150,000.[46] According to V. G. Safronov, a Soviet historian, the combined total of all Soviet and DRA forces reached 400,000. This figure doubtless included all forms of official militias, however unreliable. During the initial phase of intervention, Soviet forces included a large number of Central Asian reservists, who were probably chosen by virtue of their proximity to the theater of action and close ethnic ties to the population of Afghanistan. Scattered reports suggest that such units did not perform efficiently and that fraternization with the Afghans led to breakdowns in discipline. However, Safronov maintains that the principal cause of difficulty was the traditional hostility of Afghan Pushtuns to the more northerly tribes.[47] For the remainder of the war, most Soviet units consisted predominantly of Slavs and other European elements of the population of the USSR. One highly decorated Soviet soldier estimated that 70 percent of the troops in Afghanistan were Slavs. Although he expressed no enthusiasm for the performance of Central Asians in general, he did single out the Tajiks as capable fighters. Others reported serious disturbances between Russian and non-Russian, particularly Uzbek, troops.[48]

The bulk of Soviet motor-rifle units engaged in occupation duties and occasional sweeps, in conventional columns, into areas controlled by the

A Mujahideen artilleryman wearing a captured Soviet tanker's headphones and carrying a Soviet antiarmor weapon

resistance. According to Lieutenant General B. V. Gromov, who concluded the war as commander of the Fortieth Army, 30 to 35 percent of Soviet forces were engaged in security missions. Combat support entering Afghanistan was controlled at division level and above, thereby dulling response time in the smaller unit actions common to the theater. Airborne and assault units, employed most often for reconnaissance or forward security missions, generally proved to be better trained, more responsive to the dynamics of battle, and more capable of independent actions.[49]

Air Power

Soviet air power was perhaps the foremost element in shaping combat dynamics in Afghanistan. The Christmas 1979 shuttle to Kabul involved over 200 An-12 and An-22 transport aircraft, which moved armored vehicles, personnel carriers, and other equipment—as well as approximately 5,000 soldiers.[50] Only when the entrenched strength of the resistance became apparent, however, did the influence of combat aviation fully manifest itself. As the Mujahideen demonstrated their ability to ambush ground columns and exploit advantageous defensive positions, the Soviets realized the increased need for aggressive air support. For several years, Soviet pilots wrought devastation on rebel targets with relatively little regard for Mujahideen antiair capabilities, which consisted almost entirely of small arms and a modest stock of captured Soviet weapons. The gradual acquisition by the resistance of modern antiaircraft guns, SAM-7s, and later still, sophisticated weaponry such as Stingers and Blowpipes markedly improved the Afghans' odds in ground-to-air combat.

In the context of military development, the Soviets' employment of helicopters in a variety of tactical roles represented a significant step on their part in refining concepts of combined arms warfare. For example, their flexible use of rotor aviation for airlift, especially in rugged terrain that constricted avenues of ground movement and offered few satisfactory landing surfaces for fixed-wing aircraft, proved invaluable. The Soviets primarily used Mi-6 Hook, Mi-8 Hip, and Mi-26 Halo helicopters for the movement of men, supplies, and equipment when terrain dictated. Roads and pipelines remained the principal means of moving bulk items. The government outpost in Khowst, under siege for much of the war, survived only by virtue of aerial resupply. The Soviets engaged Mi-6s extensively in lifting heavy loads—a particularly difficult and risky affair in the thin and heated atmosphere prevailing at mountainous elevations in Afghanistan. The Soviet military press noted, on occasion, the problems of moving heavy loads, especially in the course of landing in or taking off from narrow ravines and canyons, and made them the subject of articles on pilot training. Suspended by a heavy chain or external sling, such loads war-

A self-sufficient guerrilla blacksmith fashioning pieces of steel for warfare use

ranted careful handling under any circumstances. Both cargoes and helicopters were at times lost because of winds, down drafts, air currents produced by the rotors themselves reflecting off of canyon walls, or the swaying of the aircraft straining to handle a load. One Soviet account describes the adverse effects of reflected air currents on the tail rotor of a helicopter, which forced an aircraft to swerve 180 degrees in the air and caused a loss of load.[51]

Soviet helicopters also played an important role in the escort of ground columns or the forward deployment of small forces to provide security. The placement of units in flanking positions along the intended path of column movements was a standard practice throughout much of the war. Such forces typically assumed sites on high, relatively inaccessible positions to screen the column from resistance units or to pin resistance forces from behind. Once a column was safely past, units might be lifted to a further advance position. Aircraft also laid smokescreens to cover ground forces and proved effective as forward controllers for artillery.[52]

By 1984, Soviet aerial operations clearly reflected tactical precautions against surface-to-air missiles. In a characteristic attack pattern involving six aircraft, a pair of Mi-4s would rake enemy positions with rocket and machine-gun fire, to be followed by fire from four Mi-24 Hinds. This tactic proved particularly deadly to ground forces. In the meantime, the Mi-4s would circle back over the attack area and eject decoy flares. In another observed pattern, two Mi-24s and four Mi-8s would travel in a 1-4-1 formation. In such cases, the late "D" and "E" models of the Mi-24 were armed with four-barrel 12.7-mm guns and 57-mm rockets.[53] Helicopters also assumed large responsibility for airport security. Helicopters escorted all incoming and outgoing aircraft at Kabul airport and regularly released decoys to ensure against possible missile attacks.[54] The Mi-24, by virtue of its ability to carry assault troops, was among the workhorse aircraft of the war. Mi-24 tactics evolved to permit close work in pairs, with one Mi-24 always covering the other during landing or other exposed actions. To decrease their vulnerability, pilots became increasingly skilled at maneuvering behind or close to prominent terrain features, which abounded in the Afghan landscape.[55]

Both the Soviets and Mujahideen constantly refined their tactics in the air-ground war. On 3 August 1982, Soviet Rear Admiral T. Gaidar reported in *Pravda* the capture, during one of the Panjshir campaigns, of a Mujahideen tactical guide for engaging Soviet helicopters. Actually a schematic diagram done in watercolor, the document advised rebel fighters to let the first helicopter of a pair pass through a gorge and to hold fire on the second until it began its turn to make it more difficult for the pilot to establish the source of ground fire.[56] In such situations, the Soviets learned to employ one helicopter far above a target to draw fire, the source of which would be attacked then by a second aircraft waiting nearby. Fixed-wing aircraft frequently employed the same tactic when operating in pairs.[57]

The rapid increase in the number of Soviet helicopters stationed in Afghanistan during the first half of the war was an apt indication of their growing importance. According to Western estimates, from January to September 1980, the number of Soviet helicopters swelled from 15 to 20 to 250 to 300. By one count, Soviet strength in 1984 included 132 Mi-24s, 105 Mi-8s and Mi-17s, 37 Mi-6s, and a few Mi-2s and Mi-4s. In addition, the Afghan air forces had approximately 150 Mi-8 and Mi-24 helicopters.[58]

As the Mujahideen acquired improved antiaircraft systems, the combat environment became much more dangerous for Soviet pilots. Early in the war, the Hind "A" and "B" models proved vulnerable to ground machine-gun fire in the main rotor, tail rotor assembly, turbine intakes, and oil tank below the fuselage. The "C", "D", and subsequent models flown by Soviet pilots provided greater protection to the cockpit by means of bullet-proof glass and side shields.[59] Despite their vulnerability, however, Soviet pilots often remained dangerously predictable. One Soviet journalist claims that as late as 1988 in some areas, one could keep time by observing the intervals between helicopter flights.[60]

Conventional antiaircraft weapons obtained by the resistance inflicted losses of perhaps twenty Soviet helicopters per year. Early in the war, the principal guns in the guerrilla arsenal were a Chinese copy of the Soviet ZPU-1, a 14.5-mm machine gun, and the 12.7-mm DSHK machine gun. Such weapons had been used effectively by North Vietnamese gunners against American aircraft. The Swiss-made Oerlikon 20-mm antiair cannon, in use by 1985, proved more effective and offered the advantage of rapid disassembly into portable 55-pound packages. The resistance was also known to employ rocket mortars at low-flying targets. As early as 1983, the Mujahideen acquired significant numbers of SAM-7s that produced immediate results. According to a Western report, the Soviets lost eight Mi-8s in a single operation. Within a short time, they equipped their Mi-24, Mi-8, and Mi-4 aircraft with flare dispensers and added engine shields to camouflage heat exhaust. As a more direct countermeasure, the Soviets often deployed heliborne forces to capture antiaircraft positions.[61]

Fixed-wing aircraft also occupied a vital niche in the Soviet combat scheme in Afghanistan. The MiG-21 was much in evidence early in the war but, according to one observer, did not enjoy great success. Subsequently, the MiG-23 fighter, MiG-27, Su-17, and Su-25 attack aircraft took over the lion's share of the burden. No aircraft had a greater impact than the Su-25 Frogfoot, which operated in a close support role likened by some to that of the American A-10 and was particularly favored for its ability to strike point targets. Able to cruise at subsonic speeds, it was best known to Soviet pilots in Afghanistan as the *"grach"* (rook—a black bird related to the crow). The Su-25 compiled an excellent survival record, but pilots expressed a need for improved countermeasures against SAMs.[62] The Su-25 employed "nap-of-the-earth flight" (close-to-the-ground) tactics and carried cluster bombs with drop chutes to allow dispersal of its ordnance at low altitudes. Masoud himself described the capabilities of the Su-25 as "fantastic."[63]

The Tu-16 bomber, which made its first appearance during the carpet bombing of Herat, conducted numerous high-altitude, heavy strikes, often

Afghan guerrillas in a hilltop position survey the sky for signs of Soviet helicopters

The Su-25 Frogfoot proved effective in attacks against the Mujahideen

setting the stage for follow-on attacks by fighter-bombers, helicopters, or artillery. In 1984, thirty-six Badgers carried out between thirty and forty air strikes daily in the Panjshir Valley.[64] According to some reports, pilots of Soviet fighter-bombers had difficulty at high altitudes and generally operated without forward air controllers. The inability of the planes to attack successfully at night or in adverse weather also proved a liability.[65]

All Soviet aircraft in Afghanistan were under the direct control of the Fortieth Army's headquarters in Kabul, although the operational headquarters for the Soviet Air Force was located in Termez. For reasons of security and maintenance, Soviet medium bombers were based, along with their support facilities, in Termez.[66] Major air bases within Afghanistan existed at Bagram, Mari, Karshi-Khanabad, Herat, Shindand, Farah, Lashkar Gah, Serden Band, Askargh, and Kandahar (see map 11). The Afghan air force included large numbers of older Soviet models: about 45 MiG-21s, 65 to 70 Su-7s, and 90 MiG-17s of 1953 vintage. The most modern Soviet aircraft in the Afghan stable were forty-five Su-22 aircraft of 1971 design. All Afghan pilots were under Soviet operational control.[67]

The appearance of American-made Stingers and British Blowpipes had immediate and serious consequences for Soviet and Afghan aviation. For example, the Tu-16 intermediate bomber and the Su-24, which early in the war were able to deliver their ordnance from relatively low altitudes of 2,000 to 4,000 feet, subsequently had to fly at about 10,000 feet with an attendant decrease in the accuracy of their ordnance. Likewise, Mi-24 and Mi-25 pilots became far less likely to engage in direct combat and, when they did so, resorted to low and fast passes over target areas. Ground support teams regularly engaged in measures to protect incoming and outgoing aircraft, such as launching mortar-fired flares suspended by parachutes. Still, the striking change in the combat environment for Soviet aircraft augured badly for Soviet and DRA ground forces, which now often found themselves denuded of aerial cover. According to a Western account, Stingers prevented aerial resupply to the besieged garrison at Khowst in 1987, thereby forcing a rescue campaign by ground units. During the campaign into Paktia province during the late spring of 1987, Soviet troops, for lack of air support, reportedly abandoned their personnel carriers under attack and dispersed into small units.[68]

Before the introduction of Stingers, some observers speculated that the eighteen steps involved in its firing would prove too complex for untrained guerrillas, but experience demonstrated otherwise.[69] During 1987, Soviet and DRA forces lost from 150 to 200 aircraft, and daylight flights diminished greatly.[70] On the other hand, the Mujahideen may have had difficulty mastering fire discipline with their precious Stingers. A Soviet source indicates that, at least among some groups, failure to bring down at least one aircraft with three Stingers was punishable by death.[71] The Stinger, which proved effective from a considerable distance and travels at mach 2.2 or better, was especially deadly against slow-moving helicopters.[72] The guerrillas enjoyed a further advantage in being able to fire from high altitudes, which afforded a more direct angle of fire on enemy aircraft.

Although Stingers and Blowpipes could hardly be credited with ending the war in Afghanistan (evasion from them was possible, though difficult), they forced an unmistakable reduction in Soviet aerial missions.

Ground Combat

In the course of ground combat in Afghanistan, especially small actions often performed by airborne or air assault forces, the Soviets became reacquainted with long-ignored problems associated with battle in mountainous terrain. Many of the essential principles of mountain combat had been learned by Russian fighters in the Caucasus in the nineteenth century, more recently by Red Army units in Central Asia, and by Soviet units in the Caucasus and Carpathian Mountains during the Great Patriotic War. However, during the first years of the war in Afghanistan, Soviet units in the field displayed little evidence that they had trained extensively for such conditions. At the start of the war, according to Mujahideen Commander Ali Ahmad Jalali, Soviet troops refused to dismount from their mechanized vehicles. They also lacked essential tactical reconnaissance and security skills and were easily ambushed.[73] Masoud observed in a 1983 interview that "Soviet soldiers are not trained very efficiently for mountainous conditions," noting their heavy equipment and slow movement. He was more impressed with the conduct of elite, heliborne units: "They had the courage to face us and the ability to climb mountains quickly . . . but their weakness was that they had not seen war. As soon as they came down and took losses, they evacuated."[74] Facing a tough, elusive adversary who favored ambushes to direct engagements, Soviet soldiers had to learn new skills and tactics.

Offensive combat in the mountains is extremely demanding, both psychologically and physically. A defender, especially one possessing a superior knowledge of the environment, can select his positions, to restrict available avenues of approach and direct fire on them, and remain concealed while awaiting an advancing attacker.

But as Soviet General N. N. Biazi, a successful commander in the Carpathians, observed in a study of mountain operations published shortly after the war, opportunities also await an attacker with the will and method to exploit them:

> Offensive action by small units is favored by a mountain background, with its broken ground, surface gorges, interrupted front line. . . . Such surroundings add force to even a small group of resolute, daring soldiers. . . . The success of an offensive will be assured by observing caution, stealthy movement, by intelligent initiative, a daring plan of action, sudden attack, RELENTLESS DESTRUCTION OF THE ENEMY AND IMMEDIATE CONSOLIDATION OF THE CAPTURED POSITION.[75]

Lieutenant General Gromov himself affirmed in 1989 that the lessons of mountain warfare in the Carpathians and the Caucasus had proved their relevance in Afghanistan.[76] During the Afghan War, the Soviets quickly discovered that only men with thorough preparation could hope to carry out such demanding actions, and articles on training in the military press soon reflected an emphasis on lessons central to mountain fighting.

Soviet writers readily concluded that mountain operations necessitated the cultivation of certain personal qualities in training, especially for junior and noncommissioned officers. In the tradition of Suvorov's dictum—"hard in training, easy in battle"—the Soviets stressed the virtues of physical fitness. Assorted athletic programs, including activities such as cross-country running, forced marches, running obstacle courses, and weight lifting, soon became standard training. Descriptions of training programs in the Transcaucasus and Central Asian Military Districts, each topographically similar to regions in Afghanistan, suggested numerous refinements. For example, based on the general observation that even well-conditioned soldiers would encounter difficulty in acclimatization in the mountains, soldiers were made to carry abnormally large loads in training. The aim was to produce soldiers better able to function on rugged terrain.[77] An important corollary to fitness was personal hygiene, essential in the prevention of disease in harsh climes, which was also emphasized.[78]

Another often-cited virtue closely linked to fitness was discipline. As Biazi notes, when the legendary Russian General A. V. Suvorov led his forces on their extraordinary passage through the Alps, his men had received no special training but were extremely well disciplined.[79]

Commenting on combat discipline, Soviet correspondent G. Bocharov observes that the difference between a new recruit and a veteran is that the former does not immediately believe—and thus respond to—what he sees and hears. A veteran, in contrast, knows that "in the mountains reaction decides everything." Accordingly, Soviet exercises were often accompanied by realistic combat sounds to minimize possible disorientation when troops went into combat.[80] Soviet literature on training for mountain warfare focused, above all, on "initiative"—a quality evidently in short supply, especially among junior and noncommissioned officers. As many commentators have noted, men and units in the mountains must often fight in dispersed order, and not infrequently, they will find themselves out of communication by virtue of terrain and atmospheric conditions. In such situations, junior and noncommissioned officers must be able to act independently. The execution of flanking or enveloping maneuvers, in the day or night, whether by forces advancing on the ground or in heliborne units, places a high premium on self-reliance. Accordingly, training for airborne and air-assault forces must be especially rigorous. The chief limitation of such units, in the eyes of one resistance observer, was that unlike their guerrilla counterparts, Soviet elite units could only carry on in the field for periods from three to five days without resupply. Even so, the Soviets employed these forces to advantage and maintained up to five air-assault brigades in Afghanistan.[81]

Another problem identified in Soviet training literature was teaching soldiers in Afghanistan to cope with the dynamics of mountain combat. The description of an unsuccessful company maneuver, published in 1981,

A Mujahideen guerrilla sporting a Soviet officer's jacket seized in an ambush

offers a useful perspective on the problem. The account, which does not make specific reference to Afghanistan but nonetheless depicts a scenario characteristic of conditions there, describes a motor-rifle company's encounter with an enemy defensive position in the mountains. In this encounter, the commander directed two of his three platoons to envelop the enemy from behind. However, the attempt failed because their armored personnel carriers could not negotiate the designated routes. In the meantime, the enemy recognized that it faced only a platoon in its front and counterattacked. The writer uses this case to illustrate fundamental principles of mountain combat. First, commanders must avoid stereotypical solutions in making decisions and be prepared for unforeseen developments. Second, in such circumstances, the movement of enveloping units must be concealed from the enemy. The author adds that airborne units could often conduct such an envelopment.[82]

Soviet Lieutenant Colonel A. Shulgin, in an article titled "Battle in the Mountains" (in *Voennyi vestnik* in 1985), warns that the direction of the main attack must always be masked. In addition, coordinated flank attacks, not frontal moves, were the key to advances in mountain warfare. In Afghanistan, the use of smoke was common, and Soviet airborne and air-assault units exhibited an increasing ability to conduct ambushes and night attacks.[83]

Shulgin further emphasizes the crucial importance of skillful reconnaissance and cooperation among the infantry and artillery in the attack.[84] Descriptions of reconnaissance in Afghanistan mention the use of forward detachments or the airlift of units deep into enemy territory to seize passes or dominating heights. Scout units would be charged with the identification of enemy forces and analysis of their dispositions to discover "dead ground" in the terrain or concealed routes of approach. Viewing the same problem from a defensive perspective, Soviet articles on tactics note the importance of establishing observation posts in greater numbers than would ordinarily be required on the European plain. For example, even after the seizure of a commanding height, its approaches could be difficult or impossible to observe from above, thus requiring the extension of posts outward from the heights, in echelons, to permit the observation of all lines of approach.[85]

Biazi reports that Soviet reconnaissance patrols during the Great Patriotic War often consisted of fifteen to twenty men, including a couple of sappers, who advanced in a triangular formation with a pair of two-man patrols at the head and one at the tail. If contact was made with the enemy, they were trained to give battle and then either retreat or infiltrate to the enemy rear. Recent Soviet literature on training for mountain warfare contains references to *obkhodiashchie otriady* (infiltration detachments), whose purpose is to execute a variety of missions in the enemy rear.[86]

Enveloping detachments of company and battalion size were common in Afghanistan. Airmobile units were frequently employed against passes and other tactical objectives. Typically, a combined-arms-reinforced battalion consisting of a motor-rifle battalion, a tank company, artillery, a mortar battery, an air defense company, and an antitank company undertook enveloping missions. Much like Russian columns operating in the Caucasus Mountains a century and a half earlier, the Soviets tailored a march formation to provide security against ambush. A reconnaissance patrol generally operated from fifteen to twenty kilometers in advance of the main force and was followed by a security element two or three kilometers in front of the main force. In such situations, three reinforced battalions could function as a regiment under a brigade command.[87]

In one specific instance near the Kunar River in 1980, a Soviet motor-rifle battalion moved along a ravine into the mountains to a position where a large force of Mujahideen had pinned a government battalion. Mines and obstacles impeded their progress. While sappers worked to clear the road, elements of the battalion attempted to proceed along the slope above the road without forward security. Within moments, they came under enemy fire. The battalion commander then sent a company to seize the nearest commanding height. Though burdened with weighty gear and lacking heavy fire support, the Soviets advanced. The rebels began to withdraw, and the Soviet company followed only to move into a killing zone. Without either an artillery controller or an air liaison, the company was unable to direct fire support. Only when an enveloping detachment attacked the height from the rear a day later did the Mujahideen yield the position.[88] The need for observers and liaisons at company level was one of many problems addressed as a direct result of the Afghan experience.[89] Motor-rifle companies also received additional firepower, including the AGS-17 grenade launcher, and squads and platoons gained the BG-15 grenade launcher. In addition, small units received improved communications systems and sappers. Even with this infusion of assets, however, the Soviets maintained in instructional literature that a numerical superiority as great as five to one could not assure a successful attack on a mountain strongpoint without a supporting envelopment.[90] As one Soviet military analyst observed in 1987, "Contemporary combined arms subunits, fortified with tanks, artillery, and other means, with the support of aviation, can attack from various directions, combine fire and maneuver, wide and close envelopments, support one another with enveloping detachments, tactical air assault landings . . . in such coordinated actions that the attacker always achieves success in a short time and with minimal losses."[91]

If there is little doubt about the significance of enveloping detachments in the Afghan War, the same is not true of the employment of chemicals. By far the most disputed aspect of Soviet operations in Afghanistan was their widely alleged use of chemical weapons during the early years of the war. Charges that the Soviets used disabling and lethal chemical substances—based predominantly on eyewitness reports of refugees and a few Western journalists, as well as examinations of wounded and dead by visiting physicians—did not gain universal acceptance by either the scientific or journalistic communities because of the lack of irrefutable physical proof. Furthermore, tactical descriptions of the use of such agents were scarce, and there were no reports from the Soviet side, which steadfastly denied all claims. If chemical agents or toxins were, in fact, used, their employment (aside from the incitement of terror) probably served specific tactical aims, such as securing the flanks of Soviet-DRA columns or blocking the movement of guerrillas (in general conformity with the scenario outlined by Pochter a half century before). Reports from Afghanistan also allude to the use of defoliants. Whatever the truth of the matter, reported instances of chemical use diminished greatly by the middle of the war.[92]

A more constant factor, artillery, played the central role in fire suppression against the Mujahideen. Special difficulties attending artillery support of maneuver units in the mountains, such as directing fire on elevated enemy positions, warranted special attention in Soviet training literature. At mountain centers inside the Soviet Union, tankers practiced firing from tilted vehicles, and artillerymen learned the fine points of directing fire up and down slopes. Another solution to achieve elevated fire was the employment of ZU-23 antiaircraft guns on the back of ZIL-235 and other cargo trucks.[93]

As in the Carpathians during World War II, where the Soviet 1st and 4th Ukrainian Fronts rearmed one 76-mm cannon battery per artillery regiment with 120-mm mortars and some antitank battalions with 107-mm pack howitzers, portability also influenced the Soviets' choice of weapons in Afghanistan. In Soviet units operating in Afghanistan, mortars ranging from 82-mm to 120-mm formed a key component of fire support and were prized for their ability to hit "dead ground" in the terrain. The Soviet arsenal also included 76-mm mountain howitzers, 240-mm trench mortars, and 220-mm multiple rocket launchers.[94] The Soviets often employed artillery against rebel strongpoints, sometimes in combination with air strikes. Mobile observation posts proved their worth in the direction of artillery fire, as did aircraft. Rolling fire from a range of six to eighteen kilometers frequently preceded a column attack or heliborne insertion. One resistance source asserts that the Soviets became somewhat predictable in this regard, regularly using artillery and aerial bombardment before embarking on an operation. Yet at times, the Soviets confused the resistance by pausing for up to twenty minutes during a barrage, only to resume firing while the Mujahideen were restoring their positions or evacuating wounded. In general, firepower-intensive tactics were impressive, but they often did not achieve an effect commensurate with the lavish expenditures of ordnance. According to one account, from 16 to 18 Soviet guns lobbed from 3,600 to 7,200 shells on a 6-hectare (about 15-acre) area but did relatively little damage because of the wide dispersal of Mujahideen guerrillas.[95]

Well-coordinated firepower proved invaluable not only in the mountains but in areas referred to as "green zones" (irrigated fields and vineyards forming scattered oases across Afghanistan) (see map 12). In green zones, the complex irrigation networks are fed by subterranean passages, often fifteen meters beneath the earth, that stretch up adjoining mountain slopes.[96] Mujahideen guerrillas found such zones particularly advantageous for staging ambushes and returning quickly to cover. Pursuit of guerrillas into the green zones, which were subdivided by intersecting canals and further broken by wooded patches, proved a formidable problem.

As in the mountains, Soviet forces recognized the need to maximize firepower at the lower levels also. For example, for combat in a green zone in Kandahar province, each motor-rifle company received a platoon of 82-mm mortars and each battalion a platoon of 122-mm howitzers.[97]

In May 1984, near the oasis of Fakhdzha, elements of a Soviet parachute battalion were pinned down in a green zone while on a mission to clear a nest of resistance fighters. The battalion commander directed his armored group, in coordination with sappers, artillery, airborne troops, and aviation, to fight its way in. The peril of such an advance was considerable, for the Mujahideen had flooded fields, laid mines, and created secure fire positions manned with grenade launchers to block all approaches. Moving through the checkerboard of interlocking paths and canals, past vineyards and fruit trees, sapper detachments preceded armor columns along parallel routes. Meanwhile, airborne companies moved forward on line, by platoon, to clear the flanks of the advancing armor and ensure that no guerrillas remained in the rear. At the same time, the artillery battery commander directed fire 200 meters ahead of the advance to suppress the enemy and drive them back. Air strikes by two Su-25s also destroyed an enemy obser-

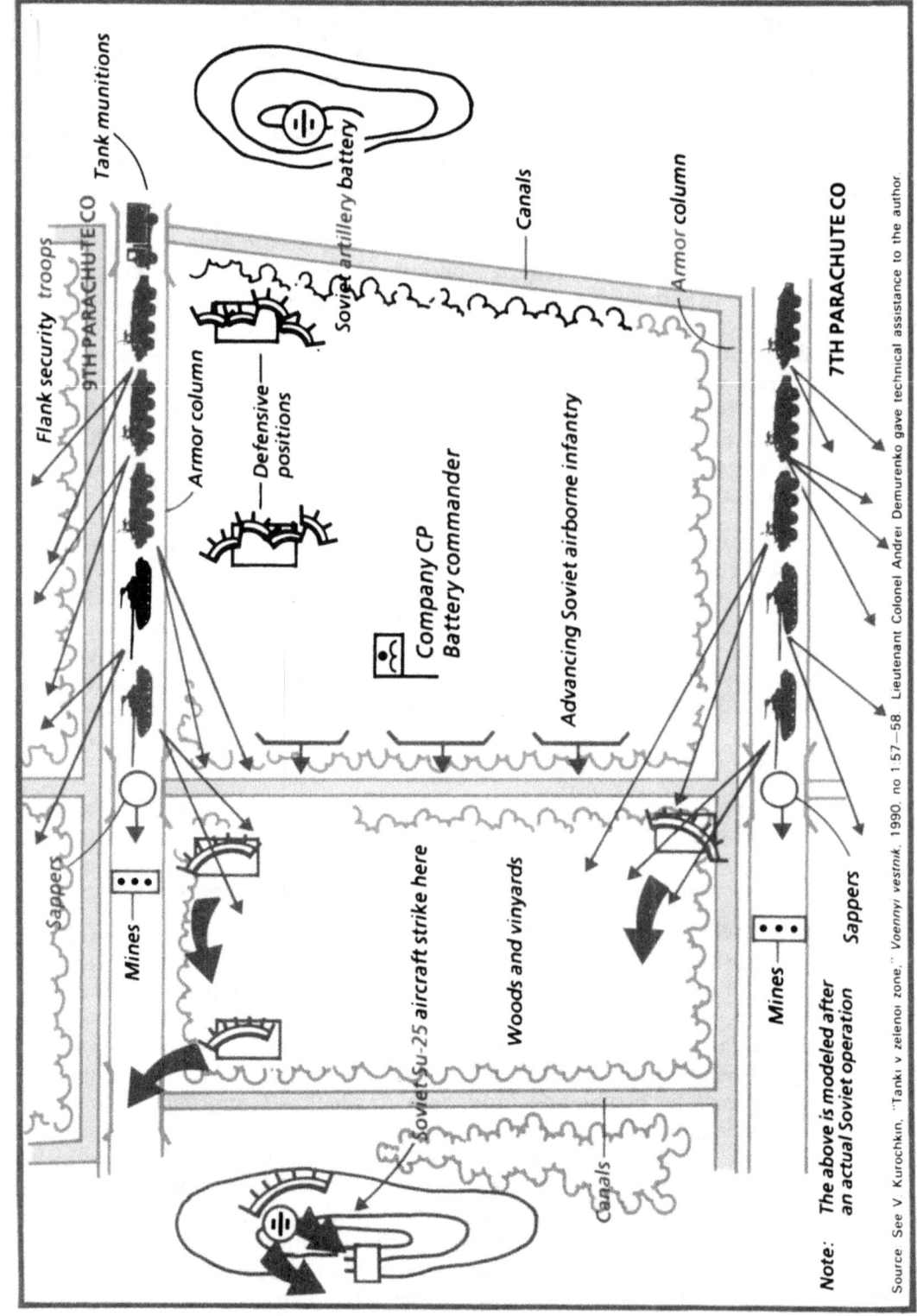

Map 12. Tactical combat in a green zone

vation post 600 meters forward. The march, slow but inexorable, proceeded at the pace of the sappers. In all, the Soviet combined arms force fought through fifteen ambushes over two days of combat but cleared the green zone, virtually without casualties.[98]

Adherence to sound combat principles, however, hardly assured success or prevented serious setbacks for the Soviet Army in Afghanistan. Writing in *Pravda* in 1982, Rear Admiral T. Gaidar candidly acknowledged the security problem for Soviet and Afghan forces operating against the Mujahideen. Discussing the spring offensive into the Panjshir Valley, he reported that although the operation was planned in secret, DRA units encountered a well-prepared enemy upon reaching the valley. Moreover, much of the population had been evacuated from the combat area, and the Mujahideen had already organized interlocking fields of fire on the route of approach. Correspondent Edward Girardet, who was with Afghan resistance forces in the field at the time, confirmed that they knew of the impending attack and added that guerrillas even managed to stage an assault on the key air base at Bagram before the operation commenced.[99]

Still other difficulties beset the Urgun operation of 1984. Urgun was a government-held outpost in the Paktia Valley that was dominated by the Mujahideen almost throughout the war. In December 1983, approximately 3,000 rebels crossed the frontier from Pakistan and attempted to overrun Urgun. While it was besieged, Soviet relief efforts sputtered because the only suitable road across the region had been heavily mined, as indeed had area airfields necessary for resupply by An-26 or Mi-6 aircraft. Eventually, with Soviet assistance, DRA units drove off the Mujahideen and seized what was reported to be a considerable stash of foreign-made military goods, including 82-mm ammunition from England, 3,383 antitank mines, 1,839 antipersonnel mines, and other assorted munitions.[100] In a similar case, when Soviet and DRA units attempted to break through to the encircled garrison at Khowst in 1987, antigovernment forces occupied all surrounding heights, covered area approaches with heavy machine-gun fire, and succeeded in closing the airfield.[101]

Defense, Movement Security, and Communications

Because Soviet units sometimes found themselves isolated and besieged, the problem of organizing defensive positions in the mountains received instructive commentary in the military press. One training scenario, based explicitly on the experience of an airborne subunit in Afghanistan, shows how a platoon in the mountains might deploy. First, the author cautions, the commander must select positions where there is no chance of a landslide or avalanche. The most desirable sites would be found on isolated heights or cliffs along a pass, where the platoon would establish a circular defense with mutually supporting positions and lay mines on all obvious paths of approach. Only well-trained soldiers possessing elementary engineering skills and entrenching tools could organize such a defense in haste.[102]

As with offensive principles, there is a close correspondence between the lessons of Afghanistan and those derived by the Soviets from mountain combat in the Carpathians during the Great Patriotic War. Biazi, in his accounts, placed special emphasis on the need for discipline and initiative when facing a threat of enemy encirclement: "It must be remembered at all times that an enemy engaged in a flanking movement can easily himself be outflanked, encircled and completely destroyed—and this is what must be aimed at."[103] Despite Soviet training efforts, at least one prominent Afghan resistance commander, Abdul Haq, asserts that defensive combat was an area in which regular Soviet troops were deficient. Haq suggests that the Soviets were so preoccupied with trying to attack that they did not know how to defend and thus reacted poorly to guerrilla initiatives.[104]

The defense of convoy units against ambush—arguably the most venerated tactic in the guerrilla repertoire—posed an enormous security problem. A standard resistance technique, described both in Soviet and Western accounts, was to attack the rear and lead vehicles of a supply or troop column so as to paralyze the column and then chop it into segments. In one such episode in June 1981, guerrillas from the Panjshir blocked a Soviet convoy on the Salang highway and forced the Soviets to destroy most of its 120 trucks, which could not be evacuated with the troops. Similarly, in the summer of 1983, the resistance routed DRA forces that had become bogged down in the mud while driving along a twisting canyon road to relieve Urgun. Writer Jim Graves, who witnessed the action, reports that two battalions of commandos were ambushed near Zhawar. About 3,000 rebels armed with machine guns, AK-47s, rocket propelled grenades, and mortars fired from elevated positions along the column flanks. The DRA column, consisting of about 800 men, 5 T-55 tanks, 12 armored personnel carriers, and 18 trucks, halted after a mine destroyed the lead tank. Heavy rain precluded timely air support, and approximately 300 soldiers perished in the engagement.[105]

The standard Soviet response in such a situation was to have combat vehicles form a shield around the column perimeter. A typical supply column consisted of from 100 to 250 vehicles, of which about 1 in 10 were infantry fighting vehicles. The use of a helicopter escort was also a standard procedure. The rapid coordination of tank and artillery fire, often called in from distant batteries, saved many pinned-down units. It was hardly coincidental that guerrilla snipers targeted communications specialists, and Soviet commanders learned to place their radios in protected positions. One account of the successful defeat of an ambush by a Soviet patrol notes the use of a company of assault troops equipped with bulletproof vests, large and small machine guns, and grenades. By 1982, Soviet companies frequently included antisniper squads.[106] In order to reduce the vulnerability of units on the road, Soviet engineers commonly cleared the sides of main routes for 200 meters in either direction. And because any delay invited peril, drivers were warned to maintain their vehicles vigilantly, clean their radiators, and be alert to the rapid evaporation of electrolytes at high altitudes.[107]

A greater impediment than the ambush to offensive movement in Afghanistan was the widespread dissemination of mines by the guerrillas. Making use of both homemade devices and large numbers of foreign-manufactured mines, the resistance rendered column movement along any known route a hazardous and ponderously slow exercise. To address this problem, the Soviet Army employed special movement-security detachments, called OODs (*otriad obespecheniia dvizheniia*), consisting of subgroups for reconnaissance, removal of mines and barricades, and road and bridge repair. Depending on the need and the size of the column, security detachments ranged in size from a platoon to a battalion. Such units possessed electronic mine detectors, tanks equipped with rollers, and trained dogs. But they found, all the same, that a meticulously laid mine could elude discovery. Indeed, one Soviet writer insisted with respect to mines encountered in the Panjshir campaign of 1984, "the guiding hand of the professional foreign instructor could be felt." The guerrillas often buried mines in shaped holes, permitting the mine to be driven deeper into the ground by the weight of a roller without detonation, which would not occur until the weight of several or more vehicles in succession had been applied. Likewise, with increasing depth, electronic detection became more difficult, and odors could be disguised to foil canine detection. To further complicate the task, decoy mines were layed that necessarily warranted the same careful attention as the genuine item, thus forcing additional delays. With experience, Soviet soldiers learned to ride on top of their vehicles, rather than inside, when the presence of mines was suspected.[108]

Another persistent problem for the Soviets in Afghanistan was the unreliability of tactical communications in the mountains. The quality of radio communications in the VHF/microwave range varied considerably with the relief of the terrain, and atmospheric conditions at high altitudes befuddled attempts at communication even by practiced operators. Furthermore, motors were less efficient, and the life span of batteries diminished at the higher altitudes.[109] Such problems often imperiled small outposts exposed to sudden attack by resistance fighters, especially on remote peaks or along the Kabul-Khairaton-Salang road. With practice and good topographic maps, signal experts learned to bounce signals off canyon walls and other terrain features. Another solution was the laying of cable between permanent posts short distances apart.[110]

At the strategic level, the Soviets established their command center in Kabul. Satellite links were maintained between Kabul, Termez, and major bases. Still, the nature of the war required heavy reliance on signal units in the field. Signal companies consisted of three platoons, one dedicated to construction and two designated to handle communications. On occasion, Soviet communications specialists were attached to Afghan subunits to improve coordination.[111]

Building the DRA Army and Regime

No dilemma confronting the Soviet Union in Afghanistan proved more politically complex or morally enervating than that of trying to forge a reliable and self-sustaining army of the Democratic Republic of Afghanistan. The weakness of Afghan units was apparent well before Soviet intervention, when the 17th Division exhibited a paralysis of will by failing to intercede effectively during the riots in Herat in 1978. In November 1979, with significant numbers of Soviet advisers on the ground and generous air support, the Afghan Army's III Corps campaigned with some success in Paktia but gave no firm indication of an ability to operate on its own.[112] From 1980, the Soviet Army found itself assuming an ever larger portion of the combat burden, while its Afghan counterpart, by all Western appraisals, suffered debilitating defections. Soviet officers directed most of the combat and probably influenced selection to command positions in the Afghan Army as well. Originally estimated at about 80,000 men in size, the Afghan Army saw its strength erode to about 50,000 by December 1979 and by as much as 50 percent more during the following year.[113]

In 1981—82, the DRA issued identity cards to curtail the problem of draft evasion, and a series of conscription laws gradually reduced the minimum service age, while extending the tour of duty from two to three years and raising the age of recall for reservists to thirty-nine. In addition, the government broke a long-standing historical precedent by attempting (without success) to impose conscription on the men of Paktia, who had been exempt, by agreement with the state, for half a century. In 1984, the standard tour of duty lengthened again to four years, and service was made mandatory for any young men who aspired to attend a university. By 1986, effective Afghan Army strength stabilized at about 40,000.[114]

The government also sought to bind the military leadership closer to the party by courting visible Khalq spokesmen for ministerial positions in the government, such as that of interior and defense. By 1985, the government proclaimed that party cells had been established in 86 percent of the army companies and batteries.[115] Equally significant, beginning in 1985, the army recruited an unspecified number of mullahs to tend to the spiritual needs of the troops upon their completion of a special indoctrination course.[116] Continued strife among army factions belied optimistic reports, and incidents of sabotage, such as the destruction of twenty aircraft at Shindand Air Base in 1985, continued. In November 1985, according to the U.S. State Department, four Afghan Army generals were arrested and executed for collaboration with the Mujahideen. The same year, a DRA unit was reported to have mutinied in Kandahar, killed its officers, and defected.[117]

In an attempt to fight fire with fire, the KHAD (the DRA security force, reported to have about 20,000 members) intensified its efforts to penetrate the resistance and, judging from the rebel response, had some success. Resistance commander Amin Wardak asserted in a March 1984 interview that his group would accept only deserters from Wardak province whose identities could be verified.[118] Meanwhile, members of the KHAD were carefully recruited and trained by Soviet experts.

Political conditions in Afghanistan pressed the government to resort to compromise measures in an effort to stabilize manpower levels in the army.

Early in the war, there had been cases of the defection of entire units, such as the 30th Mountain Brigade.[119] Thus, in light of the fragmented and tribalistic character of rural Afghan society, military authorities sanctioned the organization of units on a regional basis in some mountain areas. Adopting a ploy used by the Red Army in the 1920s, the government accepted so-called national regiments, such as the 507th formed in 1987, and included in their ranks many young men who at one time or another had served with the resistance.[120] In 1987, Soviet journalist Artem Borovik acknowledged in the youth-oriented journal *Ogonek* that the local leadership of the new unit extracted conditions from the army before agreeing to serve the DRA. Terms of the deal stipulated that none of the men of the 507th could be conscripted into the regular army, that their arms be provided by the government, and that the unit be charged with the defense of a specific territory. Borovik acknowledged the risks inherent in such arrangements and admitted that in the past some hastily created formations had accepted weapons and then rejoined the resistance at the first convenient opportunity.[121]

The government employed tribal volunteer units to prevent the free movement of guerrillas and their supply trains from Pakistan. The Afghan press made specific references to the creation of such units in Nangarhar province, Badakshan province, and in Paktia. For example, the Ahmadzar tribe in Paktia supposedly raised 1,000 fighters for a 2,500-man regiment to be supported jointly with the men of another tribe. In some instances, the DRA offered payments to tribes such as the Shinwari along the Pakistani border or sought to exploit tribal antagonisms by recruiting a given tribe to curb the activities of a traditionally hostile neighbor. This approach met with some success, especially in the north. Still, sociological shifts caused by the war apparently hampered attempts to organize the tribes. In particular, years of dislocation had undermined the traditional position of tribal chiefs, whose influence had eroded in favor of Islamic leaders of the Jihad.[122] In addition, the regime formed an urban militia, called Defense of the Revolution, consisting of well-paid (by Afghan standards) teenage youths. Urban groups were closely associated with the PDPA and the network of Sovietized governmental and social institutions. Ministry of Interior police, numbering about 30,000, also played a security role.[123]

Yet for all the Kabul regime's efforts in recruitment and indoctrination, a pathological pattern of defections continued to ravage the Afghan Army in 1987. One expedient explanation often raised by the DRA and Soviet press was that DRA soldiers, well-paid by civilian standards, were poorly paid in comparison with resistance mercenaries.[124] If pay was low, however, opportunities for promotion in the Afghan Army beckoned seductively. Soviet journalist Gennadii Bocharov provided an illuminating career profile of Colonel Muhammed Ibragim, who prior to the revolution commanded a platoon with the rank of second lieutenant and then a reconnaissance company. After the establishment of the new regime, he served as the chief of staff for a tank battalion for two years. Ibragim next rose to the positions of battalion commander, chief of the operations section of

Mujahideen warriors directing fire on a government post at Jalalabad

a division, and, finally, brigade commander—all in the span of eight years.[125] *Krasnaia Zvezda* provided a similar account in 1983 of the elevation of a common enlisted man to platoon sergeant and then to lieutenant, although he had no formal military education. Such rapid promotion, the author lamented, "is not exceptional in the current Afghan Army."[126]

Compromises in standards for promotion were matched by concessions in training and discipline. A Soviet journalist reported a minor 1986 incident in which two conscripts refused to obey an order from their lieutenant, and a colonel took it upon himself to persuade them to cooperate! Pressed for an explanation, the colonel acknowledged that such conduct was irregular but added, "we are just creating our army."[127] The lax attitude and divided loyalties of the DRA soldiers were also evident to Western journalists. In 1983, correspondent William Branigan reported spending a night on the trail and receiving breakfast in a DRA militia post.[128] In addition, some Soviet soldiers interviewed by Western writers indicated disdain for the government soldiers. One noted how press coverage of the fighting at Kandahar in 1984 vastly inflated the participation of DRA units, and another described the Afghan Army as "old men and half-wits" who "loafed about at the tail-end during our exercises and hindered us."[129]

As of 1985, the DRA Army comprised 12 divisions, each about 2,000-men strong, as well as a few independent brigades and special units for a rough total of 43,000.[130] This force proved inadequate to maintain control of the handful of major cities and roads that constituted the very foundation of the regime. Estimates of resistance strength varied widely but ranged from about 20,000 to 100,000 full-time fighters, or as many as 250,000 including part-timers.[131] If one further considers the sympathetic support extended by much of the populace, the network expands geometrically. As was evident from the Soviets' decision early in the war to limit the scale of military commitment, strategists must have hoped that airmobility, superior firepower, and advanced communications systems would enable Soviet and government forces to operate with an effectiveness far surpassing their numerical strength. Reality did not bear out such optimism. The combination of poorly trained infantry units, abysmal operational security, an unreliable Afghan Army, and declining morale constantly undermined Soviet efforts.

The Political and Cultural Dimensions of the War

Although their successes were modest, it was to the Soviets' credit that they eventually grasped the political and cultural aspects of the war in Afghanistan and encouraged the DRA to address them. Recognizing that one of the principal causes of the civil war had been the dogmatic imposition of socialist concepts on a traditional, religious culture in many ways far removed from the twentieth century, the Soviets urged general secretary of the PDPA, Babrak Karmal, and then Dr. Nadjibullah to reach out to elements of the population that were not already unalterably opposed to the regime. The central component of the DRA's attempt to bolster its legitimacy

Afghan guerrillas firing rocket propelled grenades and Kalashnikovs on the airport at Jalalabad

An Afghan father carries his wounded child, a casualty of the war

and broaden its popular following was the National Reconciliation Campaign proclaimed by Karmal in November 1985 and reaffirmed by his successor in 1986. Though not the first gesture by the government to win over a skeptical populace, the campaign offered for the first time a comprehensive program of concessions and inducements to demonstrate the benefits of cooperation and the good will of the PDPA.

Still, conduct of the war did much to undermine government programs. Military operations too often proceeded with little regard for the civilian populace or its good will. Refugees reported many incidents of looting, firing on civilians, massive aerial bombing, booby trapping, and even occasional executions. Although episodes of this type were never reported officially, the Soviet Army was doubtless aware of the problem and may, on occasion, have acted to police its own conduct. Journalist Francesco Sartori interviewed a former Soviet soldier who claimed one or more Soviet officers had been punished for a mass killing of civilians in an Afghan village.[132] Soviet journalist Borovik later reported a court-martial hearing for a similar offense in Pul-e-khumri.[133] The clearest evidence of the destructive effects of the war, to which the Mujahideen also contributed, was the extraordinary exodus of Afghan peasants to Pakistan, Iran, or even Kabul. In many areas, disaffection and dislocation were so great that the government was unable to execute basic functions such as tax collection. At the same time, the Mujahideen often raised their own revenues, sometimes by extorting road tolls from travelers.[134]

Among the first propaganda gestures by the DRA was the amnesty declared in June 1981 which, according to DRA figures, induced about 2,500 resistance fighters to lay down their arms by the fall of 1982.[135] The lack of fanfare in the official press concerning subsequent successes suggests that the achievements of the amnesty campaign were limited at best. Girardet asserted after travels in Afghanistan in 1984 that he encountered from ten to fifteen Afghan Army deserters daily. If this is a reasonable indication, the government probably lost more men than it converted.[136]

In June 1981, the government staged the founding of the National Fatherland Front, an umbrella network designed to reach beyond the ranks of PDPA followers to tribal and regional leaders. Karmal described it as "an authoritative, representative, efficient system of mass political organizations, which will allow us to coordinate and unite together the energy, enthusiasm, and working efforts of all patriots of the country." In addition, the government undertook land reform, construction projects, literacy campaigns, and attempted to promote greater civic equality for women.[137]

Efforts to reorganize Afghan life and rebuild the economy availed the government little. In 1982, the government claimed the initiation of 249 industrial projects and the distribution of land to 300,000 peasant families. However, roughly the same figure on land reform appeared in official announcements as late as 1985. Furthermore, the disruption of normal economic life created shortages and drove prices up sharply in Kabul and elsewhere. Girardet reported in 1982 the doubling of prices in the capital in the span of less than a year.[138]

Another crucial task of the government campaign was to show that the PDPA was not an implacable foe of Islam, a difficult task at best. Accordingly, official radio included in its programming readings from the Koran as well as religious services. In addition, the government restored religious instruction in the schools on the condition that the content was confined to theological matters. In 1987, the Soviet and Afghan governments announced an agreement on the cooperation between their respective official Islamic organizations.[139] By this agreement, the government made its most serious attempt yet to demonstrate its new attitude toward Islam, permitting the operation of twenty separate religious schools and releasing plans for the creation of an Islamic Institute in Kabul. Sorting out this new Soviet policy of embracing religion, Soviet journalist Bocharov commented, "Islam in an Islamic country is not merely a faith, but a way of life."[140]

Neither the Soviets nor the DRA were prepared to rely on concessions alone, and early in the war, they embarked on an ambitious program of political education, long a standard element in the building of a Communist government. In 1982, the Kabul regime founded combat-propaganda detachments (*boevye agitatsionnye otriady*) to distribute goods, circulate leaflets, organize meetings, stage films and concerts, and even offer practical medical tips. Though supposedly engaged in peaceful projects in the countryside, these detachments were prepared to fight when necessary.[141] By the end of 1983, as many as 20,000 young Afghans had traveled to the Soviet Union or other Warsaw Pact states for political indoctrination and schooling. During 1984, the government announced its intent to send several thousand young Afghans, usually between the ages of six and nine, to the USSR for extended periods of training, reportedly as long as ten years. While some of the children were the progeny of party officials, who presumably went with their parents' blessings, or orphans, others were sent off without the consent of their families.[142]

In an attempt to legitimize its rule, the regime in April 1985 convened an assembly in the image of the *loya jirga* (a traditional gathering of local leaders for the purpose of reaching decisions).[143] Though staged with much official fanfare, the meetings had little visible impact, and the general lack of success in winning converts may have been the chief cause of Karmal's removal from office.[144] In an urgent effort to find allies, Nadjibullah subsequently publicized his government's desire to seek out any political groups that might be disposed to compromise, including those of centrist or monarchist political views. As before, the government boasted of remarkable early progress. By 1986, official figures placed membership in the National Fatherland Front at almost a million and membership in the PDPA at 165,000.[145] Later in the year, Nadjibullah, in the same breath, asserted his determination to secure the revolution and made reference to a possible timetable for Soviet withdrawal.[146]

In 1987, Nadjibullah convened another *loya jirga*, which proclaimed a new constitution and renamed the state the Republic of Afghanistan. In January, he declared that representatives of 417 groups (37,000 people) had entered into negotiations with the peoples' regime and cited the effects of new programs for land and water reform. In July, the government reported that 15,000 more rebels had turned in their arms under terms of the new amnesty and reaffirmed its political flexibility: "We are ready to share power with the political opposition and have announced the creation of a multi-party system in the country."[147] Perhaps to reflect this intent, as well as to consolidate his authority, Nadjibullah in 1986 expanded the Central Committee of the PDPA, which by 1988 included not less than six ministers of pre-1978 governments. The composition of local government reflected policy changes as well. The Republic of Afghanistan claimed that over 15 percent of the employees in local organs were former rebels.[148]

The reconciliation drive helped clear the way for the Soviet Union to remove its forces from Afghanistan and, by means of a peculiar twist of reasoning, even served as a justification for the final decision. Soviet journalist Alexander Prokhanov explains it this way: "All this makes it possible to say that the original goals of the DRA were not achieved. They have been renounced by the party itself, by the revolutionary government itself. And that being so, the presence of Soviet troops in the country lost its meaning. Departure is inevitable, logical."[149] What Prokhanov seems to have

Afghan refugee children in Pakistan

been saying in circumspect language was that because Afghanistan was not about to accept socialism, the PDPA chose the inevitable path of political reconciliation, a goal that might be better served by the absence of Soviet forces. Preparations for that absence may have included the decision on 24 March 1988 to consolidate two northern Afghan provinces into one, a move viewed by some foreign observers as presaging the administrative and economic assimilation (not annexation) of the district with Soviet Central Asia.[150]

Much official good news accompanied the announcement of a Soviet withdrawal in 1988, notwithstanding the fact that the major resistance organizations still refused to deal with the Republic of Afghanistan on any terms. *Krasnaia zvezda*, for instance, reported on 22 March that approximately 120,000 refugees had returned to their homeland. It added, however, in a factual note that belied past claims, that this figure exceeded by twenty-five times the number of returnees in all previous years of the war.[151] Furthermore, in light of estimates that 5 million or more Afghans fled their homeland during the war for refuge in Pakistan or Iran, the reported flow of returnees to Afghanistan would still represent but a trickle. Yet many war-weary Afghans undoubtedly welcomed the prospect of a respite.[152]

The continuation of bitter combat in Afghanistan also suggested that official estimates of the situation were too sanguine. Soviet forces remained committed to combat operations throughout 1987. Toward the end of the year, the *Moscow News*—emerging in 1987 as one of the more outspoken and independent Soviet press organs—solicited a comment from a former Soviet commando platoon leader on the results of national reconciliation. He replied, "I honestly don't know. They are showing doushmans on TV laying down their arms, but the number of heavily wounded [Russians] is not decreasing." In a similar vein, an Afghan Army colonel told *Ogonek* that the campaign of national reconciliation was not progressing "as well as we at first calculated."[153] Soviet forces withdrew from provincial garrisons, a few quickly capitulated or were evacuated, but the collapse of the Republic of Afghanistan was not imminent. On the contrary, given its army, security apparatus, fortifications around Kabul, and generous material assistance from the USSR—not to mention the inherent disunity of the opposition—the regime's survival prospects were better than many in the West realized. Until 1992, when Russian material aid ceased and Nadjibullah fled Kabul, the possibility loomed that at least some resistance factions would find a way to coexist with a relatively weak regime stripped of its former ideological character. Even then, many servants of the DRA remained in Kabul to work on the new order.

The Soviet Home Front

For many years, the view that public opinion in the Soviet Union played no role whatsoever in the conduct of Soviet foreign affairs was almost an article of faith among Western analysts. In fact, even in the aftermath of the Afghan War, it was still difficult to ascribe any tangible influence to popular sentiment, but as the war dragged on, growing numbers of Soviet citizens began to question its purpose. Many veterans of the war returned confused and embittered, confused by the gap between what they were told to expect in Afghanistan—an appreciative citizenry and a clearly defined enemy, including Americans and Chinese at first—and what they found. They were also embittered by what they perceived as a lack of support, even duplicity, by their Afghan allies and, until the very end of the war, a lack of public gratitude at home. While few except steadfast dissidents openly questioned the moral and political merits of the cause in 1980, eight years of mounting casualties—the source of endless speculation due to the denial of any hard information from the government—and accumulating doubt about the prospects of success gnawed incessantly at public confidence. One obvious manifestation of such sentiment was the determination of many parents to shield their sons from military service in Afghanistan.

During the first years of the war, the state press presented images of Soviet soldiers protecting civilians and engaging in civic projects amidst a grateful Afghan populace committed to saving the fruits of their socialist revolution. The Mujahideen were often depicted as bandits, and comparisons were sometimes drawn to the Basmachis.[154] Only after several years did the press begin to acknowledge the reality that young Soviets were killing and being killed and that the struggle was a hard one. The tone of reporting changed markedly in 1987, reflecting General Secretary Mikhail Gorbachev's *glasnost* campaign and his frank depiction of the war as "burdensome and painful."[155] Slightly veiled admissions that the war was stalemated, that the Republic of Afghanistan had failed to rally a majority (or even a substantial plurality) of the population to its side, that unpleasant aspects of the war had not been candidly depicted in the media, and that a change of policy was necessary paved the way for an announcement that Soviet forces would be withdrawn before the achievement of a decisive resolution in Afghanistan.[156]

The disgruntlement among Soviet veterans of Afghanistan received much attention in the Soviet press beginning in 1987. By far the most striking and candid commentary was a serialized account in *Ogonek* by Artem Borovik describing the grim nature of the combat and war weariness among Soviet soldiers. Many reports described the use of alcohol and hashish among Soviet soldiers. According to one guerrilla leader in Nangarhar province, "They use alcohol all the time, and if someone gives them a little hashish, they'll give him a Kalashnikov."[157] The widespread feeling among veterans that they had not been welcomed home was especially well documented. In a particularly dramatic instance, *Krasnaia zvezda* published on 22 March 1988 the letter of the father of a veteran who returned to his homeland an invalid, utterly unprepared for an indifferent public reception and calloused treatment by the medical bureaucracy.[158] Another article in a Tajik newspaper suggested that not all veterans felt welcome and that few were admitted to the Communist Party or other responsible positions. Manifestations of official gratitude to Afghanistan veterans, such as memorials, appeared belatedly but not before many veterans protested their plight.[159] Public concern continued to mount over those who had not returned. In 1990, *Izvestiia* reported that about 100 Soviet prisoners remained in Afghanistan and Pakistan, and over 300 soldiers were officially listed as missing. Furthermore, the paper challenged the failure of the government to create an official commission to secure their return.[160]

The war also raised doubts about the fairness of conscription policies in the USSR. On 25 November 1987, *Pravda* printed the letter of a Moscow worker who complained that the sons of officials had avoided service in Afghanistan. Similar allegations appeared in *Krasnaia zvezda* and *Literaturnaia gazeta*.[161] In stark contrast to reports throughout most of the war

Soviet leader Mikhail Gorbachev reassessed his country's position in Afghanistan and sought international agreements to facilitate its military disengagement

that suggested Soviet youths were proud to perform their "internationalist duty"—the common official euphemism for military service in Afghanistan—letters published in *Sobesednik* pointed out that many young Soviets sought to avoid service in Afghanistan and could not comprehend the mission there. In fact, reports surfaced at the end of the war that Soviet personnel officers had extorted money from parents to guarantee that their sons would not serve in a combat area. In addition, a postwar opinion survey indicated that among the *afgantsy*—soldiers who served in Afghanistan—fully as many, 17 percent, considered their service a "disgrace" as were proud of it. Among the general public, 46 percent viewed such service as a "disgrace," whereas 6 percent found it a source of pride.[162] Equally troublesome to the Soviet government was the possibility that incipient nationalist tendencies emerging in some Central Asian republics of the USSR were related to the war in Afghanistan.[163] Broadcasts from Iran and Pakistan in the native languages of the region, calculated to play upon ethnic and religious sympathies, almost certainly evoked some response. Soviet press reports depicting the Afghan revolution as besieged by U.S. and Chinese mercenaries—though probably accepted at first—now met with skepticism. William Branigan interviewed a former Soviet soldier of Turkoman origin who claimed that even before his own tour of military service began, he knew such reports to be untrue. Having since cast his lot with the Afghan resistance, he said, "I am a Moslem and I am fighting against non-Moslems." Another Soviet soldier from Estonia said the Central Asians tended to "stick together" and most knew little Russian. Widespread allegations that some Central Asians serving in Afghanistan early in the war proved politically unreliable lend credence to this view.[164]

All problems notwithstanding, it would be wrong to attribute the Soviet decision to pull out of Afghanistan to the effects of public disillusionment. At no time during the war were there large-scale manifestations of organized opposition to Soviet policy. However, the government could hardly fail to notice that support was flagging. Nor did international disapproval, even among Islamic and Third World states, play a decisive role. Rather, in light of General Secretary Mikhail Gorbachev's commitment to galvanize public support in the pursuit of new national priorities, the Afghan War was an obvious liability.

Conclusion

Perhaps the fundamental Soviet problem in the war was that Afghanistan does not constitute a true nation but in a practical sense can be viewed, in the words of Anthony Arnold, as "25,000 village states."[165] Once it became clear that military action could not compensate for the inability of the DRA or Republic of Afghanistan to win popular support and that it was impractical to build a Soviet-model socialist state in Afghanistan, the Soviet Union had to choose a new course. Such a choice became possible only with the selection of Gorbachev, whose personal prestige as general secretary in 1985 was not tied to the preceding Afghan policy. Only a staggering Soviet military commitment could have forced a cessation of guerrilla resistance, and even then, there would have been no certainty that the Afghanistan government could stand on its own. Thus, continuation of the Soviet presence would necessarily have entailed a continuing, perhaps unmanageable, drain on Soviet resources. In other words, no fully satisfactory Soviet outcome could be achieved on the battlefield alone.

Indeed, the Soviet military presence may have been a liability to the Soviet cause. Soviet journalist A. Bovin, writing in *Izvestiia* in December 1988, admitted as much:

> ... the overall effect of the presence of Soviet troops and their participation in combat operations clearly proved negative. We ourselves handed the counter-revolutionary forces some powerful means of influencing public perceptions. The foreign intervention stirred patriotism, and the appearance of "infidels" spawned religious intolerance. On such a field, even a tie would have been miraculous.[166]

To the Soviets' credit, once this recognition dawned on them, they were able to reverse their policy.

Notes

Chapter 4

1. Valerii Konovalov, "Afghanistan and Mountain Warfare Training," *Radio Liberty Research Bulletin* (hereafter cited as *RL*) 118/88, 17 March 1988, 2—3. Konovalov counted over 100 articles on mountain training in *Voennyi vestnik, Sovetskii voin,* and *Aviatsiia i kosmonavtika* during the 8-year war. For the preceding eight years, he counted fifteen articles, all published in *Voennyi vestnik*. Scott McMichael, "The Soviet Army, Counterinsurgency and the Afghan War," *Parameters* (December 1989):21—35, noted the lack of attention to counterinsurgency in Soviet military literature up to the start of the war.

2. Edward Girardet, *Afghanistan: The Soviet War* (New York: St. Martin's Press, 1985), 91.

3. Ibid., 93; J. Bruce Amstutz, *Afghanistan: The First Five Years of Soviet Occupation* (Washington, DC: National Defense University, 1986), 24; Anthony Arnold, *Afghanistan: The Soviet Intervention in Perspective* (Stanford, CA: Hoover Institution Press, 1986), 39; and Graham Turbiville, "Ambush! The Road War in Afghanistan," *Army* (January 1988):34. See also Marie Broxup, "The Soviets in Afghanistan: The Anatomy of a Takeover," *Central Asian Survey*, no. 4 (1983):142.

4. L. Mironov and G. Poliakov, "Afghanistan: The Beginning of a New Life," *International Affairs* (Moscow) (March 1979):54; and Amstutz, *Afghanistan: The First Five Years*, 24.

5. Henry S. Bradsher, *Afghanistan and the Soviet Union* (Durham, NC: Duke University Press, 1985), 63—66.

6. Girardet, *Afghanistan: The Soviet War*, 101. R. Barnet and E. Ahmad, in "Bloody Games," *The New Yorker*, 11 April 1988, 59, observe that for three days after the takeover, even TASS referred to the event as a coup. Subsequently, all official references treated the event as a revolution.

7. "Sovmestnoe Sovetsko-afganskoe kommunike," *Pravda*, 8 December 1978.

8. Amstutz, *Afghanistan: The First Five Years*, 39; and Arnold, *Afghanistan*, 82—87.

9. D. Muratov, "Afghanistan," *Komsomol'skaia pravda*, 27 December 1990, as translated in JPRS USSR Report, JPRS-UMA-91-006, 4 March 1991, 61—64.

10. Girardet, *Afghanistan: The Soviet War*, 22—23; and David Isby, *War in a Distant Country, Afghanistan: Invasion and Resistance* (London: Arms & Armor, 1989), 19.

11. Girardet, *Afghanistan: The Soviet War*, 23.

12. N. Ivanov, "H-Hour" (interview with Colonel General Iu. Tukharinov), *Sovetskaia Rossiia*, 20 December 1989, as translated in JPRS-UMA-90-007, 23 March 1990, 126.

13. For relevant discussion, see the following: Fred Halliday, "The Middle East, Afghanistan and the Gulf in Soviet Perceptions," *Journal of the Royal United Services Institute for Defence Studies* (hereafter cited as RUSI) 129 (December 1984):14; Terry Hammond, *Red Flag Over Afghanistan* (Boulder, CO: Westview, 1984), 80—85, 132—37; Bradsher, *Afghan-*

istan and the Soviet Union, 153—60; Oliver Roy, "Afghanistan: A View From the Interior," *Dissent* (Winter 1981):47—48; Alex Alexiev, *Inside the Soviet Army in Afghanistan* (Santa Monica, CA: Rand, 1988), 21—27; *Special Operations: Military Lessons From Six Selected Case Studies* (New Brunswick, NJ: Center for Military Studies, 1982), 189; Joseph Collins, *The Soviet Invasion of Afghanistan* (Lexington, MA: D. C. Heath & Co., 1986), 101—3, 165—69; Selig Harrison, "Dateline Afghanistan: Exit Through Finland?" *Foreign Policy* 41 (Winter 1980—81):163—78; Mark Urban, *War in Afghanistan* (New York: St. Martin's Press, 1988); David Gibbs, "Does the USSR Have a 'Grand Strategy'? Reinterpreting the Invasion of Afghanistan," *Journal of Peace Research* 24, no. 4 (1987):366—79; Alam Payind, "Soviet-Afghan Relations From Cooperation to Occupation," *International Journal for Middle Eastern Studies* 21 (1989):107—28; and L. B. Teplinskii, *Istoriia Sovetsko-Afganskikh otnoshenii* (Moscow: Mysl, 1988), 278—79.

14. S. Kushnerev, "After Afghanistan," *Komsomol'skaia pravda*, 21 December 1989, as translated in JPRS-UMA-90-006, 20 March 1990, 21—22.

15. A. Oliinik, "Vvod voisk v afganistan: Kak prinimalos' reshenie," *Krasnaia zvezda*, 18 November 1989.

16. Ivanov, "H-Hour," 126. See also "Soobshchenie Komiteta Verkhovnogo Soveta po mezhdunarodnym delam po politicheskoi otsenke resheniia o vvode Sovetskikh voisk v Afganistan," *Krasnaia zvezda*, 27 December 1989; Igor Beliaev and Anatolii Gromyko, "This Is How We Ended up in Afghanistan," *Literaturnaia gazeta*, 20 September 1989, as translated in JPRS-UMA-89-023, 4 October 1989, 43; Oliinik, "Vvod voisk v Afganistan"; O. Yermolina and A. Zubkov, "We Were Not Preaching Evil" (interview with General V. I. Varennikov), *Sovetskii patriot*, 27 December 1989, as translated in JPRS-UMA-90-007, 23 March 1990, 123—25; Sergei Belitsky, "Authors of the USSR's Afghan War Policy," *Report on the USSR*, (RL) 195/89, 27 April 1989, 11—12; and Artem Borovik, "Afganistan: Podvodio itogi" (interview with V. I. Varennikov), *Ogonek*, no. 12 (1989):6—8.

17. Louis Dupree, *Afghanistan* (Princeton, NJ: Princeton University Press, 1980), 9—31, 58—64.

18. Gerald Guensberg, *Soviet Command Study of Iran* (Moscow, 1941) (Arlington, VA: SRI International, 1980). See also Stephen Blank, "Soviet Russia and Low-Intensity Conflict in Central Asia: Three Case Studies," in *Low Intensity Conflict in the Third World*, edited by Lewis B. Ware (Maxwell Air Force Base, AL: Air University Press, 1988), 48—49.

19. Nasrullah Safi, "Soviet Military Tactics in Afghanistan," *Central Asian Survey* 5, no. 2 (1986):103 (this article originally appeared in the *Writers Union of Free Afghanistan* 1 [no. 1]; Roy, "Afghanistan: A View From the Interior," 51; David Edwards, "Origins of the Anti-Soviet Jihad," in *Afghan Resistance: The Politics of Survival*, edited by Grant M. Farr and John G. Merriam (Boulder, CO: Westview, 1987), 40—41; and Audrey Shalinsky, "Ethnic Reactions to the Current Regime in Afghanistan," *Central Asian Survey* 3, no. 4 (1984):49—50.

20. V. G. Safronov, "Kak eto bylo," *Voenno-istoricheskii zhurnal*, no. 5 (1990):70; Alexiev, *Inside the Soviet Army in Afghanistan*, 21—22.

21. V. Salivon, "Skhvatka," *Sovetskii sport*, 10 March 1987.

22. Milton Leitenberg, "United States Foreign Policy and the Soviet Invasion of Afghanistan," *Arms Control* 7 (December 1986):283—84; Louis Dupree, "Afghanistan in 1982: Still No Solution," *Asian Survey* 23, no. 2 (1983):135, and "Afghanistan in 1983: Still No Solution," *Asian Survey* 24, no. 2 (1984):235—36; "Military Occupation of Afghanistan by Russians Is Now Heading Towards Its Fifth Year," *Afghan Realities* (Peshewar), no. 5 (16—31 December 1984):1, as cited in Amstutz, *Afghanistan: The First Five Years*, 136; and John Tagliabue, "Russians Pressing Afghan Campaigns," *The New York Times*, 21 November 1986.

23. Mark Sliwinski, "Afghanistan: The Decimation of a People," *Orbis* (Winter 1989):43—44.

24. Frederick Kempe, "Risky Mission: Supplying Guerrillas in Afghanistan Is Grueling Undertaking," *The Wall Street Journal*, 13 November 1984; Girardet, *Afghanistan: The Soviet War*, 38; Teplinskii, *Istoriia Sovetsko-Afganskikh otnoshenii*, 258; Walter Pincus, "Panel

to Probe Afghan Army Fund," *The Washington Post*, 13 January 1987; and "Afghan Rebels Excluded From US Budget," from *The New York Times* in *The Kansas City Star*, 12 May 1991.

25. V. Baikov, "V nespokoinoi provintsii," *Pravda*, 30 June 1983; V. Skrizhalin, "Byt' miru pod olivami," *Krasnaia zvezda*, 17 January 1984; Dupree, "Afghanistan in 1983," 234; and Iu. Protasov, "Vera v budushchee," *Voennyi vestnik*, no. 5 (1984):41—44.

26. Urban, *War in Afghanistan*, 44—47.

27. I. Esiutin, "Vvod voisk v Afganistan, kak eto bylo" (interview with Iu. V. Tukharinov), *Krasnaia zvezda*, 24 December 1989; Ivanov, "H-Hour," 125—26; Petr Studenikin, "Put' na Salang," in *Put' na Salang* (Moscow: DOSAAF, 1987), 10; and Urban, *War in Afghanistan*, 45—47.

28. Girardet, *Afghanistan: The Soviet War*, 34; Edward Girardet, "With the Resistance in Afghanistan," *The Christian Science Monitor*, 22 June 1982; Gerard Chaliand, *Report From Afghanistan* (New York: The Viking Press, 1981), 63; Edward Girardet, "With the Resistance in Afghanistan: Afghan Officials, Soviets at Bay," *The Christian Science Monitor*, 24 September 1981; and Bradsher, *Afghanistan and the Soviet Union*, 210.

29. Safronov, "Kak eto bylo," 68. See also Pierre Allen and Albert Shakel, "Tribal Guerrilla Warfare Against a Colonial Power," *Journal of Conflict Resolution*, no. 4 (1983):590—617.

30. Zalmay Khalilzad, "Moscow's Afghan War," *Problems of Communism*, nos. 1, 2 (1986): 4—5; Edward Girardet, "How Stubborn Tribesmen Nibble Russians to Death," *U.S. News & World Report*, 12 July 1982, 25; and Amstutz, *Afghanistan: The First Five Years*, 132. For a good profile of Ahmad Shah Masoud, see Christina Dameyer, "The Young Lion Who May Lead Guerrillas to Victory," *The San Francisco Examiner*, 24 February 1984. Dameyer reports that Masoud read the works of Mao and Che Guevara on guerrilla warfare but preferred a study by an unnamed American.

31. U.S. Department of State, Special Report no. 106, December 1982, 3—4; and Girardet, "With the Resistance in Afghanistan." Interviews in Alexiev's, *Inside the Soviet Army in Afghanistan*, 23, corroborate the pattern described by Girardet.

32. Safronov, "Kak eto bylo," 68.

33. Girardet, "How Stubborn Tribesmen Nibble Russians to Death," 25—26; Arnold, *Afghanistan*, 99; and Hammond, *Red Flag Over Afghanistan*, 161.

34. Dupree, "Afghanistan in 1982," 136; Amstutz, *Afghanistan: The First Five Years*, 132; and U.S. Department of State, Special Report, no. 106, 3—4.

35. Dupree, "Afghanistan in 1983," 235; Amstutz, *Afghanistan: The First Five Years*, 133, 145; Girardet, *Afghanistan: The Soviet War*, 85—86; William Branigan, "Bombed Village Is a Symbol of Resistance," *The Washington Post*, 19 October 1983; and "Guerrilla Leader Uses Time Versus Soviets," *The Washington Post*, 18 October 1983.

36. Aaron Trehub, "All Quiet on the Panjsher Front," *RL* 259/84, 3 July 1984, 1—2; Lee Coldren, "Afghanistan in 1984: The Fifth Year of the Russo-Afghan War," *Asian Survey* 25 (February 1985):174—76; Amstutz, *Afghanistan: The First Five Years*, 133; Jossef Bodansky, "Soviet Military Involvement in Afghanistan," in *Afghanistan: The Great Game Revisited*, edited by Rosanne Klass (New York: Freedom House, 1987), 255—56; Drew Middleton, "Key Afghan Area Is Reported Lost by the Guerrillas," *The New York Times*, 25 April 1984; and William Branigan, "Moscow's Troops Show No Zeal for Guerrilla War," *The Washington Post*, 21 October 1983.

37. Lee Coldren, "Afghanistan in 1985: The Sixth Year of the Russo-Afghan War," *Asian Survey*, no. 2 (1986):239—42; U.S. Department of State, Special Report no. 135, "Afghanistan: Six Years of Soviet Occupation" (December 1988):2; *Afghan Information Centre Monthly Bulletin*, no. 59 (1986):5 and no. 58 (1986):11—13; "Afghans Accept Both Losses and Gains in 'Holy War' Against the Russians," *The New York Times*, 1 November 1985; Tagliabue, "Russians Pressing Afghan Campaign"; William Branigan, "An Arduous Trek Along the 'Jihad Trail,'" *The Washington Post*, 17 October 1983; Frederick Kempe, "Risky

Mission: Supplying Guerrillas in Afghanistan Is Grueling Undertaking," *The Wall Street Journal*, 13 November 1984; A. Oliinik, "Vyshe gor," *Krasnaia zvezda*, 28 February 1988; Albert Stahel and Paul Bucherer, *Afghanistan 1986/87, Beilage zur Allgemeinen Schweizerishcen Militarzeitschrift*, no. 12 (1987):8—9; and Arthur Bonner, "The Slow Motion War in Afghanistan," *The New York Times*, 6 July 1986.

38. Varennikov, "Afghanistan," 6—8.

39. Anthony Cordesman, "The Afghan Chronology: Another Brutal Year of Conflict," *Armed Forces* (April 1987):158.

40. Edgar O'Ballance, "Afghanistan: Winds of Change," *Asian Defense Journal*, no. 9 (1986):84; TASS, "Bandits' Lair Wiped Out," *Pravda*, 2 May 1986, as translated in *Current Digest of the Soviet Press* (hereafter *CDSP*) 38 (no. 18):21. See also Philip Taubman, "In Kabul, Military Prowess on Parade," *The New York Times*, 19 January 1988; and Tagliabue, "Russians Pressing Afghan Campaign."

41. Branigan, "An Arduous Trek"; and Kempe, "Risky Mission."

42. O'Ballance, "Afghanistan: Winds of Change," 82—84; and TASS, "Bandits' Lair Wiped Out."

43. Safronov, "Kak eto bylo," 70; B. V. Gromov, "Zashchishchali, obuchali, stroili," *Voenno-istoricheskii zhurnal*, no. 3 (1989):11—15; *Afghan Jehad* 1 (June-July 1981):11—17.

44. A. Prokhanov, "Russian Journalist Sorts Among Ruins of Nine-Year Afghan War," *The Kansas City Times*, 5 May 1988.

45. G. Pochter, "Nekotorye osobennosti vedeniia operatsii na gorno-pustynoi teatre," *Voina i revoliutsiia*, nos. 3, 4 (1933):57.

46. An effective force of 150,000 is this author's estimate based on the order of battle compilations of others: David Isby, "Afghanistan 1982: The War Continues," *International Defense Review* (November 1982):1528; Branigan, "Moscow's Troops"; Ahmad and Barnet, "Bloody Games," 62—63; Stahel and Bucherer, *Afghanistan 1986/87*, 7; Khalilzad, "Moscow's Afghan War," 2—3; Bodansky, "Soviet Military Involvement in Afghanistan," 268—69; Urban, *War in Afghanistan*, 231—32; and U. S. State Department, Special Report no. 135, December 1985, 1—8. The military regions were as follows: 201st Motorized Rifle Division (MRD) in the northeast, 16th MRD in Balkh Province, 275th MRD in Jalalabad, 105th Artillery Battalion and 360th MRD in Kabul, 54th and 68th MRD in Herat and western Afghanistan, 357th MRD in Kandahar, plus a few air assault brigades in border regions.

47. Safronov, "Kak eto bylo," 69.

48. Ibid., *Podvig-Vypusk 34*, geroiko-patrioticheskii literaturno-khudozhestvennyi almanakh (Moscow: Molodaia gvardiia, 1989), 13; and Artem Borovik, *Afganistan eshche raz pro voine* (Moscow: Ogonek, 1990), 149.

49. Gromov, "Zashchishchali, obuchali, stroili," 13; Urban, *War in Afghanistan*, 65; Jossef Bodansky, "Bear on the Chessboard Soviet Military Gains in Afghanistan," *World Affairs*, no. 3 (1982—83):286—87; Safi, "Soviet Military Tactics in Afghanistan," 108; and Stahel and Bucherer, *Afghanistan 1986/87*, 7.

50. Denny Nelson, "Soviet Air Power: Tactics and Weapons Used in Afghanistan," *Air University Review*, no. 2 (1985):32; and Kenneth Whiting, *Soviet Air Power* (Maxwell Air Force Base, AL: Air University Press, 1985), 94.

51. B. Budnikov, "Gory ne proshchaiut oshibok," *Aviatsiia i kosmonavtika*, no. 9 (1980):8—9; "In a Ravine—From the Site," *Krasnaia zvezda*, 17 July 1984, as translated in JPRS-UMA-84-063, 10 October 1984, 94; and U.S. Department of State, Special Report no. 135, 3—4.

52. Bodansky, "Bear on the Chessboard," 286—87; John Gunston, "Su-24's, Tu-16's Support Soviet Ground Forces," *Aviation Week & Space Technology*, 29 October 1984, 40; and Isby, "Afghanistan 1982," 1524.

53. John Gunston, "Afghans Plan USSR Terror Attacks," *Jane's Defence Weekly*, 31 March 1984:481; Nelson, "Soviet Air Power," 36; and Stahel and Bucherer, *Afghanistan 1986/87*, 9.

54. Gennadii Bocharov, *Byl i videl... Afganistan 1986/87 god* (Moscow: Politizdat, 1987), 18—19.

55. A. Oliinik, "Mountains Under the Wings," *Krasnaia zvezda*, 25 April 1985, as translated in JPRS-UMA-85-038, 21 June 1985, 115—17.

56. T. Gaidar, "In the Valley of the Five Lions," *Pravda*, 2 August 1982, as translated in *CDSP* 34 (no. 32):5—7.

57. Bocharov, *Byl i videl*, 4; Nelson, "Soviet Air Power," 34—35; David Isby, "Soviet Tactics in the War in Afghanistan," *Jane's Defence Review* 4, no. 7 (1983):683; V. Tolkov, "Bomber Operations in Mountains," *Aviatsiia i kosmonavtika*, no. 10 (1989):24—25, as translated in JPRS-UAC-90-002, 1 May 1990, 22.

58. "Soviet Air Force in Afghanistan," *Jane's Defence Weekly*, 7 July 1984, 1104—5. Isby, "Afghanistan 1982," 1523, gave a substantially higher estimate in 1982, putting Soviet helicopter strength to 500 to 600, including 200 Mi-24s.

59. Jim Coyne, "Afghanistan Update, Russians Lose Battles But May Win War," *Soldier of Fortune* (December 1982):72; Nelson, "Soviet Air Power," 33; and Gunston, "Su-24's, Tu-16's," 42—43.

60. Elena Lesoto, *Komandirovka na voinu* (Moscow: Kniga, 1990), 15.

61. Stahel and Bucherer, *Afghanistan 1986/87*, 9, 18; Bodansky, "SAMS in Afghanistan: Assessing the Impact," *Jane's Defence Weekly*, 25 July 1987, 150—54; Edward Girardet, "Afghan Fighters Slowly Erode Soviet Control," *The Christian Science Monitor*, 23 December 1987; Aaron Karp, "Blowpipes and Stingers in Afghanistan: One Year Later," *Armed Forces Journal International* (September 1987):37—38; John Cushman, "Helping to Change the Course of a War," *The New York Times*, 17 January 1988; Gunston, "Su-24's, Tu-16's," 40; and Cordesman, "The Afghan Chronology," 158.

62. James Hansen, "Afghanistan: The Soviet Experience," *National Defense* (January 1982): 23—24; Nelson, "Soviet Air Power," 37—38; Jossef Bodansky, "Most Feared Aircraft in Afghanistan Is Frogfoot," *Jane's Defence Weekly*, 19 May 1984; and V. Bezborodov, "Grach—mashina nadezhnaia," *Aviatsiia i kosmonavtika*, no. 7 (1990):21—23.

63. Gunston, "Su-24's, Tu-16's," 40; and Branigan, "Moscow's Troops."

64. Nelson, "Soviet Air Power," 39; Fred Hiatt, "Soviets Use Bombers in Afghanistan," and "Soviet Troops Advance Into Key Afghan Valley," *The Washington Post*, 24 and 27 April 1984; and David Isby, "Soviets in Afghanistan, Prepared for Long Haul," *Defense Week*, 21 February 1984, 14.

65. Coyne, "Afghanistan Update," 72; and Nelson, "Soviet Air Power," 37.

66. Gunston, "Su-24's, Tu-16's," 40—42; and James Bussert, "Signal Troops Central to Afghanistan Invasion," *Defense Electronics* (June 1983):104.

67. "Soviet Air Force in Afghanistan," 1104—5.

68. Michael Mecham, "US Credits Afghan Resistance With Thwarting Soviet Air Power," *Aviation Week & Space Technology*, 13 July 1987, 26; V. Lukashin, "Hot Skies," *Izvestiia*, 1 May 1986, as translated in JPRS-UMA-86-037, 11 July 1986, 101—6; and New York Times News Service, "Stinger Missiles Aid Afghan Guerrillas," *The Kansas City Times*, 13 December 1987.

69. Cushman, "Helping to Change the Course of a War."

70. U.S. Department of State, Special Report no. 173, "Afghanistan: Eight Years of Soviet Occupation (December 1987)," 9; Girardet, "Afghan Fighters Slowly Erode Soviet Control"; and Borovik, *Afganistan eshche raz pro voine*, 132—33.

71. Lesoto, *Komandirovka na voinu*, 8—10.
72. Karp, "Blowpipes and Stingers in Afghanistan," 36—39.
73. Isby, *War in a Distant Country*, 28.
74. Branigan, "Moscow's Troops."
75. N. N. Biiazi, *Operations in Mountains*, translated by the War Office, Ottawa, Canada (Moscow: Ministry of the Armed Forces, 1947), 9.
76. B. V. Gromov, "Zashchishchali, obuchali, stroili," 11.
77. V. Golubev, "Comments Reach the School," *Krasnaia zvezda*, 12 June 1984, as translated in JPRS-UMA-84-059, 13 September 1984, 18—20; M. Sotskov, "Dlia boia v gorakh: voinskaia spetsial'nost' i fizicheskaia podgotovka," *Krasnaia zvezda*, 16 July 1983; G. Panteleev, "Ekzamen v gorakh," *Krasnaia zvezda*, 27 March 1988; "The March Training of Troops," *Krasnaia zvezda*, 31 January 1985, as translated in JPRS-UMA-85-025, 3 April 1985, 20—22; A. Arutunian, "A Mountain Concomitant: The Military Specialty and Physical Conditioning," *Krasnaia zvezda*, 14 July 1984, as translated in JPRS-UMA-84-062, 4 October 1984, 49; A. Yurkin, "Mountains Are Conquered by the Strong," *Krasnaia zvezda*, 15 May 1984, as translated in JPRS-UMA-84-053, 9 August 1984, 38—40.
78. S. Kozlovskii, "Malyi garnizon," *Voennyi vestnik*, no. 4 (1988):83.
79. V. Sosnitskii, "Desantniki v atake," *Voennyi vestnik*, no. 10 (1985): 29—30; Biiazi, *Operations in Mountains*, 1; and Isby, "Afghanistan 1982," 1524.
80. Bocharov, *Byl i videl*, 23.
81. Safi, "Soviet Military Tactics in Afghanistan," 108.
82. Iu. Tukharinov, "The Commander and Modern Combat: Maneuver in the Mountains," *Krasnaia zvezda*, 30 December 1981, as translated in JPRS-UMA-80418, 26 March 1982, 14—17.
83. A. Shulgin, "Boi v gorakh," *Voennyi vestnik*, no. 2 (1985):29—32; U.S. Department of State, Special Report no. 135, 8; and S. Tuaev, "Zasada," *Voennyi vestnik*, no. 2 (1989): 68—71.
84. Shulgin, "Boi v gorakh," 31—32.
85. S. Korobka, "Razvedka v gorakh," *Voennyi vestnik*, no. 10 (1985):13—15; and P. Drozdov, "Boi nachinaetsia s razvedkoi," *Voennyi vestnik*, no. 5 (1990):39.
86. Biiazi, *Operations in Mountains*, 1—3, 6—8; Konovalov, "Afghanistan and Mountain Warfare Training," 2—3. See also Alexiev, *Inside the Soviet Army in Afghanistan*, 31—32. Alexiev notes that *Spetsnaz* forces, often confused with airborne and air assault units, have probably played a very small role in Afghanistan.
87. I. Tretiak, "Organizatsiia i vedenie nastupatel' nogo boia v gornotaezhnoi mestnosti," *Voenno-istoricheskii zhurnal*, no. 7 (1980):42—49; V. Popov, "Usilennyi motostrelkovoi batal'on nastup aet v gorakh," *Voennyi vestnik*, no. 1 (1982):16—20; Bodansky, "Bear on the Chessboard," 283; Jossef Bodansky, "Afghanistan: The Soviet Air War," *Defense and Foreign Affairs* (September 1985):14; and Gilberto Villahermosa, "Soviet Enveloping Detachments," *Armor* (September-October 1984):13—15.
88. T. Usmanov, "Pora osmyslit' i obobshchit'," *Voennyi vestnik*, no. 5 (1990):36—37.
89. I. Antonov, "Aviatsionnyi navodchik," *Aviatsiia i kosmonavtika*, no. 8 (1990):18—19.
90. Usmanov, "Pora osmyslit' i obobshchit'," 37; Stephen Zaloga, "Soviet Infantry: Lessons From the War in Afghanistan," *Armed Forces Journal International* (October 1989):28.
91. M. Kolesnikov, "Nastuplenie v gorakh," *Voennyi vestnik*, no. 1 (1987):33.
92. Bodansky, "Bear on the Chessboard," 284—86; Isby, *War in a Distant Country*, 76; Tagliabue, "Russians Pressing Afghan Campaign"; "New Claims of Chemical Warfare in Afghanistan," *Jane's Defence Weekly*, 22 November 1986, 1206; *Afghan Information Centre Monthly Bulletin*, no. 59 (1986):2; Stuart Schwartzstein, "Chemical Warfare in Afghanistan:

An Independent Assessment," *World Affairs* 145, no. 3 (1982—83):267—72; Julianne Robinson, Jeanne Guillemin, and Matthew Meselson, "Yellow Rain: The Story Collapses," *Foreign Policy* (Fall 1987):100—117; and Pochter, "Nekotorye osobennosti," 58.

93. Nikolai M. Mulyar [Muliar], "The Fight for the Pass," *Krasnaia zvezda*, 17 March 1985, as translated in JPRS-UMA-85-034, 21 May 1985, 34—36; N. Zaitsevskii, "By a Surprise Attack," *Krasnaia zvezda*, 10 October 1984, as translated in JPRS-UMA-84-078, 62—63; Isby, "Afghanistan 1982," 1527; and Turbiville, "Ambush!" 40.

94. Stahel and Bucherer, *Afghanistan 1986/76*, 9—10; V. A. Chernukhin, "Boevoe primenenie artillerii v gorakh," *Voenno-istoricheskii zhurnal*, no. 11 (1986):28—32; and Villahermosa, "Soviet Enveloping Detachments," 14.

95. Stahel and Bucherer, *Afghanistan 1986/87*, 9—10; Safi, "Soviet Military Tactics in Afghanistan," 109; V. Litvinenko, "Pora osmyslit' i obobshchit': Ognevoe porazhenie," *Voennyi vestnik*, no. 6 (1990):45; and V. Vozovikov, "Pokorenie vershin," *Krasnaia zvezda*, 15 December 1984.

96. Lesoto, *Komandirovka na voinu*, 10, 14.

97. Litvinenko, "Pora osmyslit' i obobshchat'," 46; and "Afgan: Iz dnevnika desantnika," *Aspekt*, no. 5 (1990):5.

98. V. Kurochkin, "Tanki v zelenoi zone," *Voennyi vestnik*, no. 1 (1990):58. For an excellent discussion of the development of the *bronegruppa*, see Les Grau, "Soviet Non-Linear Combat, The Challenge of the 90's" (Pamphlet, Fort Leavenworth, KS: Soviet Army Studies Office, 1990), 9—11.

99. Gaidar, "In the Valley," 5—7; Girardet, *Afghanistan: The Soviet War*, 35; and Girardet, "How Stubborn Tribesmen Nibble Russians to Death," 25—27. Girardet points out that not all civilians were able to get out of the way of the Soviet advance and suffered extensive casualties.

100. V. Baikov, "Urgunskaia operatsiia: Iz Afganskogo dnevnika," *Pravda*, 19 March 1984; and V. Skrizhalin, "Konets banditskogo logova," *Krasnaia zvezda*, 8 March 1984.

101. Bocharov, *Byl i videl*, 37—38.

102. A. Chumichev, "Oboroniaetsia vzvod," *Voennyi vestnik*, no. 10 (1985):26—27; Mulyar, "The Fight for the Pass," 34—36; A. Shuliak, "Tekhnicheskoe obespechenie na marshe v gorakh," *Voennyi vestnik*, no. 9 (1986):16—18; and Bocharov, *Byl i videl*, 29.

103. Biiazi, *Operations in Mountains*, 15.

104. Ian Kemp, "Abdul Haq: Soviet Mistakes in Afghanistan," *Jane's Defence Weekly*, 5 March 1988, 380.

105. P. Studenikin, "Doroga v Kabul," *Pravda*, 20 September 1984; I. Zaporozhan, "Tiazhelo v uchenii—legko v boiu," *Voennyi vestnik*, no. 4 (1987):19—21; A. Oliinik, "In a Hail of Bullets," *Krasnaia zvezda*, 19 January 1985, as translated in JPRS-UMA-85-013, 45—49; Turbiville, "Ambush!" 33—36; Isby, "Afghanistan 1982," 1526; Branigan, "Guerrillas, Occupiers Bogged Down in Stalemate"; Stahel and Bucherer, *Afghanistan 1986/87*, 19—20; and Jim Graves, "Paktia Reconnaissance," *Soldier of Fortune* (December 1984):78.

106. E. Tverdokhlebov, "Okhrana na dorogakh," *Voennyi vestnik*, no. 6 (1990):47; Zaporozhan, "Tiazhelo v uchenii," 19—20; Iu. Churkin, " 'Berkut' vykhodit na sviaz'," *Voennyi vestnik*, no. 5 (1988):76—78; Iu. Dmitriev, "Battalion of Four," *Trud*, 21 February 1985, as translated in JPRS-UMA-85-021, 49; Isby, "Afghanistan 1982," 1254; and Trehub, "All Quiet on the Panjshir Front?" 3.

107. Shuliak, "Tekhnicheskoe obespechenie na marshe v gorakh," 16—18; Amstutz, *Afghanistan: The First Five Years*, 151; E. Mikhalko, "Dlia obespecheniia boia v gorakh," *Tyl i snabzhenie sovetskikh vooruzhennykh sil*, no. 10 (1986):15—19.

108. N. Starodymov, "Obespechivaia prodvizhenie kolonna," *Voennyi vestnik*, no. 10 (1986): 66—69; V. Ostankov and V. Sadovnik, "Minnaia opasnost'," *Voennyi vestnik*, no. 10 (1986):63—65; Jimmy Phillip, "On the Roads of Afghanistan: Mines, Mines and Mines,"

Armed Forces (Australia) (June 1988):11—15; E. Kaminskii, "Dushmanskie kaverzy," *Voennyi vestnik*, no. 5 (1988):80—83; A. Oliinik, "Vsego odin shans," *Krasnaia zvezda*, 26 March 1983; and V. Naugol'nyi, "Trudnyi pereval," in *Vo imia velikoi tseli* (Leningrad: Lenizdat, 1988). The Soviet press has carried many additional articles on this subject.

109. V. Goncharov, "Sviaz' na Salange," *Voennyi vestnik*, no. 8 (1987): 52—53; Churkin, " 'Berkut' vykhodit na sviaz'," 77—78; V. Zadubrovsky, "The Correct Decision," *Soviet Military Review*, no. 4 (1984):26—27; Iu. Churkin and V. Fisun, "Snaipery efira-besstrashnye boitsy," *Voennyi vestnik*, no. 10 (1986):69—71; Bussert, "Signal Troops," 104; and Nelson, "Soviet Air Power," 40. The author gratefully acknowledges the technical advice of Major James Kellet, U.S. Army.

110. Kozlovskii, "Malyi garnizon," 83—84; and Goncharov, "Sviaz' na Salange," 52—53.

111. Bussert, "Signal Troops," 104; Iu. Churkin and V. Fisun, "Snaipery efira-besstrashnye boitsy," *Voennyi vestnik*, no. 10 (1986):70.

112. Bodansky, "Bear on the Chessboard," 275.

113. Mark Urban, "A More Competent Afghan Army?" *Jane's Defence Weekly*, 23 November 1985, 1147—51; Captain Ainullah, *Afghan Realities*, November 1983; Girardet, *Afghanistan: The Soviet War*, 12; Edward Girardet, "Afghan Guerrillas Keep Soviets at Bay," *The Christian Science Monitor*, 29 June 1982; Cordesman, "The Afghan Chronology," 159; and Safi, "Soviet Military Tactics in Afghanistan," 103.

114. Khalilzad, "Moscow's Afghan War," 7; Urban, "A More Competent Afghan Army?" 1148—49; A Nearby Observer, "Afghanistan," *The Bulletin of Atomic Scientists* 39, no. 6 (1983):20; Coldren, "Afghanistan in 1984," 174; and U.S. Department of State, Special Report no. 173, 11.

115. I. Sadeki, "V edinom stroiu," *Krasnaia zvezda*, 24 December 1984; Urban, "A More Competent Afghan Army?" 1148—50; and Coldren, "Afghanistan in 1985," 238.

116. Safronov, "Kak eto bylo," 70—71; and *Afghan Information Centre Monthly Bulletin*, no. 34 (1984):18.

117. U.S. Department of State, Special Report no. 135, 7; *Afghan Realities*, 16 July 1985; Khalilzad, "Moscow's Afghan War," 7; Associated Press (Islamabad, Pakistan), "Afghans Say Four Generals Aided Rebels," *The Kansas City Times*, 8 January 1986.

118. A Nearby Observer, "Afghanistan," 22; Amstutz, *Afghanistan: The First Five Years*, 146.

119. Urban, "A More Competent Afghan Army?" 1147—48.

120. Artem Borovik, "Vstretimsia u trekh zhuravlei," *Ogonek*, no. 28 (1987):21.

121. Ibid.

122. Tashkent International Service in Uzbek, "Afghan Tribes Are Safeguarding the Revolution," 25 December 1983, as translated in JPRS-UMA-84-011, 2 February 1984, 42—43; A Nearby Observer, "Afghanistan," 20—21; Tahir Amin, "Afghan Resistance: Past, Present and Future," *Asian Survey*, no. 4 (1984):389; and Gilles Dorensboro and Chantal Lobato, "The Militia in Afghanistan," *Central Asian Survey*, no. 4 (1989):98—103.

123. Amstutz, *Afghanistan: The First Five Years*, 189; Herman Ustinov, "Guerrilla Leader Changes Sides," *New Times*, no. 12 (1985):28—30, as translated in JPRS-UMA-85-028; Dorensboro and Lobato, "The Militia in Afghanistan," 96—98; and U.S. Department of State, Special Report no. 173, 12.

124. Borovik, "Vstretimsia u trekh zhuravlei," 21; Mujahideen sources tend to confirm this view. See also *Afghan Information Centre Monthly Bulletin*, no. 63 (1986):6—9.

125. Bocharov, *Byl i videl*, 33—34.

126. A. Skrizhalin, "Boi v loshchine," *Krasnaia zvezda*, 30 June 1983; and Isby, "Afghanistan 1982," 1529.

127. Bocharov, *Byl i videl*, 36.

128. Branigan, "An Arduous Trek"; Branigan, "Moscow's Troops"; and Ahmad and Barnet, "Bloody Games," 66—67.
129. Bill Keller, "Russia's Divisive War: Home From Afghanistan," *The New York Times Magazine*, 14 February 1988, 24—28, 86; "A Soviet Estonian Soldier in Afghanistan," *Central Asian Survey* 5, no. 1 (1986):106.
130. Urban, "A More Competent Afghan Army?" 1151.
131. Branigan, "Moscow's Troops"; Safronov, "Kak eto bylo," 69; and Claude Malhuret, "Report From Afghanistan," *Foreign Affairs* (Fall-Winter 1983):428—31.
132. "Afghanistan at War" (interview with Francesco Sartori), *RL* 290/84, 5—6.
133. Borovik, *Afganistan eshche raz pro voine* (Moscow: Mezhdunarodnye otnosheniia, 1990), 170—76.
134. Coldren, "Afghanistan in 1984," 176—77; Borje Almquist, "Eyewitness to Afghanistan at War," *World Affairs* 145 (Winter 1982—83):311—14; and Borovik, "Vstretimsia u trekh zhuravlei," 22.
135. V. Skrizhalin, "Prozrenie," *Krasnaia zvezda*, 29 July 1983.
136. Girardet, *Afghanistan: The Soviet War*, 136—37; Branigan, "An Arduous Trek Along the 'Jihad Trail,'" reported a similar experience.
137. TASS, "Na novom etape," *Pravda*, 16 June 1981; and V. Baikov, "Uverennost' v budushchem," *Pravda*, 27 April 1985.
138. Collins, *The Soviet Invasion of Afghanistan*, 141; Gerard Chaliand, ed., *Report From Afghanistan*, trans. Tamar Jacoby (New York: The Viking Press, 1982), 66; S. Modenov, "The Afghan People's Resolve," *International Affairs*, no. 6 (1982):26; V. Stepanov, "Afghanistan on the Path of Revolutionary Change," *International Affairs*, no. 5 (1984): 25—33; V. Semyonov, "Revolutionary Afghanistan Eight Years Later," *International Affairs*, no. 5 (1986):47—52; and Edward Girardet, "Occupational Hazards of a Soviet Occupation," *The Christian Science Monitor*, 2 July 1982.
139. Girardet, *Afghanistan: The Soviet War*, 149; U.S. Department of State, Special Report no. 139, 1—5; Babrak Karmal, Address of 29 December 1979, in *The Truth About Afghanistan: Documents, Facts, Eyewitness Reports* (Moscow: Novosti Press, 1980), 93—96; and Ann Sheehy, "Agreement Signed Between Soviet and Afghan Official Muslim Organizations," *RL* 198/87.
140. Bocharov, *Byl i videl*, 10.
141. Abdul Vakhad and Abdul Vaki, "Boi bez vystrelov," *Krasnaia zvezda*, 1 April 1983; and *Podvig—Vypusk 34*, 131.
142. Girardet, *Afghanistan: The Soviet War*, 147; and Jeri Laber, "Afghanistan's Other War," *The New York Review of Books*, 18 December 1986, 3—7.
143. Girardet, *Afghanistan: The Soviet War*, 131.
144. Steve Sego, "Kabul Seeks National Reconciliation," *RL* 15/87, 1—2.
145. "In a Friendly Atmosphere," *Pravda*, 13 December 1986, as translated in *CDSP* 38 (no. 50):14—15.
146. Bohdan Nahaylo, "Towards a Settlement of the Afghanistan Conflict: A Chronological Overview," *RL* 16/87, 1—2.
147. "The Goal Is National Reconciliation," *Izvestiia*, 3 January 1987, as translated in *CDSP* 39 (no. 1):11; Associated Press, "Afghan Chief Touts Reconciliation Plan," *The Kansas City Times*, 22 July 1987; and Bonner, "The Slow Motion War in Afghanistan."
148. Vitaly Zhestkov, "The Afghan Revolution: Achievements and Difficulties," *Socialism: Principles, Practice, Prospects*, no. 4 (1988):33; V. Semyenov, "A New Situation in Afghanistan," *International Affairs*, no. 4 (1988):88—92; Bocharov, *Byl i videl*, 7—10; and Ann Sheehy, "Agreement Signed Between Soviet and Afghan Official Muslim Organizations."

149. A. Prokhanov, "Russian Journalist Sorts Among Ruins of Nine-Year Afghan War."
150. Steve Sego, "Will the Soviet-Afghan Border Be Redrawn?" *RL* 156/88, 1.
151. A. Oliinik, "Vremia nadezhd," *Krasnaia zvezda*, 22 March 1988.
152. D. Meshchaninov, "Dolgii i trudnyi put k miru," *Izvestiia*, 21 February 1988. One resistance commander told *Izvestiia* that he would set his misgivings aside and try to return to a normal life.
153. Viktor Turshatov, "Afghanistan Veterans: Society Owes Them," *Moscow News*, no. 50 (1987); Borovik, "Vstretimsia u trekh zhuravlei," 22; and John Kifner, "With the Afghan Guerrillas in a Heady Time," *The New York Times*, 27 May 1988.
154. Donald Mahoney, "Soviet Press Enters New Stage in Coverage of Afghan War," *RL* 34/87; "Along the River," *Ozbekistan adabiyoti va san'ati*, 21 December 1984, as translated in JPRS-UMA-85-042, 17 July 1985, 44; B. Pavlov, "Defeat of Counterrevolution in Soviet Turkestan," *Soviet Military Review*, no. 5 (1984), as translated in JPRS-UMA-84-049, 19 July 1984, 58—60; V. Sukhodolskii, "Afghanistan Profiles," *Rabochaia gazeta*, 7—8 April 1984, as translated in JPRS-UMA-84-055, 22 August 1984, 158—63; and Iu. Ivanov, "The Village Was Waiting for Bread," *Komsomol'skaia Pravda*, 24 June 1984, as translated in JPRS-UMA-84-057, 28 August 1984, 114—15.
155. Mahoney, "Soviet Press Enters New Stage"; and Dusko Doder, "Afghanistan War Saps Kremlin's Resolve," *The Kansas City Times*, 27 December 1986.
156. V. Okulov, "Afganistan zhivet v moei dushe," *Pravda*, 3 February 1988; and "Zaiavlenie General'nogo Sekretaria TsK KPSS M. S. Gorbacheva," *Krasnaia zvezda*, 9 February 1988. This item was published in *Pravda* and *Izvestiia* as well on the same date.
157. Aaron Trehub, "Popular Discontent With the War in Afghanistan," *RL* 483/87, 3; Artem Borovik, "Vstretimsia u trekh zhuravlei," *Ogonek*, no. 30 (1987):19; William Branigan, "Soviet Troops in Afghanistan Ill-Trained and Poorly Motivated," *The Washington Post*, 21 October 1983; and Bohdan Nahaylo, "Soviet Newspaper Reveals Antipathy Among Youth Towards War in Afghanistan," *RL* 23/87.
158. V. Pogrebniak, letter to the editor, *Krasnaia zvezda*, 22 March 1988; A. Turvandian, "Conscience Calls," *Kommunist* (Erevan), 24 September 1987, as translated in JPRS-UMA-87-045, 23 December 1987, 53; and N. Burbyga, "Callousness: Soldier-Internationalists Encounter it Even in a Military Hospital," *Krasnaia zvezda*, 19 January 1988, as translated in JPRS-UMA-88-008, 3 May 1988, 23—26.
159. T. Turdiiev and Iu. Tuidiiev, "The Sons of Man Are Members One Another..." *Tojikistoni soveti*, as translated in JPRS-UMA-88-002, 19 January 1988, 36; and V. Panov, "Ostavat'sia boitsami," *Znamenosets*, no. 4 (1988):25—26. See also I. M. Dynin, *Posle Afganistan* (Moscow: Profizdat, 1990).
160. N. Burbyga, "Gorkaia pravda nedavnei voiny," *Izvestiia*, 26 October 1990.
161. "Net v dushe blagodarnosti..." *Pravda*, 25 November 1987; Trehub, "Popular Discontent With the War in Afghanistan," 1—2; A. Oliinik, "Nepokorennyi: Rasskaz ob odnom iz sovetskikh voinov propavshikh bez vesti v Afganistane," *Krasnaia zvezda*, 11 June 1988.
162. Lesoto, *Komandirovka na voinu*, 85, 107—9; Nahaylo, "Soviet Newspaper Reveals Antipathy Among Youth Towards War in Afghanistan," 1—3; and Kushnerev, "After Afghanistan."
163. Taras Kuzio, "Opposition in the USSR to the Occupation of Afghanistan," *Central Asian Survey* 6, no. 1 (1987):99—100.
164. Branigan, "Moscow's Troops"; "A Soviet Estonian in Afghanistan," 103—4; Alexandre Bennigsen, "The Impact of the Afghan War on Soviet Central Asia," in Klass, *Afghanistan: The Great Game Revisited*, 292—94; A. Alexiev and S. Enders Wimbush, "Soviet Muslims in Afghanistan," in *Ethnic Minorities in the Red Army, Asset or Liability?* (Boulder, CO: Westview Press, 1987), 242—43, 251—52; Alexiev, *Inside the Soviet Army*

in Afghanistan, 43; and "The Red Army," *World*, #404 transcript (Boston: WGBH Educational Foundation, 1981), 17—18.
165. Arnold, *Afghanistan*, 97.
166. A. Bovin, "A Difficult Decade," *Izvestiia*, 23 December 1988, as translated in *CDSP* 40 (no. 51):10—11.

Bibliography

Chapter 4

Memoirs and Documents

Gorbachev, M. S. *Perestroika i novoe myshlenie dlia nashei strany i dlia vsego mira.* Moscow: Politizdat, 1988.

Guensberg, Gerald, trans. *Soviet Command Study of Iran.* Moscow, 1941. Arlington, VA: SRI International, 1980.

Vo imia velikoi tseli. Leningrad: Lenizdat, 1988.

Volkov, Y. *The Truth About Afghanistan: Documents, Facts, Eyewitness Reports.* Moscow: Novosti Press Agency, 1980.

Zvezdy slavy boevoi na zemle Afganistana. Moscow: Politizdat, 1987.

Books

Alexiev, Alex. *Inside the Soviet Army in Afghanistan.* Santa Monica, CA: Rand, 1988.

Alexiev, Alex, and S. Enders Wimbush. *Ethnic Minorities in the Red Army, Asset or Liability?* Boulder, CO: Westview Press, 1987.

Amin, Tahir. *Afghanistan Crisis: Implication and Options for Muslim World, Iran and Pakistan.* Islamabad, Pakistan: Institute for Policy Studies, 1982.

Amstutz, J. Bruce. *Afghanistan: The First Five Years of Soviet Occupation.* Washington, DC: National Defense University, 1986.

Arnold, Anthony. *Afghanistan: The Soviet Intervention in Perspective.* Stanford, CA: Hoover Institution Press, 1986.

Blank, Stephen. *Operational and Strategic Lessons of the War in Afghanistan.* Carlisle, PA: Strategic Studies Institute, 1991.

Bocharov, Gennadii. *Byl i videl... Afganistan 1986/87 god.* Moscow: Politizdat, 1987.

Bonner, Arthur. *Among the Afghans.* Durham, NC: Duke University Press, 1987.

Borovik, Artem. *Afganistan eshche raz pro voine.* Moscow: Ogonek, 1990.

Bradsher, Henry S. *Afghanistan and the Soviet Union.* Durham, NC: Duke University Press, 1985.

Chaliand, Gerard, ed. *Guerrilla Strategies: An Historical Anthology From the Long March to Afghanistan.* Berkeley: University of California Press, 1982.

_____. *Report From Afghanistan.* Trans. Tamar Jacoby. New York: The Viking Press, 1982.

Chernet, O. G. *Afganistan: bor'ba i sozdanie.* Moscow: Voennoe izdatel'stvo, 1984.

Collins, Joseph. *The Soviet Invasion of Afghanistan.* Lexington, MA: D. C. Heath & Co., 1986.

Cordesman, Anthony, and Abraham Wagner. *The Lessons of Modern War.* Vol. 3. *The Afghan and Falklands Conflicts.* Boulder, CO: Westview Press, 1990.

Dietl, William. *Bridgehead Afghanistan.* New Delhi: Lancer International, 1986.

Dupree, Louis. *Afghanistan.* Princeton, NJ: Princeton University Press, 1980.

Dynin, I. M. *Posle Afganistan.* Moscow: Profizdat, 1990.

Farr, Grant M., and John G. Merriam, eds. *Afghan Resistance: The Politics of Survival.* Boulder, CO: Westview Press, 1987.

Gankovskii, Iu. V. *Afganistan: ekonomika, politika, istoriia.* Moscow: Nauka, 1984.

Girardet, Edward R. *Afghanistan: The Soviet War.* New York: St. Martin's Press, 1985.

Gubar, Mir Gulam Mukhammad. *Afganistan na puti istorii.* Moscow: Nauka, 1987.

Guensberg, Gerald, trans. *Soviet Command Study of Iran.* Moscow, 1941. Arlington, VA: SRI International, 1980.

Hammond, Thomas. *Red Flag Over Afghanistan.* Boulder, CO: Westview Press, 1984.

Hyman, Anthony. *Afghanistan Under Soviet Domination, 1964—81.* New York: St. Martin's Press, 1982.

Isby, David. *War in a Distant Country, Afghanistan: Invasion and Resistance.* London: Arms & Armour, 1989.

_____. *Weapons and Tactics of the Soviet Army.* London: Jane's Publishing Co., 1988.

Klass, Rossanne, ed. *Afghanistan: The Great Game Revisted.* New York: Freedom House, 1987.

Lesoto, Elena. *Komandirovka na voinu.* Moscow: Kniga, 1990.

Martin, Mike. *Afghanistan: Inside a Rebel Stronghold*. London: Macmillan, 1988.

Molesworth, G. N. *Afghanistan 1919*. New York: Asia Publishing House, 1962.

Monks, Alfred. *The Soviet Intervention in Afghanistan*. Washington, DC: American Enterprise Institute for Public Policy Research, 1981.

Newell, Nancy, and Richard Newell. *The Struggle for Afghanistan*. Ithaca, NY: Cornell University Press, 1981.

Podvig-Vypusk 34, geroiko patrioticheskii literaturno-khudozhestvennyi almanakh. Moscow: Molodaia gvardiia, 1989.

Roy, Oliver. *Islam and Resistance in Afghanistan*. New York: Cambridge University Press, 1986.

Saikal, Amin, and William Maley. *The Soviet Withdrawal From Afghanistan*. Cambridge: Cambridge University Press, 1989.

Special Operations: Military Lessons From Six Selected Case Studies. New Brunswick, NJ: Center for Military Studies, 1982.

Sud'ba zovet v dorogu. Moscow: Politizdat, 1987.

Teplinskii, L. B. *Istoriia Sovetsko-Afganskikh otnoshenii*. Moscow: Mysl, 1988.

The Truth About Afghanistan: Documents, Facts, Eyewitness Reports. Moscow: Novosti Press, 1980.

Urban, Mark. *War in Afghanistan*. New York: St. Martin's Press, 1988.

Voegl, Heinrich. *Die Sowjetische Intervention in Afghanistan*. Baden-Baden, West Germany, 1980.

Ware, Lewis, ed. *Low Intensity Conflict in the Third World*. Maxwell Air Force Base, AL: Air University Press, 1988.

Whiting, Kenneth. *Soviet Air Power*. Maxwell Air Force Base, AL: Air University Press, 1985.

Special Studies

Biiazi, N. N. *Operations in Mountains*. Translated by the War Office, Ottawa, Canada. Moscow: Ministry of the Armed Forces, 1947.

Odom, William E. *The Strategic Significance of Afghanistan's Struggle for Freedom*. Occasional Papers Series, vol. 2, no. 2. Miami, FL: University of Miami, Institute for Soviet and East European Studies, 1988.

Papers From a Conference on Afghanistan and Soviet Strategies for the Muslim World, 29—30 September 1987. MacDill Air Force Base, FL: United States Central Command.

"The Red Army." *World*, #404 transcript. Boston: WGBH Educational Foundation, 1981.

Stahel, Albert, and Paul Bucherer. *Afghanistan 1986/87, Beilage zur Allgemeinen Schweizerischen Militarzeitschrift*, no. 12 (1987).

Selected Articles

Aboronov, A. "March in Mountainous and Desert Terrains." *Tekhnika i vooruzhenie*, no. 12 (1986):18—19, as translated in JPRS-UMA-87-021, 22—25.

"Afgan: Iz dnevnika desantnika." *Aspekt*, no. 5 (1990):5.

"Afghanistan at War" (interview with Francesco Sartori). *RL* 270/84, 12 July 1984, 1—9; pt. 2, *RL* 290/84, 27 July 1984, 1—9.

"Afghanistan Poses Training Problems." *Jane's Defence Weekly*, 12 March 1988, 471.

"Afghan Rebels Excluded From US Budget." From *The New York Times* in *The Kansas City Star*, 12 May 1991.

"Afghans Accept Both Losses and Gains in 'Holy War' Against the Russians." *The New York Times*, 1 November 1985.

"The Afghans Win Another Round in the Great Game." *The Economist* 61 (April 1988):37—39.

Ahmad, E., and R. Barnet. "Bloody Games." *The New Yorker*, 11 April 1988.

Akhramovich, R. "Traditsii dobrososedstva: k 60-letiiu Sovetsko-Afganskogo dogovora." *Pravda*, 19 February 1981.

Alabev, A., and A. Efimov. "Smelye liudi vertoletchiki." *Krasnaia zvezda*, 26 July 1983.

Allen, Pierre, and Albert Stahel. "Tribal Guerrilla Warfare Against a Colonial Power." *Journal of Conflict Resolution*, no. 4 (1983):590—616.

"Along the River." *Ozbekistan ababiyoti va san'ati*, 21 December 1984, as translated in JPRS-UMA-85-042, 17 July 1985, 44.

Almquist, Borje. "Eyewitnesses to Afghanistan at War." *World Affairs* 145 (Winter 1982—83):311—14.

Amin, Tahir. "Afghan Resistance: Past, Present, and Future." *Asian Survey*, no. 4 (1984):373—99.

Antonov, I. "Aviatsionnyi navodchik." *Aviatsiia i kosmonavtika*, no. 8 (1990):18—19.

APN Daily Review. "APN Informs and Comments," 29 December 1983, 1—2, in JPRS-UMA-84-011, 61.

Arnold, Anthony. *Afghanistan: The Soviet Invasion in Perspective*. Stanford, CA: Hoover Institution Press, 1985.

Arutunian, A. "A Mountain Concomitant: The Military Specialty and Physical Conditioning." *Krasnaia zvezda*, 14 July 1984, as translated in JPRS-UMA-84-062, 4 October 1984, 49—51.

Aslezov, S., and V. Grevtsev. "Dolgoe ekho." *Sovetskii patriot*, 11 August 1985.

Associated Press. "Afghan Chief Touts Reconciliation Plan." *The Kansas City Times*, 22 July 1987.

———. (Islamabad, Pakistan) "Afghans Say Four Generals Aided Rebels." *The Kansas City Times*, 8 January 1986.

———. "Up to 15,000 Troops Died in Afghan War, Soviet Says." *The Kansas City Star*, 19 May 1988.

Baikov, V. "Utro novogo dniia." *Pravda*, 24 April 1983.

———. "Urgunskaia operatsiia: Iz Afganskogo dnevnika." *Pravda*, 19 March 1984.

———. "Uverennost' v budushchem." *Pravda*, 27 April 1985.

———. "V nespokoinoi provintsii." *Pravda*, 30 June 1983.

Beliaev, Igor, and Anatolii Gromyko. "This Is How We Ended up in Afghanistan." *Literaturnaia gazeta*, 20 September 1989, as translated in JPRS-UMA-89-023, 4 October 1989, 41—46.

Belitsky, Sergei. "Authors of USSR's Afghan War Policy." *Report on the USSR, Radio Liberty Research Bulletin* (hereafter *RL*) 195/89, 27 April 1989, 11—12.

Besschetnov, E. "Our Marks Will Remain." *Aviatsiia i kosmonavtika*, no. 10 (1986), as translated in JPRS-UMA-87-017, 17—22.

Bezborodov, V. "Grach—mashina nadezhnaia." *Aviatsiia i kosmonavtika*, no. 7 (1990):21—23.

Blank, Stephen. "Soviet Russia and Low-Intensity Conflict in Central Asia: Three Case Studies." In *Low Intensity Conflict in the Third World*, edited by Lewis B. Ware. Maxwell Air Force Base, AL: Air University Press, 1988.

Bodansky, Jossef. "Afghanistan: The Soviet Air War." *Defense and Foreign Affairs* (September 1985):12—14.

———. "The Bear on the Chessboard: Soviet Military Gains in Afghanistan." *World Affairs*, no. 3 (1982—83):273—98.

———. "Learning Afghanistan's Lesson." *Jane's Defence Weekly*, 7 July 1984, 1104—5.

———. "Most Feared Aircraft in Afghanistan Is Frogfoot." *Jane's Defence Weekly*, 19 May 1984, 768.

———. "SAMs in Afghanistan: Assessing the Impact." *Jane's Defence Weekly*, 25 July 1987, 153—54.

Bonner, Arthur. "The Slow Motion War in Afghanistan." *The New York Times*, 6 July 1986.

Borovik, Artem. "Afganistan: Podvodia itogi (interview with V. I. Varennikov). *Ogonek*, no. 12 (1989):6—8.

———. "Vstretimsia u trekh zhuravlei." *Ogonek*, no. 28 (1987):20—23; no. 29:21—24; no. 30:18—21.

Bovin, A. "A Difficult Decade." *Izvestiia*, 23 December 1988, as translated in *Current Digest of Soviet Press* (hereafter *CDSP*) 40 (no. 51):10—11.

Branigan, William. "An Arduous Trek Along the 'Jihad Trail.'" *The Washington Post*, 17 October 1983.

———. "Bombed Village Is a Symbol of Resistance." *The Washington Post*, 19 October 1983.

———. "Guerrilla Leader Uses Time Versus Soviets." *The Washington Post*, 18 October 1983.

———. "Guerrillas, Occupiers Bogged Down in Stalemate." *The Washington Post*, 16 October 1984.

———. "Guerrillas' Resolve Pitted Against Kremlin's Might." *The Washington Post*, 16 October 1983.

———. "Moscow's Troops Show No Zeal for Guerrilla War." *The Washington Post*, 21 October 1983.

———. "Soviet Troops in Afghanistan Ill-Trained and Poorly Motivated." *The Washington Post*, 21 October 1983.

Breev, A. "Slagaemye uspekha." *Voennyi vestnik*, no. 11 (November 1984):27—28.

Bregman, K. "How to Improve Mountain Training, a Reader Asks." *Krasnaia zvezda*, 16 October 1981, as translated in JPRS-81426 USSR Report: Military Affairs, no. 1693, 30—31.

Brown, Robert. "SOF Inside Afghanistan. Staffers Join Siege of Russian Fort." *Soldier of Fortune* (November 1982):54.

Broxup, Marie. "Afghanistan Update." *Central Asian Survey*, no. 2 (September 1983):146—49.

———. "The Soviets in Afghanistan: The Anatomy of a Takeover." *Central Asian Survey*, no. 4 (1983):142—47.

Bruce, James. "Afghan Rebels 'Downing More Soviet Helicopters.'" *Jane's Defence Weekly*, 29 November 1986, 1258.

Budnikov, B. "Gory ne proshchaiut oshibok." *Aviatsiia i kosmonavtika*, no. 9 (1980):8—9.

Burbyga, N. "Callousness: Soldier-Internationalists Encounter It Even in a Military Hospital." *Krasnaia zvezda*, 19 January 1988, as translated in JPRS-UMA-88-008, 3 May 1988.

———. "Gorkaia pravda nedavnei voiny." *Izvestiia*, 26 October 1990.

Bussert, James. "Signal Troops Central to Afghanistan Invasion." *Defense Electronics* (June 1983):104.

Chaliand, Gerard. *Report from Afghanistan*, trans. Tamar Jacoby. New York: The Viking Press, 1982.

Chernet, O., ed. *Afganistan: bor'ba i sozidanie*. Moscow: Voenizdat, 1984.

Chernukhin, V. A. "Boevoe primenenie artillerii v gorakh." *Voenno-istoricheskii zhurnal*, no. 11 (1986):28—34.

Chumichev, A. "Oboroniaetsia vzvod." *Voennyi vestnik*, no. 10 (1985):26—29.

Churkin, Iu. " 'Berkut' vykhodit na sviaz." *Voennyi vestnik*, no. 5 (1988): 76—78.

Churkin, Iu., and V. Fisun. "Snaipery efira—besstrashnye boitsy." *Voennyi vestnik*, no. 10 (1986):69—71.

Coldren, Lee. "Afghanistan in 1984: The Fifth Year of the Russo-Afghan War." *Asian Survey* 25 (February 1985):169—79.

_____. "Afghanistan in 1985: The Sixth Year of the Russo-Afghan War." *Asian Survey*, no. 2 (1986):235—45.

Collins, Joseph. "Afghanistan: The Empire Strikes Out." *Parameters*, no. 1 (1982):32—41.

Cordesman, Anthony. "The Afghan Chronology: Another Brutal Year of Conflict." *Armed Forces* (April 1987):156—60.

Coyne, Jim. "Afghanistan Update, Russians Lose Battles But May Win War." *Soldier of Fortune* (December 1982):72.

Cushman, John. "Helping to Change the Course of a War." *The New York Times*, 17 January 1988.

Dameyer, Christina. "The Young Lion Who May Lead Guerrillas to Victory." *The San Francisco Examiner*, 24 February 1984.

Denker, Debra. "Along Afghanistan's War-Torn Frontier." *National Geographic* (June 1985):772—97.

Derleth, William. "The Soviets in Afghanistan: Can the Red Army Fight a Counterinsurgency War?" *Armed Forces and Society* 15 (Fall 1988):33—54.

Dmitriev, Iu. "Battalion of Four." *Trud*, 21 February 1985, as translated in JPRS-UMA-85-021, 48—49.

_____. "Meeting in Afghanistan." *Zvezda*, 26 February 1985, as translated in JPRS-UMA-85-035, 22 May 1985, 56—59.

Doder, Dusko. "Afghanistan War Saps Kremlin's Resolve." *The Kansas City Times*, 27 December 1986.

Dorensboro, Gilles, and Chantal Lobato. "The Militia in Afghanistan." *Central Asian Survey*, no. 4 (1989):98—103.

Doronin, A. "A Choice." *Znamenosets*, no. 4 (1984):12, as translated in JPRS-UMA-84-064, 71—74.

Drozdov, P. "Boi nachinaetsia s razvedkoi." *Voennyi vestnik*, no. 5 (1990): 39—40.

Dupree, Louis. "Afghanistan in 1982: Still No Solution." *Asian Survey* 23, no. 2 (1983):133—42.

———. "Afghanistan in 1983: Still No Solution." *Asian Survey* 24, no. 2 (1984):229—39.

Dynin, I. "Heirs to an Honored Tradition: The Overcoming Course." *Krylia rodiny*, no. 10 (1985), as translated in JPRS-UMA-86-016, 80—84.

———. "Krutye perevaly." *Krasnaia zvezda*, 26 February 1983.

Edwards, Phillip. "Daylight Raid, Freedom Fighters Batter Kabul Fort." *Soldier of Fortune* (October 1985):38—41, 76.

Emolkin, V. "Afgan: Iz dnevnika desantnika." *Aspekt*, no. 5 (1990):5.

Esiutin, I. "Vvod voisk v Afganistan, kak eto bylo" (interview with Iu. V. Tukharinov). *Krasnaia zvezda*, 24 December 1989.

———. "Zvezda soldata." *Krasnaia zvezda*, 13 March 1988.

"Equipment of a Paramilitary Obstacle Course." *Voennye znaniia*, no. 5 (1984):36, 48, as translated in JPRS-UMA-84-064, 65—70.

Fadeev, V. Vremia, newscast on Moscow Television Service, 2 January 1984, as translated in JPRS-UMA-84-011, 47 (on volunteer work in Afghanistan).

Federov, Aol. A. "Penetrating the Zone of Antiaircraft Fire." *Soviet Military Review*, no. 5 (1984):216—27, as translated in JPRS-UMA-84-049, 50—54.

Gaider, T. "In the Valley of the Five Lions." *Pravda*, 2 August 1982, as translated in *CDSP* 34 (no. 32):5—7.

Garrity, Patrick. "The Soviet Military Stake in Afghanistan: 1956—79." *Journal of the Royal United Services Institute for Defence Studies* (September 1980):31—36.

Gearing, Julian. "Chaos Likely in Afghanistan." *Jane's Defence Weekly*, 23 April 1988, 793.

"General Yazov Criticizes Military Slur." *Jane's Defence Weekly*, 6 February 1988, 397.

Gibbs, David. "Does the USSR have a 'Grand Strategy'? Reinterpreting the Invasion of Afghanistan." *Journal of Peace Research* 24, no. 4 (1987):366—79.

Girardet, Edward. "Afghan Fighters Slowly Erode Soviet Control." *The Christian Science Monitor*, 23 December 1987.

———. "Afghan Guerrilla Leader: Soviets Have Made Significant Changes in Tactics." *The Christian Science Monitor*, 31 December 1985.

———. "Afghan Guerrillas Keep Soviets at Bay." *The Christian Science Monitor*, 29 June 1982.

———. "How Stubborn Tribesmen Nibble Russians to Death." *U.S. News & World Report*, 12 July 1982, 25.

———. "New Charges of Chemical Warfare in Afghanistan." *The Christian Science Monitor*, 10 September 1982.

———. "Occupational Hazards of a Soviet Occupation." *The Christian Science Monitor*, 2 July 1982.

_____. "Resistance Successes Lure Some Afghans Back." *The Christian Science Monitor*, 22 December 1987.

_____. "With the Resistance in Afghanistan." *The Christian Science Monitor*, 22 June 1982.

_____. "With the Resistance in Afghanistan: Afghan Officials, Soviets at Bay." *The Christian Science Monitor*, 24 September 1981.

Glezdenev, V. "Assault Landing in the Mountains—On Afghanistan Land." *Krasnaia zvezda*, 16 June 1982, as translated in JPRS-82777, no. 1739.

"The Goal Is National Reconciliation." *Izvestiia*, 3 January 1987, as translated in *CDSP* 39 (no. 1).

Golubev, V. "Comments Reach the School." *Krasnaia zvezda*, 12 June 1984, as translated in JPRS-UMA-84-059, 13 September 1984, 18—20.

Goncharov, V. "Sviaz' na Salange." *Voennyi vestnik*, no. 8 (1987):52—53.

Gorbachev, Mikhail S. "Zaiavlenie General'nogo sekretaria Tsk KPSS M. S. Gorbacheva po Afganistanu." *Krasnaia zvezda*, 9 February 1988.

Grau, Les. "Soviet Non-Linear Combat, The Challenge of the 90's." Pamphlet, Fort Leavenworth, KS: Soviet Army Studies Office, 1990.

Graves, Jim. "Paktia Reconnaissance." *Soldier of Fortune* (December 1984).

Greshnov, A. "The Ranks of Army PDPA Organizations Are Swelling." *Krasnaia zvezda*, 11 February 1983, as translated in JPRS-83308 USSR Report: Military Affairs, no. 1761, 5—6.

Grintner, Lawrence. "The Soviet Invasion of Afghanistan: Its Inevitability and Its Consequences." *Parameters* (December 1982):53—61.

Gromadskii, L. J. "Dzholoi Chyntemirov's Red Star." *Sovetskaia Kirgiziia*, 23 March 1984, in JPRS-UMA-84-045, 50—55.

Gromov, B. V. "Zashchishchali, obuchali, stroili." *Voenno-istoricheskii zhurnal*, no. 3 (1989):11—15.

Gunston, John. "Afghans Plan USSR Terror Attacks." *Jane's Defence Weekly*, 31 March 1984, 481—84.

_____. "Su-24's, TU-16's Support Soviet Ground Forces." *Aviation Week & Space Technology*, 29 October 1984, 40—43.

Halliday, Fred. "The Middle East, Afghanistan and the Gulf in Soviet Perception." *Journal of the Royal United Services Institute for Defence Studies* 129 (December 1984):13—18.

Hansen, James. "Afghanistan: The Soviet Experience." *National Defense* (January 1982):20—24.

Harrison, Selig. "Dateline Afghanistan: Exit Through Finland?" *Foreign Policy* 41 (Winter 1980—81):163—87.

Hauner, Milan, and John Roberts. "Soviets Near Goal of Persian Port." *The Wisconsin State Journal*, 22 November 1987.

Hiatt, Fred. "Soviet Troops Advance Into Key Afghan Valley." *The Washington Post*, 27 April 1984.

———. "Soviets Use Bombers in Afghanistan." *The Washington Post*, 24 April 1984.

Iakutin, L. "Letters From Afghanistan." *Sovetskii voin*, no. 4 (1984):10—14, translated in JPRS-UMA-84-044, 94—102.

Ihlau, Olaf. "Inside Afghanistan." *World Press Review* (September 1981): 29—31.

Ilves, Andrew. "Soviet Admission of Failure in Afghanistan." *Report on the USSR*, RL 65/88, 18 February 1988, 1—5.

"In a Friendly Atmosphere." *Pravda*, 13 December 1986, as translated in *CDSP* 38 (no. 50):14—15.

"In a Ravine—From the Site." *Krasnaia zvezda*, 17 July 1984, as translated in JPRS-UMA-84-063, 10 October 1984.

Isby, David. "Afghanistan 1982: The War Continues." *International Defense Review* (November 1982):1523—28.

———. "Soviet Tactics in the War in Afghanistan." *Jane's Defence Review* 4, no. 7 (1983):683.

———. "Soviets in Afghanistan, Prepared for Long Haul." *Defense Week*, 21 February 1984.

———. "Resistance in Afghanistan." *Strategy and Tactics* (January-February 1985):11—15.

Ishchenko, S. "K iugu ot piandzha." *Krasnaia zvezda*, 27 March 1988.

Ivanko, A. "Vzgliad so storony: Neizvestnye stranitsy afganskoi voiny." *Izvestiia*, 11 August 1990.

Ivanov, A. "V pozornoi roli." *Krasnaia zvezda*, 29 November 1984.

Ivanov, N. "H-Hour" (interview with Colonel General Iu. Tukharinov). *Sovetskaia Rossiia*, 20 December 1989, as translated in JPRS-UMA-90-007, 23 March 1990.

Ivanov, Iu. "The Village Was Waiting for Bread." *Komsomol'skaia Pravda*, 24 June 1984, as translated in JPRS-UMA-84-057, 28 August 1984, 114—48.

Jukes, Geoffrey. "The Soviet Armed Forces and the Afghan War." In *The Soviet Withdrawal From Afghanistan*. Edited by Amin Seikal and William Maley. Cambridge: Cambridge University Press, 1989.

Kaminskii, E. "Dushmanskie kaverzy." *Voennyi vestnik*, no. 5 (1988):80—83.

Karp, Aaron. "Blowpipes and Stingers in Afghanistan: One Year Later." *Armed Forces Journal International* (September 1987):36—38.

Karp, Craig. "War in Afghanistan." *Foreign Affairs* (Summer 1986):1026—47.

Kashina, E. "Trudnyi put k miru." *Sovetskii sport*, 17 July 1987.

Kaylor, Robert, and Jeff Trimble. "Gorbachev's Problem: How to Lose a War." *U.S. News and World Report*, no. 1 (1988):400.

Keller, Bill. "Russia's Divisive War: Home From Afghanistan." *The New York Times Magazine*, 14 February 1988, 24—29, 86.

Kemp, Ian. "Abdul Haq: Soviet Mistakes in Afghanistan." *Jane's Defence Weekly*, 5 March 1988, 380—81.

Kempe, Frederick. "Risky Mission: Supplying Guerrillas in Afghanistan Is Grueling Undertaking." *The Wall Street Journal*, 13 November 1984.

Khalilzad, Zalmay. "Moscow's Afghan War." *Problems of Communism*, nos. 1, 2 (1986):1—20.

Kifner, John. "With the Afghan Guerrillas in a Heady Time." *The New York Times*, 27 May 1988.

Kline, David. "The Conceding of Afghanistan." *The Washington Quarterly* (Spring 1983):130—39.

Kolesnikov, M. "Nastuplenie v gorakh." *Voennyi vestnik*, no. 1 (1987):33—36.

Kondrashov, A. "Call Signs in Mountainous Areas." *Soviet Military Review*, 22—23, as translated in JPRS-UMA-84-047, 58—60.

Konovalov, Valerii. "Afghanistan and Mountain Warfare Training." *RL* 118/88, 17 March 1988, 1—5.

Kornilov, Iu. " 'Svoboda informatsii' ili 'svoboda provokatsii'?" *Krasnaia zvezda*, 17 October 1984.

Korobka, S. "Razvedka v gorakh." *Voennyi vestnik*, no. 10 (1985):13—15.

Kovalev, A. "Such High Mountains." *Krasnaia zvezda*, 4 May 1985, in JPRS-UMA-85-038, 21 June 1985, 110—14.

Kozlovskii, S. "Malyi garnizon." *Voennyi vestnik*, no. 4 (1988).

Kravchenko, A. "Gruppa v zasade." *Voennyi vestnik*, no. 7 (1989):45—46.

Kuchkin, Major. "For Emulation—the Feat." *Agitator armii i flota*, no. 18 (1986):24, as translated in JPRS-UMA-87-001, 74—77.

Kurochkin, V. "Tanki v zelenoi zone." *Voennyi vestnik*, no. 1 (1990):57—59.

Kushnerev, S. "After Afghanistan." *Komsomol'skaia pravda*, 21 December 1989, as translated in JPRS-UMA-90-006, 20 March 1990.

Kuzio, Taras. "Opposition in the USSR to the Occupation of Afghanistan." *Central Asian Survey* 6, no. 1 (1987):99—117.

Laber, Jeri. "Afghanistan's Other War." *The New York Review of Books*, 18 December 1986.

Leitenberg, Milton. "United States Foreign Policy and the Soviet Invasion of Afghanistan." *Arms Control* 7 (December 1986):271—94.

Litvinenko, V. "Pora osmyslit' i obobshchit': Ognevoe porazhenie." *Voennyi vestnik*, no. 6 (1990):44—46.

Lukashin, V. "Hot Skies." *Izvestiia*, 1 May 1986, as translated in JPRS-UMA-86-037, 11 July 1986, 101—6.

Mahoney, Donald. "Soviet Press Enters New Stage in Coverage of Afghan War." *RL* 34/87.

Malhuret, Claude. "Report From Afghanistan." *Foreign Affairs* (Fall-Winter 1983):428—31.

"The March Training of Troops." *Krasnaia zvezda*, 31 January 1985, as translated in JPRS-UMA-85-025, 3 April 1985, 20—22.

Martynov, V. "Polosa poiskovoi vynoslivosti." *Voennyi vestnik*, no. 10 (1988):84—86.

McCormick, Kip. "The Evolution of Soviet Military Doctrine, Afghanistan." *Military Review* (July 1987):61—72.

———. "The Soviet Army, Counterinsurgency and the Afghan War." *Parameters* (December 1989):21—35.

McMichael, Scott. "Soviet Tactical Performance and Adaptation in Afghanistan." *Journal of Soviet Military Studies* 3, no. 1 (1990):73—105.

Mecham, Michael. "US Credits Afghan Resistance With Thwarting Soviet Air Power." *Aviation Week & Space Technology*, 13 July 1987.

Meshchaninov, D. "Dolgii i trudnyi put k miru." *Izvestiia*, 21 February 1988.

———. "Insurgent's Lair Routed." *Izvestiia*, 29 August 1986, as translated in *CDSP* 38 (no. 35):14—15.

Middleton, Drew. "Key Afghan Area Is Reported Lost by the Guerrillas." *The New York Times*, 25 April 1984.

Mikhalko, E. "Dlia obespecheniia boia v gorakh." *Tyl i snabzhenie sovetskikh vooruzhennykh sil*, no. 10 (1986):15—19.

Mironov, L. "Dela Kabulskogo gorkoma." *Pravda*, 11 March 1982.

Mironov, L., and G. Poliakov. "Afghanistan: The Beginning of a New Life." *International Affairs* (Moscow) (March 1979):46—54.

Modenov, S. "The Afghan People's Resolve." *International Affairs*, no. 6 (1982):26.

Moorcraft, Paul. "Bloody Standoff in Afghanistan." *Army* (April 1985):28—34.

Mulyar [Muliar], Nikolai M. "The Fight for the Pass." *Krasnaia zvezda*, 17 March 1985, as translated in JPRS-UMA-85-034, 21 May 1985, 34—36.

Muratov, D. "Afghanistan." *Komsomol'skaia pravda*, 27 December 1990, as translated in JPRS-UMA-91-006, 4 March 1991.

Nahaylo, Bohdan. "Soviet Newspaper Reveals Antipathy Among Youth Towards War in Afghanistan." *RL* 23/87.

———. "Towards a Settlement of the Afghanistan Conflict: A Chronological Overview." *RL* 16/87.

———. "Ukrainian Mother's Protest Attracts Numerous Letters on the Afghanistan Theme." *RL*, no. 21 (27 May 1987):1—5.

Najib. "The Goal Is National Reconciliation." *CDSP* 39 (no. 1):11.

A Nearby Observer. "Afghanistan." *The Bulletin of the Atomic Scientists* 39, no. 6 (1983):16—23.

Nelson, Denny. "Soviet Air Power: Tactics and Weapons Used in Afghanistan." *Air University Review*, no. 2 (1985):31—44.

"Net v dushe blagodarnosti..." *Pravda*, 25 November 1987.

"New Claims of Chemical Warfare in Afghanistan." *Jane's Defence Weekly*, 22 November 1986, 1206.

New York Times News Service. "Stinger Missiles Aid Afghan Guerrillas." *The Kansas City Times*, 13 December 1986.

Novosti Press Agency. "The Truth About Afghanistan: Documents, Facts, Eyewitness Reports." Moscow: Novosti, 1980.

O'Ballance, Edgar. "Afghanistan: Winds of Change." *Asian Defense Journal*, no. 9 (1986):76—85.

Okulov, V. "Afganistan zhivet v moei dushe." *Pravda*, 3 February 1988.

———. " 'Belaiakniga' o chernykh delakh." *Pravda*, 20 February 1985.

———. "Uroki Kunduza." *Pravda*, 19 August 1988.

Okulov, V., and P. Studenikin. "Opalennye Kandagarom." *Pravda*, 10 August 1988.

Oliinik, A. "Courage." *Krasnaia zvezda*, 24 March 1984, as translated in JPRS-UMA-84-041, 47—54.

———. "For Courage and Heroism." *Krasnaia zvezda*, 11 July 1984, as translated in JPRS-UMA-84-057, 122.

———. "In a Hail of Bullets." *Krasnaia zvezda*, 19 January 1985, as translated in JPRS-UMA-85-013, 45—49.

———. "In the Interests of the Afghan People." *Krasnaia zvezda*, 21 January 1987, as translated in JPRS-UMA-87-035, 48—54.

———. "Mountains Under the Wings." *Krasnaia zvezda*, 25 April 1985, as translated in JPRS-UMA-85-038, 21 June 1985, 115—17.

———. "Nepokorennyi: Rasskaz ob odnom iz sovetskikh voinov propavshikh bez vesti v Afganistane." *Krasnaia zvezda*, 11 June 1988.

———. "Ognennye kilometry." *Krasnaia zvezda*, 26 May 1985.

———. "The Sending of Troops to Afghanistan: Participants in the Events Tell and Documents Attest to How the Decision Was Made." *Krasnaia zvezda*, 18 November 1989, as translated in JPRS-UMA-90-004, 8 February 1990, 74—78.

———. "Vremia nadezhd." *Krasnaia zvezda*, 22 March 1988.

———. "Vsego odin shans." *Krasnaia zvezda*, 26 March 1983.

———. "Vvod voisk v Afganistan: Kak prinimalos' reshenie." *Krasnaia zvezda*, 18 November 1989.

———. "Vyshe gor." *Krasnaia zvezda*, 28 February 1988.

Ostankov, V., and V. Sadovik. "Minnaia opasnost'." *Voennyi vestnik*, no. 10 (1986):63—65.

"Our Main Cause—The Commander Organizes Combat Training—He Who Doesn't Work Makes No Mistakes—One Must Be Competent to Teach." *Krasnaia zvezda*, 7 April 1988, as translated in JPRS-UMA-88-013, 7 July 1988, 5—6.

Panov, V. "Ostavat'sia boitsami." *Znamenosets*, no. 4 (1988):25—26.

Panteleev, G. "Ekzamen v gorakh." *Krasnaia zvezda*, 27 March 1988.

Pavlov, B. "Defeat of Counterrevolution in Soviet Turkestan." *Soviet Military Review* no. 5 (1984):53—54, as translated in JPRS-UMA-84-049, 19 July 1984, 58—60.

Payind, Alam. "Soviet-Afghan Relations From Cooperation to Occupation." *International Journal for Middle Eastern Studies* 21 (1989):107—28.

Phillip, Jimmy. "On the Roads of Afghanistan: Mines, Mines and Mines." *Armed Forces* (Australia) (June 1988):11—15.

Pincus, Walter. "Panel to Probe Afghan Army Fund." *The Washington Post*, 13 January 1987.

"Place of Service Afghanistan: You Are So Reliable." *Komsomol'skaia pravda*, 11 July 1984, as translated in JPRS-UMA-84-057, 123—24.

Pochter, G. "Nekotorye osobennosti vedeniia operatsii na gorno-pustynoi teatre." *Voina i revoliutsiia*, nos. 3, 4 (1933):50—58.

Pogrebniak, V. Letter to the editor. *Krasnaia zvezda*, 22 March 1988.

Popov, V. "Usilennyi motostrelkovoi batal'on nastup aet v gorakh." *Voennyi vestnik*, no. 1 (1982):16—20.

Portnyagin, V. "In Active Opposition." *Krasnaia zvezda*, 8 February 1984, as translated in JPRS-UMA-84-030, 9 April 1984, 34—36.

Poullada, Leon. "The Failure of American Diplomacy in Afghanistan." *World Affairs* 145, no. 3 (1982—83):230—52.

Prokhanov, A. "Russian Journalist Sorts Among Ruins of Nine-Year Afghan War." *The Kansas City Times*, 5 May 1988.

Protasov, Iu. "Vera v budushchee." *Voennyi vestnik*, no. 1 (1987):33—36.

Pugachev, F. "Bez razvedki—ni shagu!" *Voennyi vestnik*, no. 3 (1987):18—20.

Quinn-Judge, Paul. "Soviet Publication Paints Bleak Picture of War in Afghanistan." *The Christian Science Monitor*, 21 July 1988.

Rafikov, R. "Helicopters over the Battlefield." *Voennyi vestnik*, no. 9 (1986): 13—15, in JPRS-UMA-87-021, 26—29.

Rianzantsev, D. "T-72 Tank Operation in a Desert." *Soviet Military Review*, no. 12 (1982):24—26 in JPRS-82835, no. 1740.

Robinson, Julianne, Jeanne Guillemin, and Matthew Meselson, "Yellow Rain: The Story Collapses." *Foreign Policy* (Fall 1987):100—117.

Ross, William. "Primary Role for Soviet Air Forces in the Delivery of Chemical Weapons." *Jane's Defence Weekly*, 30 May 1987, 1053.

Roy, Oliver. "Afghanistan: A View From the Interior." *Dissent* (Winter 1981):47—54.

Rubin, Barnett. "Afghanistan: The Next Round." *Orbis* (Winter 1989):57—72.

Sadeki, I. "V edinom stroiu," *Krasnaia zvezda*, 24 December 1984.

Safi, Nasrullah. "Soviet Military Tactics in Afghanistan." *Central Asian Survey* 5, no. 2 (1986):103—10.

Safronov, V. G. "Kak eto bylo." *Voenno-istoricheskii zhurnal*, no. 5 (1990): 11—15.

Salivon, V. "Afganistan: zavoevano revoliutsiei." *Sovetskii sport*, 12 December 1986.

———. "Shkvatka." *Sovetskii sport*, 10 March 1987.

Samsanov, V. "Gornyi variant." *Krasnaia zvezda*, 10 September 1988.

Sautin, N. "Ispytyvaetsia tank." *Izvestiia*, 11 September 1988.

Schwartzstein, Stuart. "Chemical Warfare in Afghanistan: An Independent Assessment." *World Affairs* 145, no. 3 (1982—83):267—72.

Sego, Steve. "Kabul Seeks National Reconciliation." *RL* 15/87.

———. "US Experts Discuss Soviet Army in Afghanistan." *RL* 302/87, 24 July 1987, 1—4.

———. "Will the Soviet-Afghan Border Be Redrawn?" *RL* 156/88.

Semyonov, V. "A New Situation in Afghanistan." *International Affairs*, no. 4 (1988):88—92.

———. "Revolutionary Afghanistan Eight Years Later." *International Affairs*, no. 5 (1986):47—52.

Shalinsky, Audrey. "Ethnic Reactions to the Current Regime in Afghanistan." *Central Asian Survey* 3, no. 4 (1984):49—60.

Shcherban, V. "Desant na karavannoi trope." *Izvestiia*, 18 September 1987.

Sheehy, Ann. "Agreement Signed Between Soviet and Afghan Official Muslim Organizations." *RL* 198/87, 1—5.

Shirokov, M. "Vliianie prirodnykh uslovii gornykh raionov na vedenie boevykh deistvii." *Voennaia mysl* (December 1965):46—54.

Shulgin, A. "Boi v gorakh." *Voennyi vestnik*, no. 2 (1985):29—32.

Shuliak, A. "Tekhnicheskoe obespechenie na marshe v gorakh." *Voennyi vestnik*, no. 9 (1986):16—18.

Skrizhalin, V. "Boi v loshchine." *Krasnaia zvezda*, 30 June 1983.

———. "Byt' miru pod olivami." *Krasnaia zvezda*, 17 January 1984.

———. "Defending the Revolution, Dispatch from the DRA." *Krasnaia zvezda*, 27 December 1983, as translated in JPRS-UMA-84-011, 49—51.

———. "In a Ravine—from the Site." *Krasnaia zvezda*, 17 July 1984, as translated in JPRS-UMA-84-063, 10 October 1984, 94—95.

———. "Konets banditskogo logova." *Krasnaia zvezda*, 8 March 1984.

———. "Na vsiakii iad—protivoiadie." *Krasnaia zvezda*, 4 September 1988.

———. "Post u dorogi." *Krasnaia zvezda*, 6 July 1985.

———. "Prozrenie." *Krasnaia zvezda*, 29 July 1983.

———. "Reisy muzhestva." *Krasnaia zvezda*, 8 December 1983.

———. "The Soldiers Spoke of the Exploit. . . ." *Krasnaia zvezda*, 22 March 1983, as translated in JPRS-83308 USSR Report: Military Affairs, no. 1761, 6—10.

———. "Trassa v gorakh." *Krasnaia zvezda*, 20 October 1984.

Sliwinski, Marek. "Afghanistan: The Decimation of a People." *Orbis* (Winter 1989):39—56.

"Sluzhili na zemle Afganistana." *Krasnaia zvezda*, 9 March 1986.

"A Soldier in Afghanistan." *Central Asian Survey*, no. 1 (1986).

"Soobshchenie Komiteta Verkhovnogo Soveta po mezhdunarodnym delam po politicheskoi otsenke resheniia o vvode Sovetskikh voisk v Afganistan." *Krasnaia zvezda*, 27 December 1989.

Sosnitskii, V. "Desantniki v atake." *Voennyi vestnik*, no. 10 (1985):29—30.

Sotskov, M. "Dlia boia v gorakh: voinskaia spetsial'nost' i fizicheskaia podgotovka." *Krasnaia zvezda*, 16 July 1983.

"Soviet Air Force in Afghanistan." *Jane's Defence Weekly*, 7 July 1984, 1104—5.

"A Soviet Estonian Soldier in Afghanistan." *Central Asian Survey* 5, no. 1 (1986):101—15.

"Soviet Losses in Afghanistan: 40,000." *Jane's Defence Weekly*, 27 February 1988, 69.

"Sovmestnoe Sovetsko-afganskoe kommunike." *Pravda*, 8 December 1978.

Starodymov, N. "Obespechivaia prodvizhenie kolonna." *Voennyi vestnik*, no. 10 (1986):66—68.

Stepanov, E. "Boi v gorakh: osobye usloviia." *Voennyi vestnik*, no. 3 (1988): 22—25.

Stepanov, V. "Afghanistan on the Path of Revolutionary Change." *International Affairs*, no. 5 (1984):25—33.

Studenikin, P. "Doroga v Kabul." *Pravda*, 20 September 1984.

Studenikin, Petr. "Put' na Salang." In *Put' na Salang*, Moscow: DOSAAF, 1987.

Sukhodolskii, V. "Afghanistan Profiles." *Rabochaia gazeta*, 7—8 April 1984, as translated in JPRS-UMA-84-055, 22 August 1984.

———. "The Salang Pass." *Za rulem*, no. 2 (1986), as translated in JPRS-UMA-86-037, 11 July 1986, 111—13.

Sukhoparov, A. "Meetings on Afghan Soil." *Sovetskaia Rossiia*, 4 July 1984, as translated in JPRS-UMA-84-057, 120—21.

Tagliabue, John. "Russians Pressing Afghan Campaign." *The New York Times*, 21 November 1986.

"Tank Brigades Revived in New Role." *Jane's Defence Weekly*, 23 April 1988, 806—7.

Taranenko, I. "Trudnoe nebo." *Pravda*, 15 October 1985.

Tashkent International Service in Uzbek. "Afghan Tribes Are Safeguarding the Revolution," 25 December 1983, as translated in JPRS-UMA-84-011, 2 February 1984, 42—43.

———. "Cooperation Based on Equality and Mutual Benefit," 19 December 1983, as translated in JPRS-UMA-84-011, 44—45.

TASS. "Afganistan ustal ot voiny." *Pravda*, 24 July 1988.

———. "Bandits' Lair Wiped Out." *Pravda*, 2 May 1986, as translated in *CDSP* 38 (no. 18).

———. "Chemical Arms Seized in Afghanistan," as translated in JPRS-UMA-86-055, 48—49.

———. "Na novom etape." *Pravda*, 16 June 1981.

———. "Protest protiv vmeshatel'stva." *Pravda*, 9 February 1985.

Taubman, Philip. "In Kabul, Military Prowess on Parade." *The New York Times*, 19 January 1988.

Teplov, Iu. "That Bitter-Sweet Rice." *Krasnaia zvezda*, 23 March 1983, as translated in JPRS-83308 USSR Report: Military Affairs, no. 1761, 10—11 (attack on a convoy carrying rice).

Tolkov, V. "Bomber Operations in Mountains." *Aviatsiia i kosmonavtika*, no. 10 (1989), as translated in JPRS-UAC-90-002, 1 May 1990.

Trehub, Aaron. "Afghanistan: The Subversive War Continues." *RL* 320/84, 23 August 1984, 1—6.

———. "All Quiet on the Panjsher Front?" *RL* 259/84, 3 July 1984, 1—3.

———. "Bogomolov Reveals Opposition to Afghan Invasion." *RL* 116/88, 17 March 1988, 1—4.

———. "Popular Discontent With the War in Afghanistan." *RL* 483/87, 1—3.

Tretiak, I. "Organizatsiia i vedenie nastupatlel'nogo boia v gorno-taezhnoi mestnosti." *Voenno istoricheskii zhurnal*, no. 7 (1980):42—49.

Trusov, V. "A Special Assignment." *Krasnaia zvezda*, 5 April 1986, as translated in JPRS-UMA-86-033, 21—22.

Tuaev, S. "Zasada." *Voennyi vestnik*, no. 2 (1989):68—71.

Tukharinov, Iu. "Commitment of Troops to Afghanistan: How It Was" (interview by I. Esiutin). *Krasnaia zvezda*, 24 December 1989, as translated in JPRS-UMA-90-005, 15 February 1990, 55—57.

———. "The Commander and Modern Combat: Maneuver in the Mountains." *Krasnaia zvezda*, 30 December 1981, as translated in JPRS USSR Report: Military Affairs, no. 80418, 26 March 1982, 14—17.

Turbiville, Graham. "Airborne Troops." In *Soviet Armed Forces Review Annual*, vol. 6. Edited by David Jones. Gulf Breeze, FL: Academic International Press, 1982, 135—41.

———. "Ambush! The Road War in Afghanistan." *Army* (January 1988): 32—42.

Turdiev, T., and Iu. Tuidiiev. "The Sons of Man Are Members One Another...." *Tojikistoni soveti*, as translated in JPRS-UMA-88-002, 19 January 1988.

Turshatov, Viktor. "Afghanistan Veterans: Society Owes Them." *Moscow News*, no. 50 (1987).

Turvandian, A. "Conscience Calls." *Kommunist* (Erevan), 24 September 1987, as translated in JPRS-UMA-87-045, 23 December 1987, 53.

Tverdokhlebov, E. "Okhrana na dorogakh." *Voennyi vestnik*, no. 6 (1990): 47—48.

Urban, Mark. "A More Competent Afghan Army?" *Jane's Defence Weekly*, 23 November 1985, 1147—51.

U.S. Department of State. Special Report no. 106. "Afghanistan: Three Years of Soviet Occupation," December 1982.

———. Special Report no. 135. "Afghanistan: Six Years of Soviet Occupation," December 1988.

———. Special Report no. 139. "Soviet Influence on Afghan Youth," February 1986.

———. Special Report no. 173. "Afghanistan: Eight Years of Soviet Occupation," December 1987.

Usmanov, T. "Pora osmyslit' i obobshchit'." *Voennyi vestnik*, no. 5 (1990): 36—37.

Ustinov, G. "The Pass Is Open." *Izvestiia*, 2 February 1983, as translated in JPRS-83308 USSR Report: Military Affairs, no. 1761, 1—3.

Ustinov, Herman. "Guerrilla Leader Changes Sides." *New Times*, no. 12 (1985):28—30, as translated in JPRS-UMA-85-028, 28—30.

Vakhad, Abdul, and Abdul Baki. "Boi bez vystrelov?" *Krasnaia zvezda*, 1 April 1983.

Varennikov, V. I. "Afganistan: Podvodia itogi." *Ogonek*, no. 12 (1989):6—8.

Vasilev, Iu. "Kto sryvaet uregolirovanie." *Pravda*, 12 May 1981.

Villahermosa, Gilberto. "Soviet Enveloping Detachments." *Armor* (September-October 1984):13—15.

Volkov, M. " 'Ne khochu ubivat'!" *Pravda*, 7 February 1988.

Vorontsov, Iu. " 'Nasha tsel'—politicheskoe uregulirovanie v Afganistane." *Pravda*, 18 February 1988.

Vozovikov, V. "Miny i lozy." *Krasnaia zvezda*, 3 November 1984.

―――. "Na Afganskikh vysotakh." *Krasnaia zvezda*, 27 September 1984.

―――. "Na Afganskikh vysotakh." *Krasnaia zvezda*, 10 October 1984.

―――. "Pokorenie vershin." *Krasnaia zvezda*, 15 December 1984.

"Vruchenie vysshei nagrady Afganistana tovarishchu L. I. Brezhnevu." *Pravda*, 17 December 1981.

Warhurst, Geoffrey. "Afghanistan—A Dissenting Appraisal." *RUSI* (September 1980):31—36.

Washington Post Service. "Afghan Rebel Leader Dodges Reds' Revenge." In the *New Haven Register*, 14 November 1984.

Weintraub, Bernard. "Afghan Guerrillas Step Up Attacks on Capital Area." *The New York Times*, 28 August 1988.

Weisman, Steven. "Neighbors of Afghanistan Seek Orderly Departure by Russians." *The New York Times*, 14 February 1988.

―――. "25% of Russians in Afghan Force Will Leave in May." *The New York Times*, 15 May 1988.

Wheeler, Charles. "The Forces in Conflict: Afghanistan." *Military Review* (July 1987):55—60.

"When Is an Envelopment and a Turning Movement Used?" *Soviet Military Review*, no. 6 (1984), as translated in JPRS-UMA-84-074, 57—58.

Wilder, Bryan. "Casualties High in Afghan Battles." *Honolulu Star-Bulletin*, 8 December 1987.

Williams, E. S. "Yazov—The Darkest Horse." *Armed Forces* (January 1988): 19—20.

Winchester, Mike. "Drivin' Ivan Home." *Soldier of Fortune* (December 1988): 32—41.

"The Withdrawal of Troops from Afghanistan Can Be Stepped Up." *Moscow News*, no. 51, 28 December 1985—4 January 1986.

Yermolina, O., and A. Zubkov. "We Were Not Preaching Evil" (interview with General V. I. Varennikov). *Sovetskii patriot*, 27 December 1989, as translated in JPRS-UMA-90-007, 23 March 1990, 123—25.

Yurkin, A. "Mountains Are Conquered by the Strong." *Krasnaia zvezda*, 15 May 1984, as translated in JPRS-UMA-84-053, 9 August 1984.

Zadubrovsky, V. "The Correct Decision." *Soviet Military Review*, no. 4 (1984):26—27.

"Zaiavlenie General'nogo Sekretaria TsK KPSS M. S. Gorbacheva." *Krasnaia zvezda*, 9 February 1988.

Zaitsevskii, N. "By a Surprise Attack." *Krasnaia zvezda*, 10 October 1984, as translated in JPRS-UMA-84-078, 62—64.

Zaloga, Stephen. "Soviet Infantry: Lessons From the War in Afghanistan." *Armed Forces Journal International* (October 1989):28.

Zaporozhan, I. "Tiazhelo v uchenii—legko v boiu." *Voennyi vestnik*, no. 4 (1987):19—21.

Zhestkov, Vitaly. "The Afghan Revolution: Achievements and Difficulties." *Socialism: Principles, Practice, Prospects*, no. 4 (1988):32—34.

Lectures and Briefings

Briefings on Afghan War at the U.S. Army Command and General Staff College, 27—28 October 1986.

Newsletters and Bulletins

Afghan Information Centre Monthly Bulletin, Peshawar.

Afghanistan Reports. The Institute of Strategic Studies, Islamabad, Pakistan.

Afghan Jehad.

Afghan Realities.

The Letter from the BIA, Bureau International Afghanistan, Paris.

Conclusions

The evidence of historical continuities in the style of Russian and Soviet warfare on the southern, predominantly Muslim periphery of the old Russian Empire and, subsequently, the USSR, probably says as much about the rough congruence of conditions involved in the successive wars in the Caucasus, Central Asia, and Afghanistan as it does about recurring patterns of Russian military behavior. Obvious circumstantial parallels can be found in cultural factors, particularly religion, and geographical influences.

Although, for example, the intensity of religious reaction to the Russians ranged from Shamil's holy war to the less-fervent tribal war waged by the Basmachis, the Russians, in each instance, confronted peoples whose political and social development, culture, and world view reflected far more similarities than differences. Furthermore, each encounter reflected a collision of cultures where the antagonists peered at one another across a gaping divide carved by many centuries of separate and divergent development. Thus, each Muslim society, whether intruded upon by imperial Russian or Soviet forces, was readily galvanized by the alien presence. The mobilization of resistance, however, did not necessarily bring about unity among the resisters, and the fractious nature of tribal politics prevented the creation of strong and durable alliances. Indeed, even the short-lived Muslim polity forged by Shamil in the Caucasus was eventually torn asunder, in part, by internal strife.

In addition to general similarities in the cultural setting, the geographical backdrop for each war also presented some fundamental parallels. The Caucasus mountains, like the most rugged areas of northern and eastern Afghanistan, posed distinct strategic and tactical problems for the Russians and Soviets. In particular, they restricted maneuver and increased the difficulties in sustaining regular, European-style forces. In the same manner, the vast steppes and desert tracts of Central Asia demanded the careful articulation of strategic and tactical priorities and their consequent implementation, such as the securing of positions from which to control river and land traffic or, above all, the obtaining of sources of drinking water. Nature, it may be said, constituted the predominant factor in Central Asian defenses. In fact, the difficulty of movement by any but small armed groups had so insulated the tribes of Central Asia from external armed predators, and even from one another, that it probably impeded their military and political development. Thus, in the Caucasus, Central Asia, and Afghanistan, the Imperial Army, the Red Army, and the later, more technologically advanced, Soviet Army discovered that nature, in substantial measure, dictated the terms of battle.

Within the context described above, many similarities emerge—in varying degrees to be sure—between Russian conduct of past wars and that in Afghanistan. In all four cases considered in this study, the Russians committed initial errors in their military and political assessments of their adversary. Such were quite understandable during the imperial period given the Russians' limited knowledge of the peoples and lands with which they were coming into contact. The sluggish response to local conditions in the Caucasus, where a fundamental adaptation to the prevailing conditions of warfare occurred only after decades of Russian futility, can only be explained by command inertia and institutional rigidity. There, and in the Central Asian campaigns to follow, military adjustments depended inordinately on the diagnostic talents and influence of a few key personalities, such as Bariatinskii, Miliutin, Skobelev, and Kaufman. Consequently, although there can be no doubt that the Russian Army was capable of correcting its errors, it nevertheless failed to preserve its acquired knowledge from conflict to conflict. Its collective wisdom was never codified in the form of tactical regulations for unconventional warfare. As Russian participants in the unconventional wars passed from the scene, so, too, did the lessons of their experience. Aside from a handful of ponderous histories, and articles in old issues of the official military journal, *Voennyi sbornik*, little but undigested documentary collections remained to inform future generations of soldiers.

The Red Army's experience in Central Asia while Russia was in the midst of a civil war and in the act of self-creation hardly merits a harsh appraisal for its early shortcomings. Later, the speed with which leaders like Frunze revised the political approach to the war in Central Asia and Red Army analysts came to grips with tactical problems ignored for half a century was remarkable. On the other hand, the Soviet intervention in Afghanistan was predicated upon the mistaken assumption that the country could be ruled from Kabul and that modern military might would cow any opposition. That such an abysmal misconception of Afghan conditions should prevail after over twenty years of direct Soviet involvement in that country's affairs reflects little credit on Leonid Brezhnev's regime.

In the Caucasus and Central Asia, the decisive campaigns of imperial Russian forces depended upon a preparatory phase based on systematic consolidation of vital traffic arteries and strategic points. Once the Russians were in a position to sustain their forces—and understood the importance of method in their approach to conquest—their power was all but irresistible. Likewise, the Red Army seized the strategic initiative early in its struggle with the Basmachis. A logical question follows: why, then, did Soviet control of cities and roads yield such meager gains in Afghanistan? The answer lies, in part, in the ferocity of the Afghan resistance and the Soviet decision to limit its commitment of forces. In all probability, at the time of their initial intervention in 1979, the Soviets intended only to stabilize their client regime and to restore order. Inadequate Soviet political analysis and enormous infusions of foreign aid to the resistance, however, led to Soviet failure.

When the Soviets found that their initial strategic assessment of Afghanistan was incorrect, they also discovered that their conventional tactics in the field in Afghanistan were more appropriate for a war in Europe. But the Soviet Army in Afghanistan gradually relied less on motorized infantry forces in favor of specially trained heliborne units. Descriptions of large, conventional sweeps by Soviet and DRA forces bear an astonishing likeness to those of imperial offensives in the Caucasus, where main columns became overextended along narrow trails; advance and rear guards, as well as supply trains, were cut off; and lines of communication were subjected to frequent interdiction. The Caucasian mountaineers, like the Afghan Mujahideen, gave battle only on their own terms, choosing to yield before superior forces—but always exacting a stiff price for each enemy advance.

Another characteristic common to each of the four cases considered in this study is the Russians' and Soviets' blending of military and nonmilitary elements in their applications of power: the old fashioned "carrot-and-stick" approach. For example, Shamil's alliance and the Basmachis' resistance both succumbed to a mixture of inducement and force, the former consisting of political and administrative measures calculated to temper the most provocative aspects of Russian rule and the latter relating to the progressive destruction of the economy, villages, and crops upon which the resistance subsisted. Even during the imperial conquest of Central Asia, the Russians made flexible use of diplomacy, local administration, and commercial inducements to head off outbursts of native anger.

Frunze also showed great flexibility in undermining support for the Basmachis. Drawing on this tradition, Soviet analyst and Deputy Chief of the General Staff M. A. Gareev (in a veiled commentary on Afghanistan in 1987), fully embraced Frunze's emphasis on "specific situational conditions."[1] Accordingly, Soviet practice in Afghanistan reflected increasing awareness of the importance of manipulating local conditions as the war progressed. For example, the Soviets induced their client regime to adopt a tolerant policy toward Islam and also to change the name of the state from the Democratic Republic of Afghanistan to the Republic of Afghanistan. The Soviets also influenced the Afghan regime to undertake economic and social reform to mitigate the negative effects of ruthless socialist policies implemented during the preceding decade. At the same time, of course, Soviet and DRA forces wrought tremendous destruction on insubordinate tribes and regions.

Particularly in Afghanistan and the Caucasus, and to a lesser extent in Central Asia, population control—at least as related to the separation of submissive and unsubmissive elements—was a central Russian objective of coercion. Thus, forced relocation of a substantial portion of the populace was essential for victory in the Caucasus and Afghanistan. The simple aim of forcible relocation whether by capture and removal or through terror bombing was to deny the resistance any benefits local populations might provide, especially recruits and means of subsistence. Co-opted populations, in turn, could form the human infrastructure for a new social and political order, whether as soldiers, officials, or farmers.

Both the Russians and Soviets drew significant military manpower from the native populations or from ethnically and linguistically related tribal groups that had been assimilated during previous conquests—a fact of symbolic as well as practical importance. In the Caucasus, some local tribes, including Muslims as well as Christian Georgians, contributed forces to the Russian cause. During the conquest of Central Asia, large numbers of Kazakhs and even Turkomans served as camel drivers, scouts, and laborers. The Red Army went even further in Central Asia during the 1920s and formed national military units—although with mixed success. In turn, the early employment by the Soviets of large numbers of Soviet Tajik and Uzbek reservists in Afghanistan, though in part the simple result of their proximity to the theater, was no doubt calculated to make a positive impression on the Afghans. As fellow Central Asians, they would seem a less alien presence among the Afghans than would Russian troops. Unfortunately, the Soviet reservists may have identified too closely with the Afghans, and their reliability was subsequently called into question. Even native Afghan units in the DRA Army proved as impermanent as sand castles at high tide—their ranks dissolving in waves of defections. Though that army survived and even included some battleworthy units by the date of the Soviet withdrawal, its resilience in the absence of active Soviet support remained suspect.

All parallels notwithstanding, some circumstances in Afghanistan differed markedly from those of the past. For primarily political reasons, the Soviet forces in Afghanistan never enjoyed the advantage of strategic envelopment, used to such good effect in prior cases. The annexation of Georgia in 1801 placed Russian forces on both the southern and northern flanks of the Caucasian mountaineers. Similarly, Russia engulfed Central Asia in a series of encirclements. A great pincer movement with one prong advancing along the Syr River in the west and the other slicing southward from Siberia in the east swallowed the Kazakh steppe and the khanate of Kokand during the 1850s and 1860s. An offensive on four converging axes brought the submission of Khiva in 1873. Henceforth, Russian control of the Caspian Sea and the sealing off of the southern frontier with Persia by diplomatic means left the Turkomans in virtual encirclement. With the outbreak of the Basmachi resistance after the October Revolution, most cities and major lines of communications throughout Central Asia were already under Russian control. Although many Central Asians fled across the Afghan border, which remained porous, only briefly did the Basmachis wrest large portions of the region from Soviet control. In contrast, the Soviet march into Afghanistan came from the north, and following the seizure of Kabul, the Soviet Army sought to extend control from the center outward toward the periphery of that nation.

The availability of Pakistan and Iran as sanctuaries, both for the Mujahideen and their families, made it impossible for the Soviets to corner and liquidate the resistance. With their kin safely beyond the frontier, the guerrillas could seldom be forced to defend their homes, nor would their movement in the country be encumbered by spouses, children, and possessions. Further, the inability of the Soviets to seal the frontiers meant that the Mujahideen enjoyed sustained foreign support and were free to fight or withdraw as circumstances dictated. Short of a vastly greater commitment of military force, these conditions, which had no precedent in past wars, doomed the Soviet Union to a stalemate in Afghanistan.

Two other political factors, not present in previous cases, influenced events as well. First, unlike the Russian public of bygone years, which stoically bore past burdens, many Soviet citizens came to doubt the purpose of years of fighting in Afghanistan. Although no organized opposition to the war ever surfaced, dampened enthusiasm—as manifested in the attempts of many Soviet parents to keep their sons from serving in the Army—no doubt made the decision to extricate Soviet soldiers from their predicament a popular one. More important, the reform movement led by Mikhail Gorbachev marked the most dramatic peaceful turn in political direction since Peter I. Cognizant of the costs, international and domestic, of indefinite pursuit of a futile war, Gorbachev had every reason to seek a political accommodation that would enable him to focus his resources more fully on a new agenda at home.

Shortly after the Soviet intervention in Afghanistan began, some Western observers attempted to draw analogies between the Soviet experience and that of the United States in Vietnam. In fact, the truth or falsehood of such comparisons is less important than the light such debates can shed on the complexity and confusion attending the involvement of modern military powers in the affairs of Third World states. Furthermore, important questions emerge concerning the definition of victory and defeat in such interventions—and even whether such terms are strictly relevant in some contexts.

Many of the specific circumstances in Vietnam and Afghanistan are hardly comparable. Vietnam was formally a divided state, whereas Afghanistan was not. Nevertheless, the Communist opposition to the Republic of Vietnam—which operated in the south but to an appreciable degree was sustained from the north—was far more unified in its political goals than the Afghan resistance, which could agree on little more than a common desire to force a Soviet withdrawal. In Vietnam, Communist bloc states supported a war against an American client regime, whereas in Afghanistan, Western and Islamic states helped sustain opposition to a Soviet-sponsored regime. But even those who compare the Soviet and American experiences acknowledge such obvious differences. Rather, it is more in their general contours that the cases of Vietnam and Afghanistan bear a striking, though perhaps facile, likeness.

One American analyst of the Vietnam War, Harry Summers, observes that both the Americans and the Soviets failed to discern the enemy's "center of gravity"—its true source of strength, deprived of which it could not continue.[2] Obviously, given their limited economic development, possession of foreign sanctuaries, and massive materiel support from outside, both the Vietnamese Communists and the Afghan Mujahideen were not dependent on a domestic military-industrial infrastructure. Furthermore, no single city or position on a map assumed great significance to either resistance movement. Therefore, the Mujahideen were not intimidated by Soviet occupation of their capital city, and it is by no means certain that the loss of Hanoi would have been fatal to the North Vietnamese (who themselves had been guerrillas without a capital within recent memory). In addition, to the extent that each waged a guerrilla war, they did not offer their forces in large formations to be destroyed at the hands of a superior power. Their true "center of gravity" lay as much in their conception of the struggle as in any strategic objective. Each resistance movement was nourished by a powerful mix of motivational factors, be they religion, nationalism, xenophobia, ideology, or ethnicity. Thus, each war was in a fundamental sense political and psychological, grounded in specific factors of history and culture.

The question of a strategic "center of gravity" or point of crucial vulnerability is better raised with regard to the American and Soviet positions. Both the United States and the Soviet Union probably possessed the military means to destroy their opponent—if they were willing to pay a high enough price. Neither, however, realistically estimated that price before committing itself. Nor did either comprehend fully the inherent weakness and instability of the regime it sought to preserve and the absolutely essential role that regime must play in the achievement of a political victory. Only a strong client regime would in time become self-sufficient and cease to rely on the outside power. The failure of the Republic of Vietnam to command the loyalty of a solid majority, or even a cohesive plurality, of the population vitiated its efforts on the battlefield. Similarly, a lack of popular legitimacy plagued the Democratic Republic of Afghanistan, and even as they began their withdrawal, the Soviets were not sanguine about its future. Yet in the absence of Soviet forces, the Kabul regime gained an opportunity—however fleeting—to establish its own credibility and, perhaps, reach a *modus vivendi* with at least some of the resistance factions.

Ultimately, the Soviets pulled out of Afghanistan not because they were unable to meet the price of victory, but because the prize seemed less and less worth the expenditure. The inescapable irony of Afghanistan is that the presence of Soviet forces gave the opposition a cohesion it could never have achieved on its own. Meanwhile, the Soviet-backed regime made minimal progress either in building its legitimacy or intimidating its enemies. Thus, in Afghanistan, the Soviets were willing to settle for less than their predecessors obtained in the other cases considered in this study. In some instances, however, less may be more. Ethnic unrest in the Caucasus and Central Asia, not to mention the dissolution of the USSR in 1991, suggests that, whatever their lasting strategic value, the bill for those conquests has not yet been paid in full. Inasmuch as the struggle in Afghanistan not only failed to further Soviet policy objectives but impeded progress in many specific foreign and domestic policies, it was best abandoned.

www.ingramcontent.com/pod-product-compliance
Lightning Source LLC
Chambersburg PA
CBHW082118230426
43671CB00015B/2733